T0192047

Web Application Development with Streamlit

Develop and Deploy Secure and Scalable Web Applications to the Cloud Using a Pure Python Framework

Mohammad Khorasani
Mohamed Abdou
Javier Hernández Fernández

Apress®

Web Application Development with Streamlit: Develop and Deploy Secure and Scalable Web Applications to the Cloud Using a Pure Python Framework

Mohammad Khorasani
Doha, Qatar

Mohamed Abdou
Cambridge, United Kingdom

Javier Hernández Fernández
Doha, Qatar

ISBN-13 (pbk): 978-1-4842-8110-9   ISBN-13 (electronic): 978-1-4842-8111-6
https://doi.org/10.1007/978-1-4842-8111-6

Managing Director, Apress Media LLC: Welmoed Spahr
Acquisitions Editor: James Robinson-Prior
Development Editor: James Markham
Coordinating Editor: Jessica Vakili

Distributed to the book trade worldwide by Springer Science+Business Media New York, 233 Spring Street, 6th Floor, New York, NY 10013. Phone 1-800-SPRINGER, fax (201) 348-4505, e-mail orders-ny@springer-sbm.com, or visit www.springeronline.com. Apress Media, LLC is a California LLC and the sole member (owner) is Springer Science + Business Media Finance Inc (SSBM Finance Inc). SSBM Finance Inc is a **Delaware** corporation.

For information on translations, please e-mail booktranslations@springernature.com; for reprint, paperback, or audio rights, please e-mail bookpermissions@springernature.com.

Apress titles may be purchased in bulk for academic, corporate, or promotional use. eBook versions and licenses are also available for most titles. For more information, reference our Print and eBook Bulk Sales web page at http://www.apress.com/bulk-sales.

Any source code or other supplementary material referenced by the author in this book is available to readers on the Github repository: https://github.com/Apress/Web-Application-Development-with-Streamlit. For more detailed information, please visit http://www.apress.com/source-code.

Printed on acid-free paper

*To my parents Yeganeh and Daryoush and to
my departed grandparents Ghamar and Reza.*

—Mohammad Khorasani

To my family, friends, and the open source community.

—Mohamed Abdou

To my family and friends for their support.

—Javier Hernández Fernández

Table of Contents

About the Authors

Mohammad Khorasani is a hybrid of an engineer and a computer scientist with a Bachelor of Science in Mechanical Engineering from Texas A&M University and a master's degree in Computer Science from the University of Illinois at Urbana-Champaign. Mohammad specializes in developing and implementing software solutions for the advancement of renewable energy systems and services at Iberdrola. In addition, he develops robotic devices using embedded systems and rapid prototyping technologies. He is also an avid blogger of STEM-related topics on Towards Data Science – a Medium publication.

linkedin.com/in/mkhorasani/

Mohamed Abdou is a software engineer with diverse academic and industrial exposure, a graduate of Computer Engineering from Qatar University, and currently an Software Development Engineer at Amazon. Mohamed has built a variety of open source tools used by tens of thousands in the Streamlit community. He led the first Google Developer Student Club in Qatar and represented Qatar University in national and international programming contests. He is a cyber security enthusiast and was ranked second nationwide in bug bounty hunting in Qatar in 2020 among under 25-year-olds.

linkedin.com/in/mohamed-ashraf-abdou/

ABOUT THE AUTHORS

 **Javier Hernández Fernández** specializes in the area of technology innovation and brings over 20 years of practical experience in overseeing the design and delivery of technological developments on behalf of multinational companies in the fields of IT, telecom, and utilities. He publishes extensively, speaks at conferences around the world, and spends his days wading through piles of academic papers in the hope of finding something interesting. He holds master's degrees in both Energy Management and Project Management, in addition to a BSc in Computer Science from the Faculty of Engineering of the University of Ottawa.

linkedin.com/in/javier-hernandezf/

About the Technical Reviewers

Rosario Moscato has a master's degree in Electronic Engineering (Federico II University, Naples) as well as a master's degree in Internet Software Design (CEFRIEL, Milan). He also has a Diploma in Apologetics (Pontifical Athenaeum Regina Apostolorum, Rome) and a master's degree in Science and Faith (Pontifical Athenaeum Regina Apostolorum, Rome). Rosario has gained over 20 years of experience, always focusing his attention on the development and fine-tuning of the most innovative technologies in various international companies in Europe and Asia, covering various highly technical, commercial, and business development roles.

In recent years, his interest has focused exclusively on artificial intelligence and data science, pursuing, on one hand, the goal of enhancing and making every business extremely competitive by introducing and supporting machine and deep learning technologies and on the other hand, analyzing the ethical-philosophical implications deriving from the new scenarios that these disciplines open up.

Rosario has authored two books, and he is a speaker at international research centers and conferences as well as a trainer and technical/scientific consultant on the huge and changing world of AI.

Currently, he is working as Senior Data Scientist with one of the biggest multinational IT companies in the world.

Randy Zwitch is a data science and analytics professional with broad industry experience in big data and data science. He is also an open source contributor in the R, Python, and Julia programming language communities.

Acknowledgments

This undertaking would not have been possible without the support and efforts of a selfless few. Individuals and entities who in one way or another have made a contribution to the contents of this book are named as follows in no particular order:

- *Streamlit*: The folks who created the framework itself, empowering countless developers

- *Iberdrola*: Which provided the inspiration and time for us to put Streamlit to a very noble use

- *Iberdrola Innovation Middle East*: The folks who served as a test bed for our very first Streamlit ventures and had to put up with our constant pitching of Streamlit's formidability

- *Qatar Science & Technology Park*: Which has fostered an environment conducive to innovation and research

- *Daniel Paredes, Jerome Dumont, Ana Martos, and Gustavo López-Luzzatti*: For being our very first Streamlit users

- *Dr. Nikhil Navkar*: For being another trailblazing Streamlit user

In addition, a tangible part of our careers and personal endeavors would have simply been inconceivable without the spirit of the open source community. It is therefore in order to give a special tribute to Python and its respective developers, in addition to the multitude of other online forums who are silent heroes. Without their efforts, all-nighters would be every other night and our works not nearly as neat as they are.

Preface

It was an inconspicuous night like any other. I was about to doze off, but right before that happened, my phone buzzed, and being a millennial, I just could not resist the temptation to check. However, much to my disdain, it was just another pesky email advertisement recommending an online course in something called "Streamlit." I am a strong disbeliever in email lists, and, honestly, I would have investigated no further had it not been for the aesthetically pleasing Streamlit logo. In retrospect, I am glad I clicked on the ad. Since then, my programming life has one way or another been intertwined with a framework that I had been yearning for someone to create for years – the formidable Streamlit.

I noticed early on in my career that there is a plethora of seasoned Python developers that are adept with backend and server-side programming but cannot develop frontend user interfaces and client-side software to save their lives, myself included. While there were noble efforts made by the teams in Flask and Django, both frameworks solicit an abundance of exposure and technical know-how of HTML, CSS, and HTTP, which effectively rendered them as no-fly zones. I found myself making do with the likes of Tkinter and PyQt, thereby limiting myself to local desktop software with no means of deploying my work to the cloud. This is the predicament that I and a multitude of other programmers faced. What all of us Python loyalists needed was a pure Python web framework with an intuitive API that enabled the prompt creation and deployment of web applications while allowing the developer to focus on the backend. Similar perhaps to what ReactJS is to JavaScript. And when I clicked on that pesky ad mentioned earlier, that is exactly what I found. It was a sort of eureka moment!

Mind you, this anecdote of mine occurred in the summer of 2020, and Streamlit had only been released to the public in the fall of 2019. But less than a year of development by their team had rendered exactly the sort of framework and API that I had hoped for. And ever since then, this product has only been moving in one direction – upward, with a steep incline. For myself personally, I could not have discovered it at a more auspicious time. I had just been hired by Iberdrola and tasked with the audacious goal of creating and deploying a Python-based application to the Web. In a pre-Streamlit world, I would have fervently resisted the notion of deploying applications to the Web, but armed with my new friend, I found myself routinely advocating for the development of web applications while passionately brandishing Streamlit's untethering capabilities. Overnight, I had been transformed into a trailblazing member of sorts within our development team.

With all good things in the world, it just does not feel right to proceed without sharing the goodness with the world at large. Consequently, I have made it a subtle goal in life to inform the online and offline software development community of the empowerment that Streamlit ushers in. This book is the culmination of that effort, and more specifically it is intended for those who have faced the same hurdles as I have, and it will provide a holistic overview of Streamlit. This book will guide the reader through the life cycle of creating scalable web applications of their own, from the most basic use cases to crafting complex and distributed applications on the cloud.

In addition to learning all the ins and outs of Streamlit itself, after perusing this book, readers should be able to interface their web applications with robust server-side infrastructure like MongoDB, PostgreSQL, Linux, Windows Server, and Streamlit's own deployment platform. In a nutshell, you should be able to walk away from this book feeling empowered enough to unleash your ideas and to embody them on the Internet. Perhaps this could be the beginning of your next startup for the curious inner entrepreneur in you.

Mohammad Khorasani
September 2021

Acronyms

aaS As a service

API Application programming interface

BLOB Binary large object

CLI Command-line interface

CPU Central processing unit

CRUD Create, read, update, and delete

CSP Cloud service provider

CSRF Cross-site request forgery

CSS Cascading Style Sheet

DI Dependency injection, a coding pattern

DG Delta Generator, a core module in Streamlit

DOM Document Object Model

DTW Dynamic time warping

GPU Graphics processing unit

HTML Hypertext Markup Language

IDE Integrated development environment

ISP Internet service provider

JSON JavaScript Object Notation

JWT JSON Web Token

MLaaS Machine learning as a service

NAT Network address translation

ORM Object-relational model

OS Operating system

PID Process identifier

RCE Remote Code Execution

RDP Remote Desktop Protocol

REST Representational state transfer

SaaS Software as a service

SCADA Supervisory Control and Data Acquisition

SQL Structured query language

SQLI SQL injection

SSH Secure Shell

TPU Tensor processing unit

UI User interface

URI Uniform Resource Identifier

URL Uniform Resource Locator

UX User experience

VPN Virtual private network

XSS Cross-site scripting

Intended Audience

This book assumes that you have no less than a basic level of exposure and understanding in the following areas:

- Object-oriented programming

- Data structures and algorithms

- Python and the following bindings:

  - Pandas

  - Numpy

  - Plotly

- SQL (both relational and nonrelational databases)

- Git version control frameworks

- Cloud computing

In order to materialize on the concepts divulged in this book, it is imperative that you possess sufficient experience in programming. If you have little to no prior experience in the areas mentioned previously, then you should consider first enrolling in an online crash course of your choice that would offer at the least an introductory level of exposure. Other than that, by no means must you be an expert of any sort in the aforementioned concepts, although experts also stand to gain from the contents of this book. Even if you have the ability to develop applications with a more sophisticated stack, you may still appreciate the amount of time and energy that is saved by utilizing Streamlit. With Streamlit, you can render a robust web application in hours what would have previously taken you weeks to produce in Flask or Django. In simpler terms, it offers a lot more bang for the buck.

Notwithstanding, it is important to clarify that for those who are looking for a means to deliver highly bespoke and tailored frontend user interfaces, perhaps Streamlit is not what you should be scouting for. Not that it will not address your needs someday, it is just that "someday" is not today. Streamlit is a work in progress, and while their team perseveres relentlessly, we should remain patient and expect a greater degree of customizability alongside a multitude of additional features to be released in the near future. Should you need something more amenable, then you may find that Django is a more suitable option. Mind you, Django lands you back in the realm of the predicament mentioned earlier, as you will need to be a more advanced programmer to create web applications with it.

Hopefully upon completion of this book, you should be equipped with the tools that you will need to produce a scalable web application deployed to the cloud from inception to deployment and operation. You will become confident in addressing the functional and performance requirements of developing both server-side and client-side software. You will be able to create both backend functionality and frontend user interfaces. In addition, you will learn to interface your software with relational and nonrelational database systems such as PostgreSQL and MongoDB in order to scale your application on demand. And finally, you will acquire the technical know-how to orchestrate and provision your scalable application on the cloud using Microsoft Server, Linux containers, and Streamlit's own cloud service.

While this book will go into great depth and breadth of the required concepts, a degree of self-learning and research is still expected of any reader. There will be gaps in tutorials, and perhaps some of the tools used will be deprecated or obsolete by the time you are reading this book; therefore, a great deal of intuition and sound judgment is solicited. Furthermore, this book will not attempt to provide any explanation for the source code used by Streamlit or any other binding/API. Our scope will be solely limited to the application of the objects, classes, and functions included in each of the tools used. Each tutorial included will address a separate use case or application with the corresponding code provided. All original source codes published in this book are released under the MIT License and are open source. It is anticipated that you will utilize the whole or part of the methodology of the provided book to fulfill your own technical requirements.

Additional Material

This book is accompanied with an abundance of online material including repositories, datasets, libraries, APIs, and their corresponding documentation. Wherever necessary and possible, the URL to the material will be provided. All tutorials and source code included in this book will be available at the following repository: `https://github.com/`. Finally, any reference made to the Streamlit API can be additionally found on `https://docs.streamlit.io/library/api-reference`.

CHAPTER 1

Getting Started with Streamlit

With the inundation of data, and the pace at which it is created, traditional computing methods possess limited means to deliver results. On the other hand, cloud computing acts as an enabler, allowing one to overcome the limitations of the former. With increased scalability, reduced costs, and enhanced adaptability, cloud service providers, developers, and users alike stand to gain from the fruits of migrating to the cloud.

Given that Python is currently the scripting language of choice for most of the software development community, it is absolutely vital to provide a web framework for developers that would bridge their skills gap. While legacy frameworks such as Flask and Django solicit a firm understanding of HTML and CSS, Streamlit is the first major framework that is all pure Python, thereby reducing development time from weeks to hours.

1.1 Why Streamlit?

Limiting oneself to local computing options is simply a figment of the distant past, given that the cloud unlocks a host of advantages and allows developers to leave a tangibly greater impact on the world. It is for this very reason that an entire new echelon of developers are beginning to embrace everything cloud, and the rapid transition toward this new

© Mohammad Khorasani, Mohamed Abdou, Javier Hernández Fernández 2022
M. Khorasani et al., *Web Application Development with Streamlit*,
https://doi.org/10.1007/978-1-4842-8111-6_1

paradigm of computing is a testament to that fact. And this is exactly where a pure Python web framework such as Streamlit can deliver a lot of value to developers who want to make the transition but who need an enabler to do so.

1.1.1 Local vs. the Cloud

The cloud is rapidly becoming synonymous with data itself. Quite literally, wherever there is an abundance of data, it is somehow intertwined with cloud computing. Put into layman's terms, it is simply inconceivable to harness the value of big data without utilizing the resources of the cloud. Gone are the days where one would brandish Microsoft Excel to create a 1990s style dashboard for their dataset. With the sheer magnitude of data exposed to us, local computing will not make the cut.

Even still, there are certain tangible benefits to local computing, namely, prototyping an idea is considerably faster, and latency between nodes and servers is several orders of magnitude smaller. This is why edge computing still holds an "edge" over the cloud, no pun intended. In addition, there are applications for which security is sacrosanct and/ or regulations are inhibiting, and in that case, one may be better off disconnecting themselves from the world at large. Other than that, there is not much else that one can attribute to the list of benefits of local computing. However, there is a plethora of reasons why you should steer clear of it. To name a few, the bottom line will be quite lower with the overheads solicited to run the infrastructure at hand. There will also be very limited adaptability to fluctuating traffic; imagine the half-time surge in traffic during the Super Bowl, you simply will not be able to scale to meet demand.

On the other hand, cloud computing is cheaper to provision, exceedingly adaptable to demand, highly robust against failure, and supremely reliable to run. In addition, cloud computing platforms enable scalability in two dimensions – horizontal and vertical. Horizontal for when you need multiple instances of the same computing resources and vertical for when you need bespoke resources, the likes of GPUs, TPUs, database systems, and more. Perhaps, the single most salient factor about the cloud is that it expands your horizons and allows you to offer your product as a service on the World Wide Web. The latest paradigm shift in tech is to offer quite literally anything as a service. The as-a-service model (aaS) can be applied to software (SaaS), machine learning (MLaaS), and any other product that can be offered as a web application on the Internet. And this is precisely where a web framework such as Streamlit fits the bill. Streamlit is a cloud enabler for those of us in the software development community that have been unable to deploy our value to the Internet due to a hefty skills gap that has thus far impeded us from doing so. Concisely put, Streamlit is a means of empowerment for developers at all levels.

1.1.2 A Trend Toward Cloud Computing

Cloud computing is north, south, east, and west. Academia, the corporate world, governments, and even spy agencies are shifting from local to the cloud at a breathtaking pace. With legacy software providing limited means for growth and return on investments, organizations are increasingly migrating to cloud service providers who in turn offer agility, economies-of-scale, and advanced computing resources. Even CSPs themselves are jumping on the bandwagon, with the likes of Google and Microsoft offering their legacy applications on the cloud with Google G Suite and Microsoft Office 365.

Evidently, from a business perspective, the justification is even more so robust. Disruptive businesses are as pervasive as they have ever been and have wholly championed what others had so far been reluctant to accept. Therefore, embracing the cloud is no longer a subjective decision but rather a means for survival. With reduced lead time, scalability, limited capital investments, and increased innovation, businesses stand to gain a great deal. From a CSP perspective, this proposition is possibly even

3

more enticing. Equipped with the cloud, CSPs are able to pool resources together, increase resource elasticity, and reduce maintenance and overheads. And perhaps most importantly, from a consumer's point of view, the cloud is the best thing that ever happened since the Internet itself. As a consumer, the SaaS model offers unparalleled flexibility, price granularity, and plenty more bang for the buck. In other words, the cloud is win-win-win; everyone stands to gain.

While the trend toward cloud computing was already on a healthy trajectory, a once-in-a-century pandemic doubled as a booster toward everything cloud. The pandemic all but destroyed the stigma associated with remote learning, online examinations, working from home, and other dogma that decades of noble efforts by the tech community had failed to make a dent into. It is fair to assume that from here onward, the progression toward everything cloud will exceed the prediction of pundits. And if numbers alone can serve to indicate where we are heading, then one should feast themselves on the omen of Figure 1-1.

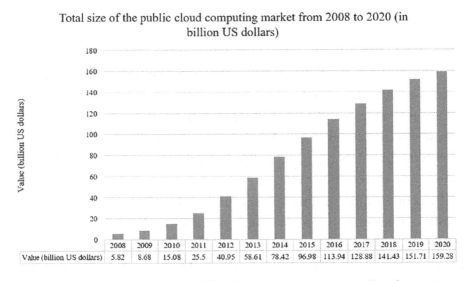

Figure 1-1. *Growth of the public cloud computing market from 2008 to 2020. Source: statista.com [13]*

1.1.3 History of Web Frameworks in Python

Web development can be quite an arduous task, soliciting a multidisciplinary team with expertise in frontend, backend, and server-side software development. It is for this very reason that full-stack developers who brandish the know-how for the entire development process are in surplus demand and are often in receipt of a handsome compensation.

Traditionally, these developers would resort to using JavaScript, PHP, or Perl to develop web applications, with Python being sidelined as a local scripting language. This was due to the fact that Python is not inherently designed to run on the Internet and requires a web framework to interface with web servers and browsers. Over the years however, the community has developed several novel frameworks that allow Python to be utilized effectively for the Internet. And given Python's emphasis on simplicity, readability, rich ecosystem of libraries, and being open source, it has steadily transformed into one of the main web scripting languages of choice for many developers. Python has even gained enough traction to being adopted by heavyweights, the likes of Google and Instagram.

Generally, such web frameworks come in two types, full-stack and nonfull-stack. They manage everything from communications and infrastructure to other lower-level abstractions required by web applications. Nontrivial applications require a slew of functionalities including but not limited to interpreting requests, producing responses, storing data, and rendering user interfaces. For such applications, one would often utilize a full-stack framework that provides an in-house solution for all the technical requirements. This contrasts with nonfull-stack frameworks otherwise known as microframeworks that provide a bare minimum level of functionality, typically limited to routing HTTP requests to the relevant controllers, dispatching the controller, and subsequently returning a response. Such frameworks are usually stacked with other APIs and tools in order to create applications. Some of the most popular examples of each type are listed in the following sections.

1.1.4 Flask

Flask was developed in 2010 by Armin Ronacher from what was allegedly an April fool's joke to begin with. Flask is a nonfull-stack or microframework that provisions an application server without offering much else in terms of components. Flask is composed of two main elements: *Werkzeug*, a tool that lends support for HTTP routing, and *Jinja*, a template engine used to render basic HTML pages. In addition, Flask uses *MarkupSafe* as a string handling library and *ItsDangerous* as a secure data serialization library to store session data as cookies.

Flask is a minimalistic framework that is equipped with the bare minimum of the components required to render a web application. Consequently, the developer is afforded a great deal of autonomy and also responsibility to create their own application. As a result, Flask is best suited for static websites and for experienced developers who are able to provision most of their own infrastructure and render their own interfaces.

1.1.5 Django

Django was developed by a group of web programmers in 2003 who used Python to build web applications. It allows developers to create complex applications with relatively less overhead in comparison to Flask. Specifically, Django enables programmers to render dynamic content with enhanced scalability and with in-house capabilities to interface with database systems using object-relational mapping.

In addition, there are a host of other modules including but not limited to ecommerce, authentication, and caching packages that allow the developer to readily provision extended services. Bundled with a multitude of other third-party packages, Django allows the developer to focus mainly on the idea while not having to worry much about the implementation.

1.1.6 Dash

Dash is a web framework developed by Plotly to render enterprise-grade web applications in Python, R, and even Julia. Given that Plotly predominantly develops data analytics and visualization tools, similarly Dash is more often used to create dashboards. Even still, it is indeed possible to create a host of general-purpose applications with due to its extended customizability.

Dash has the ability to natively support D3.js charts and provides default HTML and CSS templates to use. However, for more tailored interfaces, developers must be well versed with frontend programming themselves. Furthermore, Dash tenders an enterprise package that enables experienced developers to deploy their applications on the cloud with production-grade capabilities such as authentication and database systems.

1.1.7 Web2Py

Web2Py is a full-stack web framework for Python which like Django makes use of the model view controller architectural paradigm. It allows developers to create primitive yet dynamic content with relative ease and interfaces natively with database systems. The novelty of this framework as opposed to others is that it comes with its own web-based integrated development environment equipped with a ticketing system for error tracking and management.

The main disadvantage however is that Web2Py executes objects and controllers via a single global environment that is initiated at each HTTP request. While this has its benefits, it does also carry the pitfalls of experiencing compromised performance and incompatibility issues with certain modules.

7

1.1.8 The Need for a Pure Python Web Framework

Previously, the community of Python developers would have to suffice with deploying their software locally as desktop applications unless they commanded adept knowledge of HTML, CSS, and JavaScript. With Tkinter and PyQt, programmers can indeed produce complex, dynamic, and aesthetically pleasing interfaces, albeit with the heartbreak of not being able to render it on the Web. And this has largely been the predicament of many Python loyalists, who, up until recently, had no pure Pythonic way of migrating to the cloud.

It was always quite demeaning to peruse through repository after repository of awesome applications developed by people who had no other way of exposing their goodness to the world than sharing the source code with others hoping that they would be able to replicate it locally. Oh, and forget about the nontechnical users who had no hope whatsoever of executing even as much as that. Countless noble efforts were left largely unutilized in vain as a result. In other words, the community was in desperate need of a major framework that would solicit no additional expertise other than the knowledge of writing your average Python script and being able to deploy it instantly to a cloud server. Then came along Streamlit and freed developers from the shackles of HTML, CSS, and JavaScript. The rest will be history.

1.1.9 Academic Significance

Being able to create web apps directly from Python easily has made Streamlit a valuable tool for academia [1]. Despite its recent creation, the first beta release is dated April 2019; research teams worldwide have started adopting the framework to showcase the outcomes of their projects. Today, many publications already mention Streamlit as their visualization framework covering a wide range of fields. Some of these areas include health [2, 3, 4, 5], computer science [6, 7, 8, 9], economics [11, 10], and civil engineering [12], to mention a few.

1.2 Firing It Up

Being the highly versatile and accommodating framework that it is, Streamlit allows the developer to utilize it with a variety of computing resources and technical stack. Even still, there are some recommended best practices to follow for greater ease and usability.

1.2.1 Technical Requirements

While there is no one-size-fits-all solution when it comes to running Streamlit, the following computing and system requirements or greater are recommended for developing and running applications smoothly.

Table 1-1. *Hardware requirements*

CPU	RAM	Storage	Internet/Network access
2 x 64-bit 2.8 GHz	4 GB 1600 MHz DDR3	120 GB	1 Mbps

Table 1-2. *System requirements*

Operating System	Database
Ubuntu 16.04 to 17.10	PostgreSQL 9.6 or higher
Windows 7 to 11	pgAdmin v4.0 or higher
Mac OS X 10.11 or higher	
Linux: RHEL 6/7	

Table 1-3. *Software requirements*

Streamlit	Anaconda
1.9 or higher	With Python 3.8 or higher

Table 1-4. *Network requirements*

Inbound Ports	Outbound Ports
HTTP: TCP 8080, 8443	HTTPS: TCP 443
SSH: TCP 22	SMTP: TCP 25
	LDAP(s): TCP 389/636

1.2.2 Environment Installation with Anaconda

In order to create a web application run on a local Streamlit server for prototyping and testing, we first need to install and create a Python runtime environment with all the dependencies required for our server. In this regard, we will be making use of Anaconda which is one of the most widely used and supported Python distributions available. First, proceed with downloading and installing a compatible version of Anaconda. Once the installation has been successfully completed, you may then create a virtual environment that will be used to download and install the packages necessary to run your web application.

Programmatic Installation

To create an Anaconda environment through the console, please follow these steps:

1. To create and install your environment programmatically, enter the following commands in Anaconda Prompt sequentially:

    ```
    conda create -n <environment name>
    python=<version number>
    ```

    When conda asks you to proceed, select *y*.

    ```
    proceed ([y]/n)?
    ```

Subsequently, the new environment will be created in the environments folder within the root directory of Anaconda as *C:/ProgramData/Anaconda3/envs/*.

2. Activate your environment by typing the following:

```
conda activate <environment name>
```

3. If you have a list of dependencies, *dependencies. yml*, place it in your newly created environment's directory: `C:/ProgramData/Anaconda3/envs/ environment name/`

4. Change your root directory to your environment's directory by typing the following:

```
cd C:/ProgramData/Anaconda3/envs/<environment name>/
```

5. Ensure that the first line in the *dependencies.yml* is written correctly as the name of your environment, *name: environment name*; otherwise, the environment may not be installed.

6. Update your environment by installing all the dependencies listed in the file *dependencies.yml* by typing the following:

```
conda env update -f dependencies.yml
```

7. If prompted by Anaconda, proceed with updating your version of conda by typing the following:

```
conda update -n base -c defaults conda
```

8. To check the list of environments, type the following:

```
conda info -envs
```

9. To check the list of dependencies in your environment, type the following:

```
conda list
```

10. To install additional dependencies that may be required later, please type the following:

```
conda install <dependency name>
```

11. Some dependencies may not be available for download via *conda install*; in this case, download pip and subsequently use pip install as shown in the following:

```
conda install pip
pip install <dependency name>
```

12. To deactivate your environment, you may type the following:

```
conda deactivate
```

Graphical Installation

Alternatively, you may use Anaconda Navigator to create and maintain your environments as follows:

1. Launch Anaconda Navigator.

2. Click the *Environments* tab.

Figure 1-2. *Opening the Environments tab in Anaconda*

3. Click the *Create* button and enter the desired name
    and Python version for your environment.

Figure 1-3. *Creating an environment in Anaconda*

4. Next, follow steps 2–12 in the previous section to
    install the dependencies. Subsequently, as shown
    in Figure 1-4, the *test_environment* environment
    will appear activated with all the required packages
    installed.

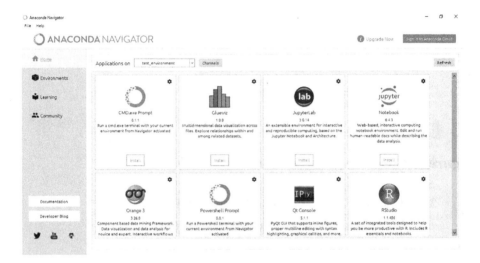

Figure 1-4. *Newly created environment in Anaconda*

5. Finally, you will be able to launch any of the
    available code editors in Anaconda within your
    newly created environment in the *Home* tab.

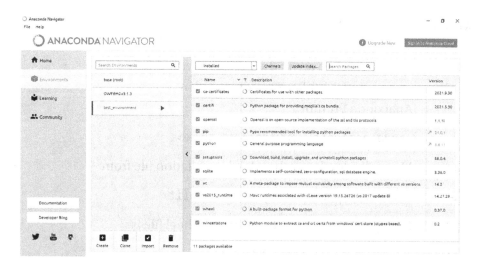

Figure 1-5. *Selection of code editors in Anaconda*

1.2.3 Downloading and Installing Streamlit

There are multiple ways to download and install the Streamlit library for use, and in this section, we will cover one of the most commonly used types of installation.

Direct pip Installation

1. To download and install Streamlit, first ensure that you are in the correct environment by entering the following command in Anaconda Prompt:

   ```
   conda activate <environment name>
   ```

2. Subsequently, you may download and install Streamlit by entering the following command:

   ```
   pip install streamlit
   ```

Manual Wheel File Installation

1. Ensure that you are in the correct environment by entering the following command in Anaconda Prompt:

    ```
    conda activate <environment name>
    ```

2. Manually download the wheel installation file from

    https://pypi.org/project/streamlit/

3. Change the directory to where the wheel file is located:

    cd `C:/Users/.../`

4. Subsequently install the downloaded wheel file by entering the following command:

    ```
    pip install streamlit-1.0.0-py2.py3-none-any.whl
    ```

If the installation has been successful, you may proceed with creating your script. For good measure, restart Anaconda before you do so.

Importing Streamlit

To import Streamlit into your Python script, ensure that the following line precedes the rest of your code:

```
import streamlit as st
```

Subsequently, any Streamlit method can be invoked by appending **st** to it as follows:

```
st.write('Hello world')
```

1.2.4 **Streamlit Console Commands**

When Streamlit is installed, the Streamlit command-line (CLI) tool is also installed. The command line can help you run, operate, and diagnose issues related to your Streamlit application.

To get additional help, enter the following command:

```
streamlit --help
```

To run your application, ensure that you have changed the directory to where your script is located:

```
cd C:/Users/.../script directory/
```

Then enter the following to run your script:

```
streamlit run <script.py> [--script args]
```

Subsequently, your application's local URL and network URL will be displayed. Simultaneously, your application will automatically appear on your default web browser. You may use the local URL to connect to your application locally and the network URL to connect on any other device over the local area network.

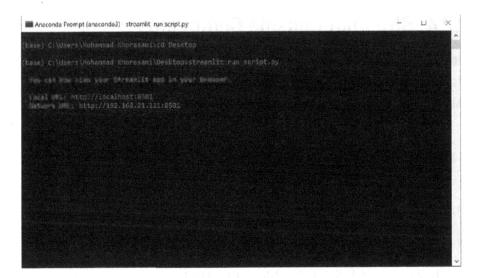

Figure 1-6. *Console while running the Streamlit application*

To clear the cache, enter the following command:

```
streamlit cache clear
```

To open Streamlit's documentation on a web browser, enter the following command:

```
streamlit docs
```

To display Streamlit's version, enter the following command:

```
streamlit --version
```

Configuring Streamlit Through the Console

You may pass config options to *streamlit run* to configure options such as the port the application is being run on, disable run-on-save, and others.

For an exhaustive list of configuration options, enter the following command:

```
streamlit run --help
```

You can view the list of configured options by entering the following command:

```
streamlit config show
```

You may configure these options using one of the four following methods:

1. Using a global config file at *.streamlit/config.toml*:

    ```
    [server]
    port = 80
    ```

2. Using a config file for each project in your project's directory: *C:/Users/.../.streamlit/config.toml*.

3. Using *STREAMLIT_** environment variables as shown in the following:

    ```
    export STREAMLIT_SERVER_PORT=80
    ```

4. Using flags in the command line when running your script as shown in the following:

    ```
    streamlit run <script.py> --server.port 80
    ```

1.2.5 Running Demo Apps

To run Streamlit's demo applications, enter the following command:

```
streamlit hello
```

Subsequently, the following application will be displayed on your default web browser. You may use the menu on the sidebar to visit the four following demo applications.

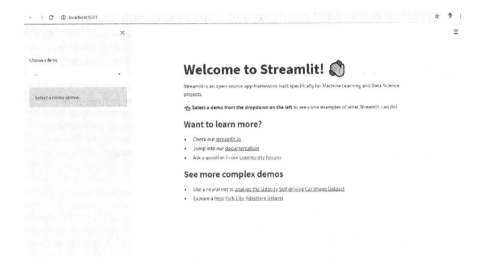

Figure 1-7. *Streamlit demo application home page*

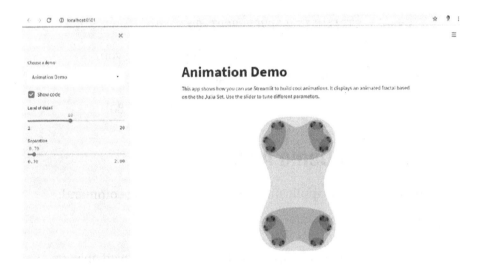

Figure 1-8. *Streamlit animation demo application*

1.2.6 Writing and Testing Code with PyCharm

Generally speaking, code expands over time, whether by making new modules in the original code base or integrating it with third-party services. As a step toward making sure the code performs flawlessly, testing can be utilized. Code testing can be broken down to two methods: unit testing and integration testing, where both can be used to test independent modules and the whole system end to end, respectively. For the sake of this example, we will cover unit tests, but the same concept can be applied to the other option. Either way, we need to give inputs and compare expected outputs against actual ones. For a simple Streamlit application which enables the user to calculate the sum of any two numbers, we can test two main parts, one being if the web application is rendered according to our expectations and the other to verify the summation logic is correct. These are two different unit tests to do, but the first is a common thing to do when developing any frontend work. Listing 1-1 is the sample application we are trying to test in this example with output of Figure 1-12 when ran with Streamlit. Listing 1-2 tests both rendering and summation logic of the mentioned example.

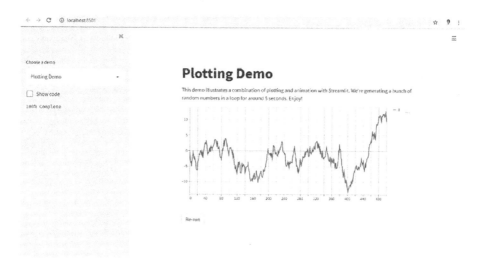

Figure 1-9. *Streamlit plotting demo application*

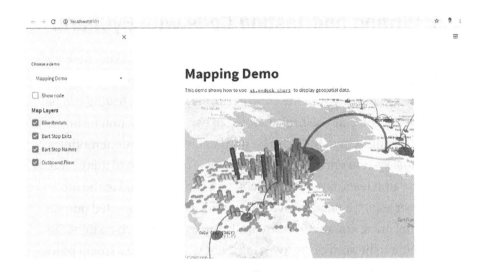

Figure 1-10. *Streamlit mapping demo application*

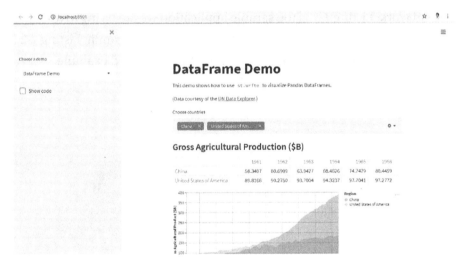

Figure 1-11. *Streamlit dataframe demo application*

Listing 1-1. main.py

```python
import streamlit as st

def calculate_sum(n1, n2):
    return n1 + n2

st.title("Add numbers")

n1 = st.number_input("First Number")
n2 = st.number_input("Second Number")

if st.button("Calculate"):
    st.write("Summation is: " + str(calculate_sum(n1, n2)))
```

Listing 1-2. Unit_test.py

```python
from main import calculate_sum
from selenium import webdriver
from selenium.webdriver.chrome.options import Options
import time

def test_user_interface():
    # Path to chromedriver. Can end with .sh if on (Li/U)nix
    environments
    driver_path = r"----------\chromedriver.exe"
    options = Options()
    options.add_argument("--headless") # To not open a real
                                         chrome window
    with webdriver.Chrome(driver_path, chrome_options=options)
    as driver:
        url = "http://127.0.0.1:8501"
        driver.get(url)
        time.sleep(5)
        html = driver.page_source
```

```python
    assert "Add numbers" in html
    assert "First Number" in html
    assert "Second Number" in html

def test_logic():
    assert calculate_sum(1, 1) == 2
    assert calculate_sum(1, -1) == 0
    assert calculate_sum(1, 9) == 10

if __name__ == "__main__":
    test_logic()
    test_user_interface()
```

Figure 1-12. *Output of Listing 1-1*

To test rendering, we first need the application to be running, so it can be accessed by selenium's driver, which is Chrome in this example. To automate launching the application before running the tests, we might need to use an advanced IDE. PyCharm can do the required job for us.

First, we need to set up a running configuration to run Streamlit on a button click as seen in Figure 1-13. Now as we have a configuration used to run Streamlit, we can use it as a prerun command in another configuration which shall be used for running the unit tests (Figure 1-14).

1.3 How Streamlit Works

Unlike other web frameworks which send static files to the browser, Streamlit modifies the real DOM and its state to render the final web document from the server side. There shall be no security concerns under normal user behavior. Like PHP, this can be RCE (Remote Code Execution) susceptible, if it was poorly coded, where user input is not sanitized where it can be used to execute OS-level code.

Having a Streamlit web application starts from executing the binary, whether *streamlit.exe* on Windows or *stream-lit.sh* on MacOS or Linux, against the target document using the default Python interpreter. This will initialize the application configuration such as secrets, settings, themes, and, most importantly, the Delta Generator (DG for short) which acts as the middleman between the Python script and the ReactJS web application served by Streamlit.

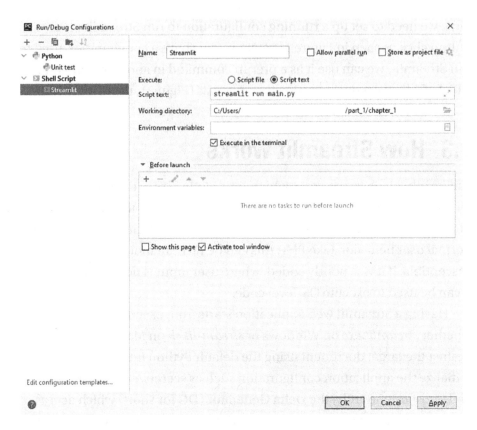

Figure 1-13. *Making a shell command to run once the current configuration is chosen and ran*

1.3.1 The Streamlit Architecture

The DG takes care of efficiently transferring HTML components to be rendered on the client side and retrieving back their state. The initial render starts from the beginning of the Python document and ends at the last line. The next render does not start from the beginning of the file executed, but from the component which had been interacted with by the user or changed state; this will be covered in detail in later chapters. Every new render of a component will be queued in the DG, which will later be replaced with a new HTML snippet or be newly placed between other rendered HTML components on the final DOM.

Streamlit components are queued and rendered individually to avoid negatively affecting the user's experience with a blank page if renders take too long. Such delays can occur from an extensive ongoing computation, waiting for API responses, or even sleep functions, as shown in Listing 1-3.

Listing 1-3. Code snippet to display random text with a delay within the execution

```python
import streamlit as st
import time

# User sees this first
st.title("My Title")

time.sleep(2)
```

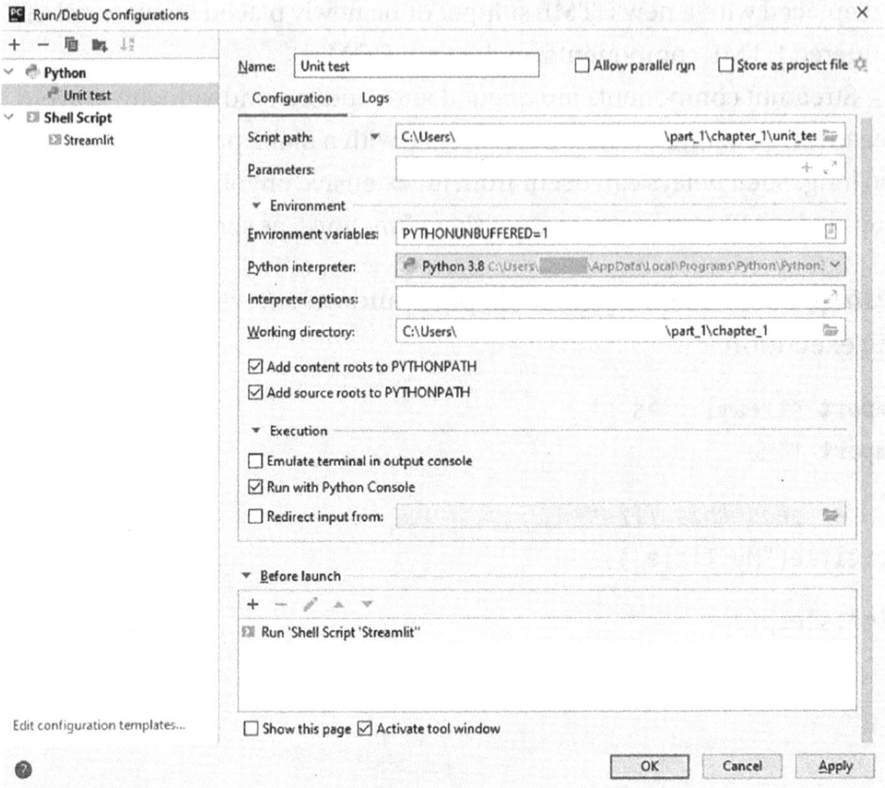

Figure 1-14. *Choosing a Python interpreter to run the unit test file but after running the configuration in Figure 1-13*

```
# User sees this second after 2 seconds
st.write("My *markdown* text in **Streamlit**")
```

The end user will notice the page updates to include the **st.write** message within two seconds to what seems like a fully loaded page.

1.3.2 ReactJS in Streamlit

For simplicity purposes, we kept mentioning that Streamlit inserts HTML onto the clients' browser. But in reality, it uses ReactJS's virtual DOM to insert elements and manage their state. This can be verified by using Chrome's "React Developer Tools" extension as shown in Figure 1-17.

Knowing this fact and Streamlit's source code, we can conclude that Streamlit uses built-in ReactJS components grouped to make a fully fledged JavaScript web application with Python! In addition to that, we can leverage Streamlit's generic treatment of components to build custom and complex ones that are not provided out of the box in later chapters.

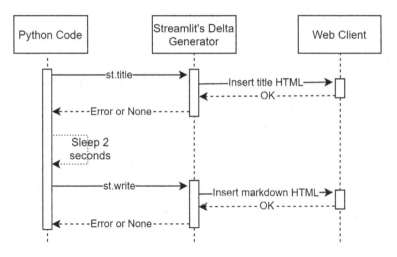

Figure 1-15. *End-to-end execution sequence for Listing 1-3*

My Title

My *markdown* text in **Streamlit**

Figure 1-16. *Streamlit output for Listing 1-3*

Figure 1-17. Streamlit output for Listing 1-3

1.4 Summary

A tangible part of this chapter covered the trend toward cloud computing and the advantages that it provides to developers, users, and cloud service providers alike. In addition, we listed the four most commonly used web frameworks for Python, including one microframework – Flask – and three full-stack frameworks, Django, Dash, and Web2Py. Subsequently, Streamlit was introduced as a pure Python framework, and we learned how this poses a competitive advantage over its competitors as it bridges the skills gap and reduces development time from weeks to hours. The reader was then acquainted with installing and utilizing Streamlit to render basic applications on demand. In the next chapter, we will cover the basic building blocks of Streamlit, offer an exhaustive overview of its application programming interface, and show how it can be employed to produce our own customized applications.

CHAPTER 2

Streamlit Basics

Streamlit has made it thoroughly simple to create interfaces, display text, visualize data, render widgets, and manage a web application from inception to deployment with its convenient and highly intuitive application programming interface showcased in the Appendix. With the techniques covered in this chapter, one will learn how to create input forms, implement conditional flow, manage errors, mutate dataframes, and render basic charts. And upon completion of Streamlit basics, a developer should be able to produce, manage, and control a variety of trivial web applications and to deploy them locally. Such applications include but are not limited to data explorer, machine learning, multimedia, data wrangling, and other general-purpose applications. Once the developer has mastered the basics of Streamlit, they may then begin to develop more advanced and nontrivial applications that will be addressed in subsequent chapters.

2.1 Creating a Basic Application

Putting Streamlit's mighty API to use, we can render a variety of applications. From the simplest use cases catering to microservices to complex applications with distributed systems, Streamlit enables us to accommodate to our users' diverse set of requirements. To begin with however, we will peruse the more trivial types of applications in this section before proceeding to more complex ones in subsequent sections.

© Mohammad Khorasani, Mohamed Abdou, Javier Hernández Fernández 2022
M. Khorasani et al., *Web Application Development with Streamlit*,
https://doi.org/10.1007/978-1-4842-8111-6_2

2.1.1 Generating User Input Forms

Creating forms in Streamlit can be as simple as bundling several text, number, and other input widgets together on a page coupled with a button that triggers an action such as recording the entries on a database or saving it to the session state. The caveat with this approach is that each time the user interacts with any of the widgets, Streamlit will automatically rerun the entire script from top to bottom. While this approach provides the developer with a logical and seamless flow to their program, it may sometimes be useful to bundle input widgets together and have Streamlit rerun the script only when prompted by the user. This can be done using the *st.form* command.

Listing 2-1. input_form.py

```python
import streamlit as st

with st.form('feedback_form'):
    st.header('Feedback form')

    # Creating columns to organize the form
    col1, col2 = st.columns(2)
    with col1:
        name = st.text_input('Please enter your name')
        rating = st.slider('Please rate this app',0,10,5)
    with col2:
        dob = st.date_input('Please enter your date of birth')
        recommend = st.radio('Would you recommend this app to
        others?',('Yes','No'))

    submit_button = st.form_submit_button('Submit')

if submit_button:
    st.write('**Name:**', name, '**Date of birth:**', dob,
    '**Rating:**', rating,'**Would recommend?:**', recommend)
```

A Streamlit form can be called within a *with* statement and using the *st.form* command. In Listing 2-1, we initially create columns with the *st. columns* command to organize the widgets within our form into two columns of equal width. In the first column, we place a text input and slider widget using the *st.text_input* and *rating* commands, respectively, and in the second column, we place a date input and radio button widget using the *st.date_input* and *st.radio* commands.

Subsequently, within the same *with* statement, we add a form submit button using the *st.form_submit_button* command. When this button is clicked, it will submit the entries of all the widgets collectively at once regardless of how many items are included in the form. It is important to note that *st.form_submit_button* is not the same as *st.button*, and without a form submit button, Streamlit will throw an error.

As shown in Figure 2-1, all of the widgets will be bundled together in one form with the *st.form* command. Once the form submit button is clicked, all of the entries will be processed collectively at once and the output processed as shown in Figure 2-2.

Figure 2-1. *Streamlit input form (output of Listing 2-1)*

Figure 2-2. *Instantiated Streamlit input form (output of Listing 2-1)*

2.1.2 Introducing Conditional Flow

It may be necessary to introduce conditional flow to your Streamlit applications whereby certain actions will be dependent on prior actions or on the state of widgets. This is especially useful for prompting the user to correctly fill in forms and/or use the application correctly. Without implementing conditional flow, your application will be prone to throwing errors should the user make incorrect use of it.

Example 1

Listing 2-2. conditional_flow_1.py

```python
import streamlit as st

def display_name(name):
    st.info(f'**Name:** {name}')

name = st.text_input('Please enter your name')
```

```
if not name:
    st.error('No name entered')

if name:
    display_name(name)
```

In Listing 2-2, to ensure the user has entered an input into the name field, we are using an *if* statement to check whether this field is not empty. If it is empty, the user will be prompted with an error message (Figure 2-3), and if it is not empty, a function will be invoked to display the entry (Figure 2-4).

Example 2

Listing 2-3. conditional_flow_2.py

```
import streamlit as st

def display_name(name):
    st.info(f'**Name:** {name}')

name = st.text_input('Please enter your name')

if not name:
    st.error('No name entered')
    st.stop()

display_name(name)
```

In Listing 2-3, similarly we are using an *if* statement to check whether the name field is not empty. The only difference here is that we are utilizing the *st.stop* command to stop the execution of the script if the name field is empty. And if it is not empty, we are proceeding with the rest of the script that displays the entered name. The benefit of this method is that it eliminates the need for an additional if statement and simplifies your script; otherwise, in terms of utility, both examples are identical.

Please enter your name

No name entered

Figure 2-3. *Implementing conditional flow (output of Listing 2-2)*

Conditional flow programming can be applied to both trivial and nontrivial applications. Indeed, this technique can be scaled and implemented with nested if statements, while loops, and other methods if required.

Please enter your name

John Smith

Name: John Smith

Figure 2-4. *Implementing conditional flow continued (output of Listing 2-2)*

2.1.3 Managing and Debugging Errors

If you are running Streamlit in development mode and have configured *showErrorDetails = True* as shown in Table 3-1 in Section 3.1, then Streamlit will natively display runtime exceptions on the web page similar to how any other IDE would display such messages on the console. This is far from ideal as the user will not be able to make much sense of it and will be left confused. More importantly, leaving exceptions mismanaged can trigger a chain of fatal errors in subsequent parts of your code that can have a cascading effect on other systems. In addition, Streamlit will display the errorsome segment of your code that is causing the exception to the user, which may infringe on intellectual property rights, should your source code be subject to such restrictions.

Listing 2-4. without_try_and_except.py

```
import streamlit as st

col1, col2 = st.columns(2)

with col1:
    number_1 = st.number_input('Please enter the first
    number',value=0,step=1)
with col2:
    number_2 = st.number_input('Please enter the second
    number',value=0,step=1)

st.info(f'**{number_1}/{number_2}=** {number_1/number_2}')
```

Running Listing 2-4, we can create a trivial application where one number is divided by another. If the user divides by any number other than zero, the application will work just fine and display an output similar to Figure 2-5. However, should the user decide to divide by zero, logically Python will throw a zero division error that will be displayed by Streamlit as shown in Figure 2-6.

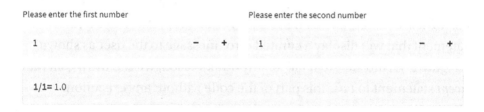

Figure 2-5. *Running Streamlit without a try and except block without an error (output of Listing 2-4)*

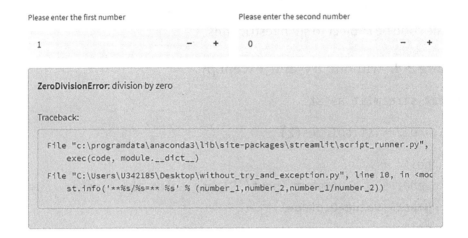

Figure 2-6. *Running Streamlit without a try and except block with an error (output of Listing 2-4)*

Example 1

You can indeed limit the range of input values for the *st.number_input* widget, but let us assume for a moment that you could not. Then the remedy for this would be to make use of try and except blocks in your code as shown in Listing 2-5 wherever there is a likelihood of running into an unforeseen issue. In this instance, we attempt to run the troublesome part of the script with the *try* statement. Should it fail due to a *ZeroDivisionError*, we will handle it with an *except ZeroDivisionError* statement that will display a curated error message to the user as shown in Figure 2-7. And should it fail for any other reason, we can use a general *except* statement to *pass* this part of the code without any execution.

Listing 2-5. try_and_except_1.py

```
import streamlit as st

col1, col2 = st.columns(2)

with col1:
    number_1 = st.number_input('Please enter the first
    number',value=0,step=1)
with col2:
    number_2 = st.number_input('Please enter the second
    number',value=0,step=1)

try:
    st.info(f'**{number_1}/{number_2}=** {number_1/number_2}')
except ZeroDivisionError:
    st.error('Cannot divide by zero')
```

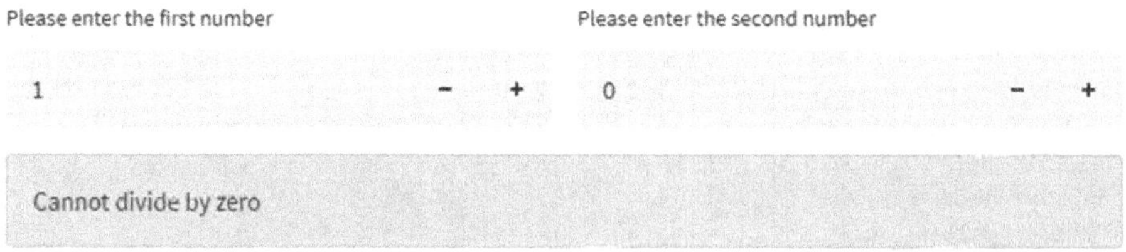

Please enter the first number	Please enter the second number
1 − +	0 − +

Cannot divide by zero

Figure 2-7. *Running Streamlit with a try and except block with an error (output of Listing 2-5)*

Example 2

Another way of managing exceptions is to use a general *except* statement, and within it displaying a curated message of the actual error occurring as shown in Figure 2-8. This can be particularly useful for debugging the script for the developer themselves while not compromising on the user experience.

Listing 2-6. try_and_except_2.py

```python
import streamlit as st

col1, col2 = st.columns(2)

with col1:
    number_1 = st.number_input('Please enter the first
    number',value=0,step=1)
with col2:
    number_2 = st.number_input('Please enter the second
    number',value=0,step=1)

try:
    st.info(f'**{number_1}/{number_2}=** {number_1/number_2}')
except Exception as e:
    st.error(f'Error: {e}')
```

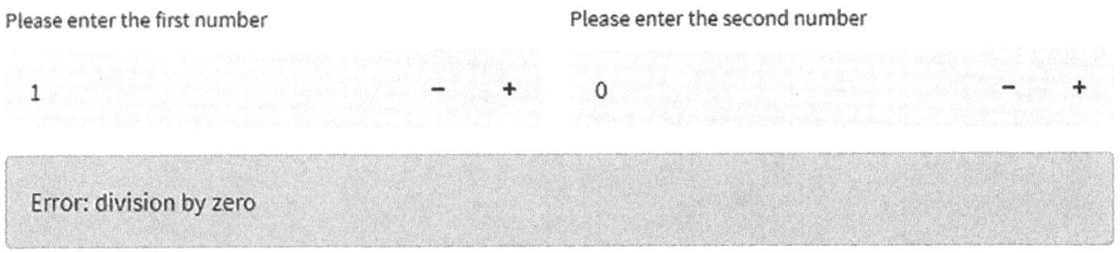

Please enter the first number		Please enter the second number	
1	− +	0	− +

Error: division by zero

Figure 2-8. *Running Streamlit with a try and except block with an error (output of Listing 2-6)*

2.2 Mutating Dataframes

Given Streamlit's emphasis on developing machine learning and data science applications, as a developer you will often need to mutate dataframes in response to a user input or need. In this section, we will introduce a non-exhaustive list of some of the most commonly used methods of mutating Pandas dataframes.

2.2.1 Filter

Dataframes can be filtered by using the method shown in Listing 2-7. We can simply specify a condition for a column numerical and/or string, that is, *df[df['Column 1'] > -1]*, and filter the rows based on that as shown in Figure 2-9.

Listing 2-7. mutate_dataframe_filter.py

```python
import streamlit as st
import pandas as pd
import numpy as np

np.random.seed(0)

df = pd.DataFrame(
    np.random.randn(4, 3),
    columns=('Column 1','Column 2','Column 3')
              )
st.subheader('Original dataframe')
st.write(df)

df = df[df['Column 1'] > -1]
st.subheader('Mutated dataframe')
st.write(df)
```

Original dataframe

	Column 1	Column 2	Column 3
0	0.4153	0.8148	1.6891
1	0.7829	-0.7485	-0.1621
2	0.0207	-2.2372	0.3849
3	-1.1700	0.5403	0.5729

Mutated dataframe

	Column 1	Column 2	Column 3
0	0.4153	0.8148	1.6891
1	0.7829	-0.7485	-0.1621
2	0.0207	-2.2372	0.3849

Figure 2-9. *Filtering Pandas dataframes (output of Listing 2-7)*

2.2.2 Select

Dataframe columns can be selected by using the method shown in
Listing 2-8. We can specify which columns to keep by their names, that
is, *df[['Column 1,' 'Column 2']]*, and remove other columns as shown in
Figure 2-10. Alternatively, the exact same function can be achieved by
using the *drop* command, that is, *df.drop(columns=['Column 3']).*

Listing 2-8. mutate_dataframe_select.py

```python
import streamlit as st
import pandas as pd
import numpy as np

np.random.seed(0)

df = pd.DataFrame(
    np.random.randn(4, 3),
    columns=('Column 1','Column 2','Column 3')
            )
st.subheader('Original dataframe')
st.write(df)

df = df[['Column 1', 'Column 2']]
st.subheader('Mutated dataframe')
st.write(df)
```

Original dataframe

	Column 1	Column 2	Column 3
0	-0.0481	-0.7764	0.0165
1	-1.1647	0.2303	0.8265
2	0.9110	-0.1735	0.4024
3	2.0134	1.4145	0.8714

Mutated dataframe

	Column 1	Column 2
0	-0.0481	-0.7764
1	-1.1647	0.2303
2	0.9110	-0.1735
3	2.0134	1.4145

Figure 2-10. *Selecting Pandas dataframe columns (output of Listing 2-8)*

2.2.3 Arrange

Dataframe columns can be arranged and sorted in ascending and/or descending order based on the numerical or nominal value of a specified column by using the method shown in Listing 2-9. We can specify which column to sort and in which order, that is, *df.sort_values(by='Column*

1,ascending=True), as shown in Figure 2-11. Once the column has been sorted, the index will be modified to reflect the new order. If necessary, you may reset the index by using the *df.reset_index(drop=True)* command to restart the index from zero.

Listing 2-9. mutate_dataframe_arrange.py

```python
import streamlit as st
import pandas as pd
import numpy as np

np.random.seed(0)

df = pd.DataFrame(
    np.random.randn(4, 3),
    columns=('Column 1','Column 2','Column 3')
                )
st.subheader('Original dataframe')
st.write(df)

df = df.sort_values(by='Column 1',ascending=True)
st.subheader('Mutated dataframe')
st.write(df)
```

Original dataframe

	Column 1	Column 2	Column 3
0	-0.9856	1.6419	0.4121
1	0.6446	-1.0611	-0.9746
2	0.6027	-1.6802	1.6636
3	1.6305	0.6703	-0.5791

Mutated dataframe

	Column 1	Column 2	Column 3
0	-0.9856	1.6419	0.4121
2	0.6027	-1.6802	1.6636
1	0.6446	-1.0611	-0.9746
3	1.6305	0.6703	-0.5791

Figure 2-11. *Sorting Pandas dataframe columns (output of Listing 2-9)*

2.2.4 Mutate

Dataframe columns can be mutated by assigning new columns based on the value of another column by using the method shown in Listing 2-10. We can specify a simple *lambda* function to apply to the values of an existing column, that is, *Column_4 = lambda x: df['Column 1]*2*, to compute the output shown in Figure 2-12.

Listing 2-10. mutate_dataframe_lambda.py

```python
import streamlit as st
import pandas as pd
import numpy as np

np.random.seed(0)

df = pd.DataFrame(
    np.random.randn(4, 3),
    columns=('Column 1','Column 2','Column 3')
                )
st.subheader('Original dataframe')
st.write(df)

df = df.assign(Column_4 = lambda x: df['Column 1']*2)
st.subheader('Mutated dataframe')
st.write(df)
```

Original dataframe

	Column 1	Column 2	Column 3
0	-1.4070	0.5518	-0.8536
1	0.8926	-0.8607	0.6242
2	2.7735	0.5299	1.7047
3	1.7536	0.9111	0.1194

Mutated dataframe

	Column 1	Column 2	Column 3	Column_4
0	-1.4070	0.5518	-0.8536	-2.8139
1	0.8926	-0.8607	0.6242	1.7851
2	2.7735	0.5299	1.7047	5.5470
3	1.7536	0.9111	0.1194	3.5073

Figure 2-12. *Mutating Pandas dataframes (output of Listing 2-10)*

2.2.5 Group By

Sometimes, it may be necessary to group or aggregate the values in a column or several columns in a dataframe. This can be done in Pandas using the method shown in Listing 2-11. We can specify which column or columns to group by with the *df.groupby(['Column 1', 'Column 2'])* command. This will reindex the dataframe and group the relevant rows together as shown in Figure 2-13.

Listing 2-11. mutate_dataframe_groupby.py

```python
import streamlit as st
import pandas as pd
import numpy as np

df = pd.DataFrame(
    np.random.randn(12, 3),
    columns=('Score 1','Score 2','Score 3')
            )
df['Name'] = pd.DataFrame(['John','Alex','Jessica','John','Alex',
'John', 'Jessica','John','Alex','Alex','Jessica','Jessica'])

df['Category'] = pd.DataFrame(['B','A','D','C','C','A',
'B','C','B','A','A','D'])

st.subheader('Original dataframe')
st.write(df)

df = df.groupby(['Name','Category']).first()
st.subheader('Mutated dataframe')
st.write(df)
```

2.2.6 Merge

Multiple dataframes can be merged together with Pandas utilizing a common column as a reference using the method shown in Listing 2-12. We can specify which column to merge on and whether the merge should be a union or intersection of both dataframes with the *df1.merge(df2,how ='inner,'on='Name')* command. This will create a combined dataframe as shown in Figure 2-14.

Listing 2-12. mutate_dataframe_merge.py

```python
import streamlit as st
import pandas as pd

df1 = pd.DataFrame(data={'Name':['Jessica','John','Alex'],
'Score 1':[77,56,87]}
               )

df2 = pd.DataFrame(data={'Name':['Jessica','John','Alex'],
'Score 2':[76,97,82]}
               )

st.subheader('Original dataframes')
st.write(df1)
st.write(df2)

df1 = df1.merge(df2,how='inner',on='Name')
st.subheader('Mutated dataframe')
st.write(df1)
```

Original dataframe

	Score 1	Score 2	Score 3	Name	Category
0	0.8551	0.6345	0.9989	John	B
1	-0.2270	0.5825	0.3430	Alex	A
2	0.3788	0.4579	0.7396	Jessica	D
3	0.6724	-0.5880	0.2884	John	C
4	-0.3496	0.1938	-0.9714	Alex	C
5	0.6412	0.4649	1.1796	John	A
6	0.9674	-1.0133	-1.3107	Jessica	B
7	-0.2369	-0.2820	0.4142	John	C
8	-0.8134	-0.2197	0.7172	Alex	B
9	1.4496	-1.4238	1.2059	Alex	A

Mutated dataframe

		Score 1	Score 2	Score 3
Alex	A	-0.2270	0.5825	0.3430
Alex	B	-0.8134	-0.2197	0.7172
Alex	C	-0.3496	0.1938	-0.9714
Jessica	A	1.3468	-0.4117	-1.4019
Jessica	B	0.9674	-1.0133	-1.3107
Jessica	D	0.3788	0.4579	0.7396
John	A	0.6412	0.4649	1.1796
John	B	0.8551	0.6345	0.9989
John	C	0.6724	-0.5880	0.2884

Figure 2-13. *Grouping Pandas dataframes (output of Listing 2-11)*

2.3 Rendering Static and Interactive Charts

Data visualization is quite literally where Streamlit shines the most. The ease at which a variety of static and interactive charts can be invoked and rendered is quite remarkable. Streamlit natively supports a host of charts including but not limited to bar, line, and area charts as well as graphs, maps, and other types of interactive and noninteractive visuals. In addition, there is a multitude of third-party plots that can also be used with Streamlit. In this section, we will develop several instances of static and interactive charts using data from a Pandas dataframe.

2.3.1 Static Bar Chart

A static bar chart can be generated by inputting a Pandas dataframe into a Matplotlib figure by using the method shown in Listing 2-13. We can specify the chart type by setting *kind='bar'*. Other Matplotlib parameters can be found at `https://matplotlib.org/stable/api/_as_gen/matplotlib.pyplot.plot.html`. The generated chart is shown in Figure 2-15.

Listing 2-13. static_bar_chart.py

```
import streamlit as st
import pandas as pd
import matplotlib.pyplot as fig

df = pd.DataFrame(data={'Name':['Jessica','John','Alex'],
'Score 1':[77,56,87],'Score 2':[76,97,82]}
                  )
df.set_index('Name').plot(kind='bar',stacked=False,xlabel='Name',
ylabel='Score')
st.pyplot(fig)
```

Original dataframes

	Name	Score 1
0	Jessica	77
1	John	56
2	Alex	87

	Name	Score 2
0	Jessica	76
1	John	97
2	Alex	82

Mutated dataframe

	Name	Score 1	Score 2
0	Jessica	77	76
1	John	56	97
2	Alex	87	82

Figure 2-14. *Merging Pandas dataframes (output of Listing 2-12)*

2.3.2 Static Line Chart

Similarly, a static line chart can be generated by inputting a Pandas dataframe into a Matplotlib figure by using the method shown in Listing 2-14. We can specify the chart type and the option of having subplots by setting *kind='line,' subplots=True*.

Other Matplotlib parameters can be found at *https://matplotlib. org/stable/api/_as_gen/matplotlib.pyplot.plot.html*. The generated chart is shown in Figure 2-16.

Listing 2-14. static_line_chart.py

```
import streamlit as st
import pandas as pd
import matplotlib.pyplot as fig

df = pd.DataFrame(data={'Exam':['Exam 1','Exam 2','Exam 3'],
'Jessica':[77,76,87],'John':[56,97,95],'Alex':[87,82,93]}
                 )

df.set_index('Exam').plot(kind='line',xlabel='Exam',ylabel=
'Score',subplots=True) st.pyplot(fig)
```

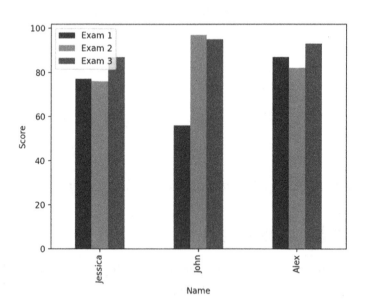

Figure 2-15. *Generating a static bar chart (output of Listing 2-13)*

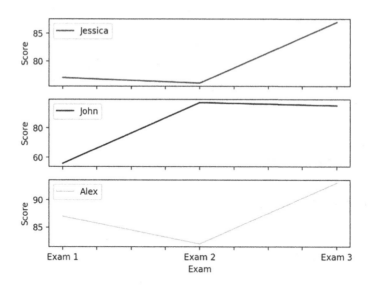

Figure 2-16. *Generating a static line chart (output of Listing 2-14)*

2.3.3 Interactive Line Chart

An interactive line chart can be generated by inputting a Pandas dataframe into a Plotly figure by using the method shown in Listing 2-15. We can simply declare the chart type and its associated properties by using the JSON notation used with all Plotly charts and figures. Other Plotly parameters can be found at *https://plotly.com/python/line-charts/*; we will cover Plotly line charts in greater depth in Section 4.2. The generated chart is shown in Figure 2-17.

Listing 2-15. interactive_line_chart.py

```python
import streamlit as st
import pandas as pd
import plotly.graph_objects as go

df = pd.DataFrame(data={'Exam':['Exam 1','Exam 2','Exam 3'],
'Jessica':[77,76,87],'John':[56,97,95],'Alex':[87,82,93]}
                  )
```

```
fig = go.Figure(data=[
    go.Line(name='Jessica', x=df['Exam'], y=df['Jessica']),
    go.Line(name='John', x=df['Exam'], y=df['John']),
    go.Line(name='Alex', x=df['Exam'], y=df['Alex'])
])

fig.update_layout(
    xaxis_title='Exam',
    yaxis_title='Score',
    legend_title='Name',
)

st.plotly_chart(fig)
```

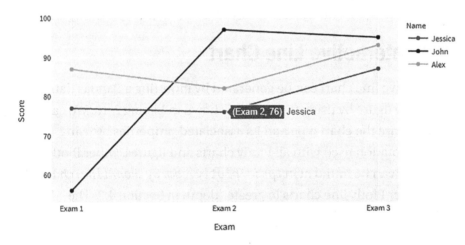

Figure 2-17. *Generating an interactive line chart (output of Listing 2-15)*

2.3.4 Interactive Map

Likewise, an interactive geospatial map can be generated by inputting a Pandas dataframe containing the longitude and latitude of a set of points into a Plotly figure by using the method shown in Listing 2-16. In addition, we can declare the exact geospatial location to zoom into by setting *geo_scope='usa'*. Other Plotly parameters can be found at *https://plotly.com/python/scatter-plots-on-maps/*; we will cover Plotly geospatial charts in greater depth in Section 4.2. The generated map is shown in Figure 2-18.

Listing 2-16. interactive_map.py

```python
import streamlit as st
import pandas as pd
import plotly.graph_objects as go

df = pd.DataFrame(data={'university':['Harvard
University','Yale University',
'Princeton University','Columbia University','Brown
University',
'Dartmouth University','University of Pennsylvania','Cornell
University'],
'latitude':[42.3770,41.3163,40.3573,40.8075,41.8268,
43.7044,39.9522,42.4534],
'longitude':[-71.1167,-72.9223,-74.6672,-73.9626,-71.4025,
-72.2887, -75.1932,-76.4735]}
               )

fig = go.Figure(data=go.Scattergeo(
        lon = df['longitude'],
        lat = df['latitude'],
        text = df['university'],
        ))
```

```
fig.update_layout(
        geo_scope='usa',
    )

st.plotly_chart(fig)
```

Figure 2-18. *Generating an interactive map (output of Listing 2-16)*

2.4 Developing the User Interface

Typically, developing a user interface for a web application requires a separate skill set that pertains to graphical design and usability studies. A frontend developer will begin by conceptualizing their idea with a wireframe diagram that disposes the elements of a page. This will then iteratively be converted to an actual user interface through testing and refinements. Streamlit has largely eliminated that undertaking with its intuitive, responsive, and standardized interface, whereby the developer can render a web page without having to worry about the intricate details of design.

In other words, Streamlit interfaces are plug and play, allowing the developer to focus on the logic of their program while leaving the visual implementation to Streamlit. Should the user require something more bespoke and customized, they are indeed welcome to integrate their own HTML and/or JavaScript components. Customizability and external components will be addressed in subsequent chapters.

In this section, we will be developing an application similar to the *dataframe demo* application shown in the previous chapter as an example of how to create a basic user interface.

Listing 2-17. dataframe_demo.py

```python
import streamlit as st
import pandas as pd
import plotly.express as px

program = st.sidebar.selectbox('Select program',['Dataframe
Demo','Other Demo'])
code = st.sidebar.checkbox('Display code')

if program == 'Dataframe Demo':
    df = px.data.stocks()
    st.title('DataFrame Demo')
    stocks = st.multiselect('Select stocks',df.columns[1:],
    [df.columns[1]])
    st.subheader('Stock value')

    # Mutating the dataframe to keep selected columns only
    st.write(df[['date'] + stocks].set_index('date'))

    # Creating a Plotly timeseries line chart
    fig = px.line(df, x='date', y=stocks,
            hover_data={"date": "|%Y %b %d"}
            )
```

```
st.write(fig)

if code:
    st.code(
        """

import streamlit as st
import pandas as pd
import plotly.express as px

df = px.data.stocks()
st.title('DataFrame demo')
program = st.sidebar.selectbox('Select
program',['Dataframe Demo'])
code = st.sidebar.checkbox('Display code')
stocks = st.multiselect('Select stocks',df.columns[1:],[df.
columns[1]])
st.subheader('Stock value')
st.write(df[['date'] + stocks].set_index('date'))

fig = px.line(df, x='date', y=stocks,
            hover_data={"date": "|%Y %b %d"}
            )

st.write(fig)
        """
        )
elif program == 'Other Demo':
    st.title('Other Demo')
```

As always, we initially import the stack of dependencies that we will be using for this application, namely, Streamlit itself, Pandas for dataframe handling, and Plotly Express to plot a simple time-series chart of the value of several blue chip stocks over time. We then download a dataset from Plotly's list of available open source datasets and initiate our user interface by invoking a title using the *st.title* command. We then add a *st.sidebar. selectbox* command to define a list of programs/pages for this application. This is followed by a checkbox on the sidebar to display our code using the *st.sidebar.checkbox* command. Widgets can be added to the sidebar by appending the *st.sidebar* prefix if applicable. We then use a *st.multiselect* command to select the list of stocks we want to visualize. The selection will be used to filter the dataframe containing the stock values and will then be displayed using the *st.write* command.

Subsequently, we will use the filtered dataframe to create a time-series line chart with Plotly using the reference at `https://plotly.com/python/ time-series/`. Once the figure has been generated, it can be displayed using *st.write*, otherwise known as the pocket knife command due to its versatility in rendering virtually anything. And last but not least, we will use a *st.code* command to present our snippet of code if the checkbox is preselected by the user. And there you have it (Figures 2-19 and 2-20), a basic dataframe application in a little over 40 lines of code.

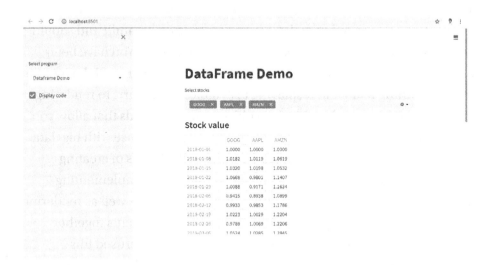

Figure 2-19. *Dataframe demo application (output of Listing 2-17)*

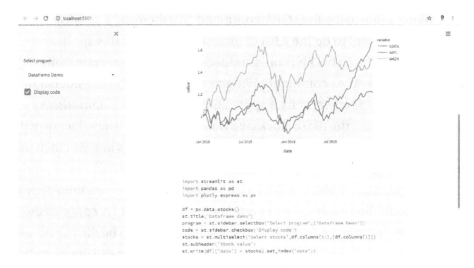

Figure 2-20. *Dataframe demo application continued (output of Listing 2-17)*

2.5 Summary

This chapter has been a rigorous one indeed. At this point, you should have gotten up to speed with the gist and essence of Streamlit and should have also developed a fairly clear idea of its capabilities. You have been introduced to the diverse set of commands in the Streamlit API that pertain from everything related to displaying text, tables, and charts to rendering interactive widgets, and multimedia objects, to commands that allow you to organize the page and optimize Streamlit for efficient use with big data.

In the latter part of this chapter, we covered the basics of creating a trivial web application. This included creating forms, implementing conditional flow, managing exceptions, mutating data, as well as rendering a variety of visualizations, and bundling all of these elements together in the form of one user interface. In short, after having perused this chapter, you should feel confident enough to proceed with developing a straightforward web application of your own in Streamlit.

CHAPTER 3

Architecting the User Interface

With Streamlit, the developer is able to focus on implementing their backend logic while leaving the frontend implementation largely to the framework itself. In addition, using Streamlit you can render responsive interfaces for PC, tablet, and mobile platforms at your fingertips with no added overhead. However, should one need to develop more bespoke and tailored applications, Streamlit affords a considerable degree of customization of its frontend design to the developer without soliciting any knowledge of HTML, CSS, or JavaScript. One may configure their application using a multitude of color schemes, fonts, and appearances both graphically and programmatically.

Furthermore, Streamlit gives you the ability to immaculately structure and organize the web page using a combination of a sidebar, columns, expanders, and containers. Together, these elements can offer the user an enhanced experience while making efficient use of the space on the page. Furthermore, with placeholders and progress bars, you can render dynamic content on demand or in response to an event. And most importantly, with Streamlit you can create as many pages and nested subpages as required for your application in a highly modularized and scalable way.

© Mohammad Khorasani, Mohamed Abdou, Javier Hernández Fernández 2022
M. Khorasani et al., *Web Application Development with Streamlit*,
https://doi.org/10.1007/978-1-4842-8111-6_3

3.1 Designing the Application

While designing a Streamlit application, we can make use of the multitude of native methods it provides to customize our page to be exactly the way we want. From color schemes and themes to columns, expanders, sidebar, and placeholders, the number of design permutations we can achieve is endless.

3.1.1 Configuring the Page

With Streamlit, you have the ability to configure several attributes of the web page, namely, configuring the page layout, initial sidebar state, page title (displayed on the browser), icon, hamburger menu state, footer, and more. While some of these items can be configured within your script, the rest must be set within the global config file */.streamlit/config.toml* that was discussed in Section 1.2.

Basic Page Configuration

Listing 3-1 can be used to configure the page title, icon, layout, initial sidebar state, and menu items as shown in Figure 3-1. Please note that the page icon supports *.ico* files. You may use the package *Pillow* to import and handle images. The page layout can be *'centered'* or *'wide'*, and the initial sidebar state can be *'auto'*, *'expanded'*, or *'collapsed'*. In addition, you may choose to customize one or more of the following pages in the hamburger menu: *'Get help'*, *'Report a bug'*, or *'About'*. The *Get help* and *Report a bug* pages can only be instantiated with a URL that will redirect the user to another web page. The *About* page can be instantiated as a modal window that will appear as shown in Figure 3-2.

Listing 3-1. page_config.py

```python
import streamlit as st
from PIL import Image
icon = Image.open('favicon.ico')

st.set_page_config(
    page_title='Hello world',
    page_icon=icon,
    layout='centered',
    initial_sidebar_state='auto',
    menu_items={
        'Get Help': 'https://streamlit.io/',
        'Report a bug': 'https://github.com',
        'About': 'About your application: **Hello world**'
        }
)

st.sidebar.title('Hello world')
st.title('Hello world')
```

Figure 3-1. *Streamlit page configured with Listing 3-1*

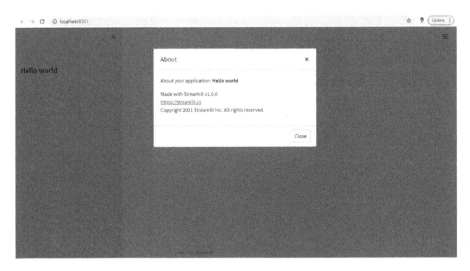

Figure 3-2. *Displaying the About modal window*

Removing Footer and Hamburger Menu

You may choose to remove the default footer provided by Streamlit as well as the entire hamburger menu by adding the commands shown in Listing 3-2. The output is shown in Figure 3-3. Please note that while modifications to the CSS may work in the current version of Streamlit, this exact method however is not guaranteed to work in subsequent versions, should the internal implementation be changed.

Listing 3-2. remove_footer_menu.py

```
hide_footer_style = "'
<style>
.reportview-container .main footer {visibility: hidden;}
"'

st.markdown(hide_footer_style, unsafe_allow_html=True)

hide_menu_style = "'
<style>
#MainMenu {visibility: hidden;}
</style>
"'


st.markdown(hide_menu_style, unsafe_allow_html=True)
```

Figure 3-3. *Removed footer and hamburger menu from the page*

Adding a Customized Footer

Furthermore, you may add your own customized footer by adding the markdown command shown in Listing 3-3. The output is shown in Figure 3-4.

Listing 3-3. footer.py

```
st.sidebar.markdown(
    f"'<div class="markdown-text-container stText"
    style="width: 698px;">
    <footer><p></p></footer><div style="font-size: 12px;">
    Hello world v 0.1</div>
    <div style="font-size: 12px;">Hello world LLC.</div>
    </div>"', unsafe_allow_html=True)
```

Advanced Page Configuration

Aside from the basic configurable settings of a Streamlit web page, there is a multitude of other parameters that can be configured as required by modifying the global config file */.streamlit/config.toml* discussed earlier in Section 1.2. Parameters that can be configured pertain to the global, logger, client, runner, server, browser, mapbox, deprecation, AWS S3, and theme settings as shown in Tables 3-1, 3-2, and 3-3. For further information, please refer to *https://docs.streamlit.io/library/advanced-features/configuration*. An example of configuring the theme used for the web page is shown in Listing 3-4.

Table 3-1. *config.toml file parameters*

Configuration Options

[global]

- *disableWatchdogWarning = false*

  Streamlit watchdog will check for changes in the source code. If this parameter is disabled, Streamlit will not display a warning message if the watchdog is unavailable.

- *showWarningOnDirectExecution = true*

  Streamlit will display a warning when you try to run a script using python script.py when this parameter is set to true.

- *dataFrameSerialization = 'arrow'*

  Setting this parameter to legacy will serialize dataframes using Streamlit's slower custom format; setting this parameter to arrow will serialize dataframes with the much faster Apache Arrow.

(continued)

Table 3-1. (*continued*)

Configuration Options

[logger]

- *level = 'debug'*

  Available options include error, warning, info, and debug.

- *messageFormat = "%(asctime)s %(message)s".*

  This parameter will specify the string format for logging messages.

[client]

- *caching = true*

  Setting this parameter to true will enable st.cache.

- *displayEnabled = true*

  Setting this parameter to true will ensure your script is drawn to a Streamlit application.

- *showErrorDetails = true*

  Setting this parameter to true will display runtime exceptions on the Streamlit application; if set to false, a generic error message will be shown instead.

[runner]

- *magicEnabled = true*

  Setting this parameter to true will allow you to write strings and variables outside of a *st.write* command.

(continued)

Table 3-1. (*continued*)

Configuration Options

- *installTracer = false*

  Setting this parameter to true will allow you to stop the execution of your script at any specified point.

- *fixMatplotlib = true*

  Setting this parameter to true will set the *MPLBACKEND* environment variable to *Agg* within Streamlit to prevent Python from crashing.

- *postScriptGC = true*

  Setting this parameter to true will run the Python garbage collector module which helps avoid excess memory usage.

- *fastReruns = false*

  Setting this parameter to true will handle script rerun requests immediately, making applications far more responsive.

Table 3-2. *config.toml file parameters (continued – 1)*

Configuration Options

[server]

- *folderWatchBlacklist = [ ]*

  This parameter specifies the list of folders that should not be inspected by Streamlit for any changes.

(*continued*)

Table 3-2. (*continued*)

Configuration Options

- *fileWatcherType = 'auto'*

  Setting this parameter to auto will ensure Streamlit uses the watchdog module if it is available, the watchdog will force Streamlit to use the watchdog module, the poll forces Streamlit to use polling, and none will stop Streamlit from inspecting files.

- *cookieSecret = 'key'*

  This parameter specifies the key to use to produce cookies; if not set, Streamlit will randomly assign a value.

- *headless = false*

  Setting this parameter to false will force Streamlit to start the application on a browser window.

- *runOnSave = false*

  Setting this parameter to true will force Streamlit to automatically run the script upon resaving the script.

- *address =*

  This parameter will specify the address where the server will listen to for client and/or browser connections.

- *port = 8501*

  This parameter will specify the port where the server will listen to for browser connections.

(*continued*)

Table 3-2. (*continued*)

Configuration Options

- *baseUrlPath = 'URL'*

  This parameter will specify the base path for the URL from where the Streamlit application will be served.

- *enableCORS = true*

  Setting this parameter to true will enable cross-origin request sharing protection.

- *enableXsrfProtection = true*

  Setting this parameter to true will enable cross-site request forgery protection.

- *maxUploadSize = 200*

  This parameter specifies the maximum uploadable file size in megabytes.

- *enableWebsocketCompression = false*

  Setting this parameter to true will enable support for WebSocket compression.

[browser]

- *serverAddress = 'localhost'*

  This parameter specifies the URL which users should enter into their browsers to connect to the Streamlit application, can be an IP address or DNS with path.

- *gatherUsageStats = true*

  Setting this parameter to true will enable sending usage statistics to Streamlit.

- *serverPort = 8501*

  This parameter sets the port at which users should point their browsers to, in order to connect to the Streamlit application.

Table 3-3. *config.toml file parameters (continued – 2)*

Configuration Options

[mapbox]

- *token = ' '*

    This parameter specifies the token for custom Mapbox elements; for further information, please refer to `www.mapbox.com/`.

[deprecation]

- *showfileUploaderEncoding = 'True'*

    Setting this parameter to true will enable the deprecation warning message for the file uploader encoding.

- *showPyplotGlobalUse = 'True'*

    Setting this parameter to true will enable the deprecation warning message for the global Pyplot element.

[s3]

- *bucket =*

    This parameter specifies the name of the AWS S3 bucket to use with your Streamlit application.

(continued)

Table 3-3. (*continued*)

Configuration Options

- *url =*

  This parameter specifies the URL root for the external viewing of your Streamlit application.

- *accessKeyId =*

  This parameter specifies the access key to write to your AWS S3 bucket.

- *secretAccessKey =*

  This parameter specifies the secret access key to write to the AWS S3 bucket.

- *keyPrefix =*

  This parameter specifies the subdirectory within the AWS S3 bucket to use with your Streamlit application.

- *region =*

  This parameter specifies the AWS region where your S3 bucket is located.

- *profile =*

  This parameter specifies the AWS credentials to use for the S3 bucket.

[theme]

- *base =*

  This parameter specifies the Streamlit theme to use with your custom theme, can be one of 'light' or 'dark'.

(*continued*)

Table 3-3. (*continued*)

Configuration Options

- *primaryColor =*

  This parameter specifies the color HEX to use for the interactive Streamlit elements.

- *backgroundColor =*

  This parameter specifies the color HEX to use for the main content of the Streamlit page.

- *secondaryBackgroundColor =*

  This parameter specifies the color HEX to use for the sidebar.

- *textColor*

  This parameter specifies the color HEX to use for the text.

- *font*

  This parameter specifies the font to use for the text, can be 'sans serif', 'serif', or 'monospace'.

Figure 3-4. *Adding a customized footer*

3.1.2 Developing Themes and Color schemes

Streamlit gives both the developer and the user the ability to customize the theme and color scheme of the application both graphically and programmatically.

Customizing the Theme Graphically

You may select one of the available theme appearances, *Light* or *Dark*, from the settings menu located within the hamburger menu as shown in Figure 3-5. In addition, you may select colors for each of the following areas: *Primary color, Background color, Text color*, and *Secondary background color*, and select one of the available fonts, *Sans serif, Serif,* or *Monospace*, as shown in Figure 3-6.

Table 3-4 provides more information about each color setting and the Streamlit elements that each one alters. Please note that the interactive widgets such as *st.slider* will use the *Secondary background color* as their background color when the widget is used within the body of the application; however, when the widget is called within the sidebar, the *Background color* is used instead, as shown in Figure 3-7.

Table 3-4. *Theme color settings*

Color Parameter	Altered Elements
Primary color	Interactive widgets such as *st.slider*.
Background color	Main body of application.
Text color	All text elements.
Secondary background color	Sidebar background color.

Figure 3-5. *Customizing the theme's appearance from the settings menu*

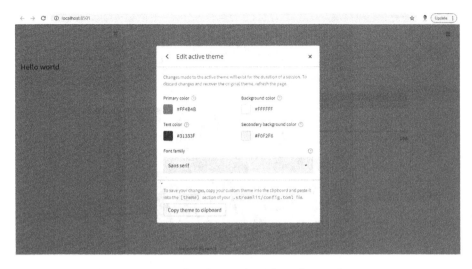

Figure 3-6. *Customizing the theme's colors from the settings menu*

Customizing the Theme Programmatically

Alternatively, you may choose to customize the theme's appearance and colors programmatically by modifying the global config file */.streamlit/config.toml* discussed earlier in Section 1.2. You may specify the theme settings by modifying the *[theme]* parameters as shown in Listing 3-4. Please note that the color convention used is *color HEX*. For further information regarding this convention, please refer to www.w3schools.com/colors/colors_hexadecimal.asp *HEXadecimal.asp*.

Figure 3-7. *Customized theme's colors*

Listing 3-4. config.toml

```
[theme]

base = 'light'
primaryColor = '#7792E3'
backgroundColor = '#273346'
secondaryBackgroundColor = '#B9F1C0'
textColor = '#FFFFFF'
font = 'sans serif'
```

Using Themes with Custom Components

If you are developing your own custom Streamlit components, it may be necessary to pass the application's theme settings to your component. Please ensure that you have installed the latest version of *streamlit-component-lib* by using the following command:

```
npm install streamlit-component-lib
```

This package will automatically update the colors of your custom component to reflect the theme settings of your Streamlit application. In addition, it will allow you to read the theme settings in your JavaScript and/or CSS script as shown in the following.

As CSS variables, the object settings can be exposed as follows:

```
--primary-color
--background-color
--secondary-background-color
--text-color
--font
```

Accordingly, these settings can be accessed as follows:

```
.mySelector {
  color: var(--primary-color);
}
```

Alternatively, you may choose to expose the object settings as a ReactJS prop, which may be accessed as follows:

```
{
  "primaryColor": ""
  "backgroundColor": "",
  "secondaryBackgroundColor": "",
  "textColor": "",
  "font": "",
}
```

3.1.3 Organizing the Page

Streamlit provides several methods to organize and customize the frontend design of an application. Namely, as a developer you have the ability to enable a sidebar, divide the web page into columns, display expander boxes to hide content, and create containers to bundle several widgets together. Combined with one another, these features allow you to customize your application to a tangibly high degree and offer a tailored experience to your users.

Sidebar

With Streamlit, you have the ability of subdividing your page with an elegant sidebar that can be expanded and contracted on demand with the *st.sidebar* command. In addition, as shown in Section 3.1, you may configure Streamlit to keep the sidebar expanded, contracted, or automatically adjusted at the start based on the screen size. Practically, every Streamlit element and widget with the exception of *st.echo* and *st. spinner* can be invoked within the sidebar. You may even render other features related to page organization such as *st.columns*, *st.expander*, and *st.container* within the sidebar as shown in Listing 3-5 and Figure 3-8.

Expanders

With Streamlit, you have the ability to collapse content into expanders, should you wish to make more efficient use of the space on the main body or sidebar of your application. Expanders can be expanded and contracted on demand or can be set to either state at the start. In addition, expanders can contain any element including columns and containers but not nested expanders. An example of using expanders is shown in Listing 3-5 and Figure 3-8.

Columns

Similarly, you can divide the main body and sidebar with Streamlit's columns feature that can be called with the *st.columns* command. You may specify the number of columns you require by writing *st.columns(2)*, or alternatively you may use a list to set the number and width of each column arbitrarily by writing *st.columns([2,1])*. Columns can be invoked within a *with* statement and can be used concurrently with expanders and containers; however, they may not be nested within one another. An example of using columns is shown in Listing 3-5 and Figure 3-8.

Containers

Should you require to bundle several widgets or elements together, you can do so with Streamlit's container feature that can be called with the *st.container* command in the main body or sidebar. Containers can be invoked within a *with* statement and can be used with columns, expanders, and even nested containers. They can also be altered out of order, for instance, if you display some text out of the container and then display some more text within the container, the latter will be displayed first. An example of using containers is shown in Listing 3-5 and Figure 3-8.

Listing 3-5. page_organization.py

```python
import streamlit as st
from datetime import datetime

#Expander in sidebar
st.sidebar.subheader('Expander')
with st.sidebar.expander('Time'):
    time = datetime.now().strftime("%H:%M:%S")
    st.write('**%s**' % (time))

#Columns in sidebar
st.sidebar.subheader('Columns')
col1, col2 = st.sidebar.columns(2)
with col1:
    option_1 = st.selectbox('Please select option 1',['A','B'])
with col2:
    option_2 = st.radio('Please select option 2',['A','B'])
```

```
#Container in sidebar
container = st.sidebar.container()
container.subheader('Container')
option_3 = container.slider('Please select option 3')
st.sidebar.warning('Elements outside of container will be
displayed externally')
container.info('**Option 3:** %s' % (option_3))

#Expander in main body
st.subheader('Expander')
with st.expander('Time'):
    time = datetime.now().strftime("%H:%M:%S")
    st.write('**%s**' % (time))

#Columns in main body
st.subheader('Columns')
col1, col2 = st.columns(2)
with col1:
    option_4 = st.selectbox('Please select option 4',['A','B'])
with col2:
    option_5 = st.radio('Please select option 5',['A','B'])

#Container in main body
container = st.container()
container.subheader('Container')
option_6 = container.slider('Please select option 6')
st.warning('Elements outside of container will be displayed
externally')
container.info('**Option 6:** %s' % (option_6))
```

Placeholders

A placeholder is one of the most versatile and powerful features brandished by Streamlit. By using the *st.empty* or *st.sidebar.empty command*, you have the ability to quite literally reserve space at any location on the main body or sidebar of your application. This can be particularly useful for displaying content out of order or on demand after a certain event or trigger. A placeholder can be invoked by writing *placeholder = st.empty()*, and subsequently any widget or element can be attached to it whenever required. For instance, you may attach text to it by writing placeholder. info*('Hello world')*, and then the same placeholder can be replaced by equating it to another element. And finally when it is no longer needed, the placeholder can be cleared using the *placeholder.empty()* command.

3.2 Displaying Dynamic Content

To display dynamic content such as a constantly updating map, chart, or clock, you may place an element within a placeholder and invoke it within a for loop or while loop to iterate over many instances of that element. As a result, the element will appear to be dynamic with a constantly changing state with each iteration of the loop. An example of dynamic content is the clock application built using a placeholder as shown in Listing 3-6 and Figures 3-9 and 3-10. A while loop is being used to constantly update the st.info element to display the current time until the time reaches a predefined point, at which the placeholder is cleared and the while loop is ended.

Listing 3-6. placeholder.py

```
import streamlit as st
from datetime import datetime
st.title('Clock')
clock = st.empty()
```

```
while True:
    time = datetime.now().strftime("%H:%M:%S")
    clock.info('**Current time: ** %s' % (time))

    if time == '16:09:50':
        clock.empty()
        st.warning('Alarm!!')
        break
```

Figure 3-8. *Organizing the page using Listing 3-5*

Clock

Figure 3-9. *Output of Listing 3-6*

Clock

Alarm!!

Figure 3-10. *Output of Listing 3-6 (continued)*

3.2.1 Creating a Real-Time Progress Bar

When working with big data, it may be helpful to visualize the amount of progress made with regard to downloading, uploading, and/or performing computations that may take a long time. Specifically, users need to tangibly feel how much progress has been made in an operation and how much longer they can expect to wait to complete the process. For this purpose, we can make use of Streamlit's *st.progress* widget that will render a progress bar showing the value provided to it between 1 and 100 as an integer or 0.0 and 1.0 as a float. As an example, in Listing 3-7 we will visualize the progress made in downloading a file from a URL using the package *wget*. If you have not already done so, please proceed by downloading and installing it using *pip install wget*. From *wget*, we can read the total size of a file in bytes and the current amount downloaded in bytes which we will then feed to our progress bar for visualization as shown in Figure 3-11.

Listing 3-7. progress_bar.py

```
import streamlit as st
import wget

progress_text = st.empty()
progress_bar = st.progress(0)

def streamlit_progress_bar(current,total,width):
    percent = int((current/total)*100)
```

```
progress_text.subheader('Progress: {}%'.format(percent))
progress_bar.progress(percent)
```

```
wget.download('file URL',
bar=streamlit_progress_bar)
```

Progress: 40%

Figure 3-11. *Output of Listing 3-7*

3.3 Provisioning Multipage Applications

Pagination and scalability are inherent needs for any web application, and with Streamlit there are indeed multiple ways to address such needs in intuitive and accessible ways. Simply put, the limit to the breadth of an application when using Streamlit is really the limit of one's desires.

3.3.1 Creating Pages

The need to create pages within any web application is inherent, and with Streamlit you have the option of creating your own pages to organize your content accordingly. To begin with, you will require one main script that will house the main page of your application with routes to all the other pages as shown in Listing 3-8. In this main script, you will initially import all of the other pages' scripts (Listings 3-9 and 3-10) by writing *from pages.page_1 import main_page_1*. Please note that if the scripts for the pages are located within another folder, then you will need to append the name of the folder to the script name to import it, that is, *from pages.page_1*. Subsequently, you will create a drop-down menu using a widget such as *st. selectbox* with the names of each page and create a dictionary that contains the name of each page as the key and the function to render the page as the value. When the user selects a page from the menu, the name is passed to the dictionary to acquire the corresponding function for that page, and then that function is invoked to render the page as shown in Figure 3-12.

Listing 3-8. main_page.py

```python
import streamlit as st
from pages.page_1 import func_page_1
from pages.page_2 import func_page_2

def main():

    st.sidebar.subheader('Page selection')
    page_selection = st.sidebar.selectbox('Please select a
page',['Main Page',
    'Page 1','Page 2'])

    pages_main = {
        'Main Page': main_page,
        'Page 1': run_page_1,
        'Page 2': run_page_2
    }

    # Run selected page
    pages_main[page_selection]()

def main_page():
    st.title('Main Page')

def run_page_1():
    func_page_1()

def run_page_2():
    func_page_2()

if __name__ == '__main__':
    main()
```

Listing 3-9. page_1.py

```
import streamlit as st

def func_page_1():
    st.title('Page 1')
```

Listing 3-10. page_2.py

```
import streamlit as st

def func_page_2():
    st.title('Page 2')
```

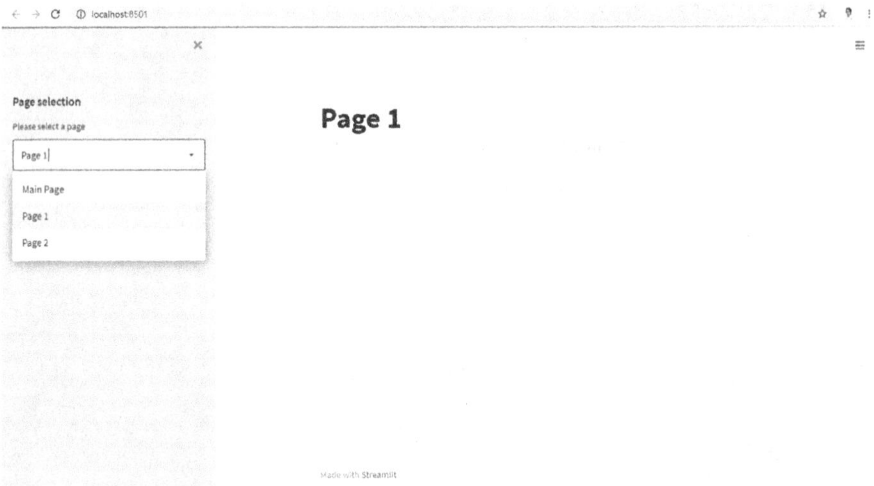

Figure 3-12. *Multipage Streamlit application*

Enabling URL Paths

You may add unique URL paths for each page within your multipage Streamlit application if you download and use the *Extra-Streamlit-Components* package that will be divulged in great depth in Section 10.4. An example of such URL paths is shown in Figure 3-13.

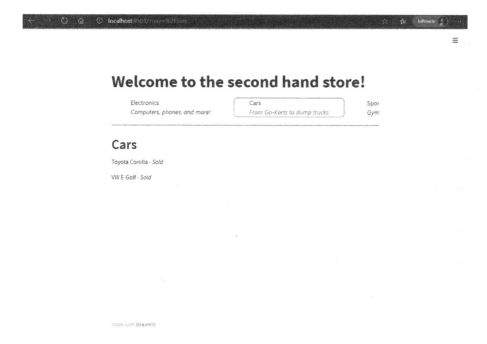

Figure 3-13. *Enabling URL paths for multipage applications*

3.3.2 Creating Subpages

With Streamlit, you also have the ability to create nested subpages within other pages to as many levels as you possibly need. The process for creating subpages is in fact very similar to that of creating pages discussed earlier in Section 3.3. Once again, you will need to begin by importing the scripts for all of the pages and subpages into your main script. Once that is done, you will create a separate dictionary of subpages for each page; the dictionary contains the name of the subpage as the key and the associated function to run it as the value. Subsequently, you will create a drop-down menu for the pages using the *st.selectbox* widget, and then you can use a series of *if* and *elif* statements to determine which page has been selected by the user. Within each *if* statement, you will then create another drop-down menu for the subpages. Once the user has selected a subpage, it will be passed to the dictionary to acquire the associated function to invoke and render the subpage as shown in Figure 3-14. Please refer to Listings 3-11, 3-12, and 3-13 for further information.

Listing 3-11. main_page_subpage.py

```python
import streamlit as st
from pages.page_1 import func_page_1
from pages.subpages_1.subpage_1_1 import func_subpage_1_1
from pages.subpages_1.subpage_1_2 import func_subpage_1_2
def main():

    st.sidebar.subheader('Page selection')
    page_selection = st.sidebar.selectbox('Please select a
page', ['Main Page','Page 1'])

    pages_main = {
        'Main Page': main_page,
        'Page 1': run_page_1
    }

    subpages_page_1 = {
        'Subpage 1.1': run_subpage_1_1,
        'Subpage 1.2': run_subpage_1_2
    }

    if page_selection == 'Main Page':
        # Run selected page
        pages_main[page_selection]()

    elif page_selection == 'Page 1':
        st.sidebar.subheader('Subpage selection')
        subpage_selection_1 = st.sidebar.selectbox("Please
select a subpage", tuple(subpages_page_1.keys()))
```

```python
    # Run selected subpage
        subpages_page_1[subpage_selection_1]()
def main_page():
    st.title('Main Page')

def run_page_1():
    func_page_1()

def run_subpage_1_1():
    func_subpage_1_1()

def run_subpage_1_2():
    func_subpage_1_2()

if __name__ == '__main__':
    main()
```

Listing 3-12. subpage_1_1.py

```python
import streamlit as st

def func_subpage_1_1():
    st.title('Subpage 1.1')
```

Listing 3-13. subpage_1_2.py

```python
import streamlit as st

def func_subpage_1_2():
    st.title('Subpage 1.2')
```

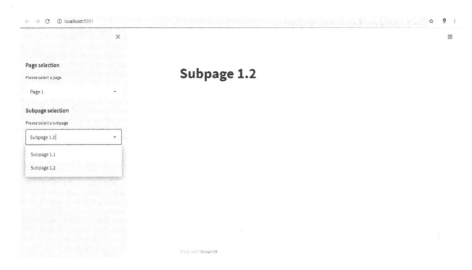

Figure 3-14. *Multipage Streamlit application with subpages*

3.4 Modularizing Application Development

In almost every web project, there is a need for visual components and code parts that manages the overall experience which is not directly seen by the end user, rather experienced. This is what is usually referred to as the business logic of the application that is responsible for controlling and managing intermodule communication, specifically whenever there is a reaction to be made upon user action, or to initiate an action by the user such as prompting the user to sign in .

3.4.1 Example: Developing a Social Network Application

For instance, a simple social network application such as the one shown in Figure 3-15 will need components to make a post and to read fields. These two seemingly simple requirements can be broken down into three main parts: views, action handling services, database connection or API (application programming interface) client of another backend service. For that example, everything will be post-centric, which means this should be a reusable, shared resource. A basic application as such shall have an architecture similar to Figure 3-16.

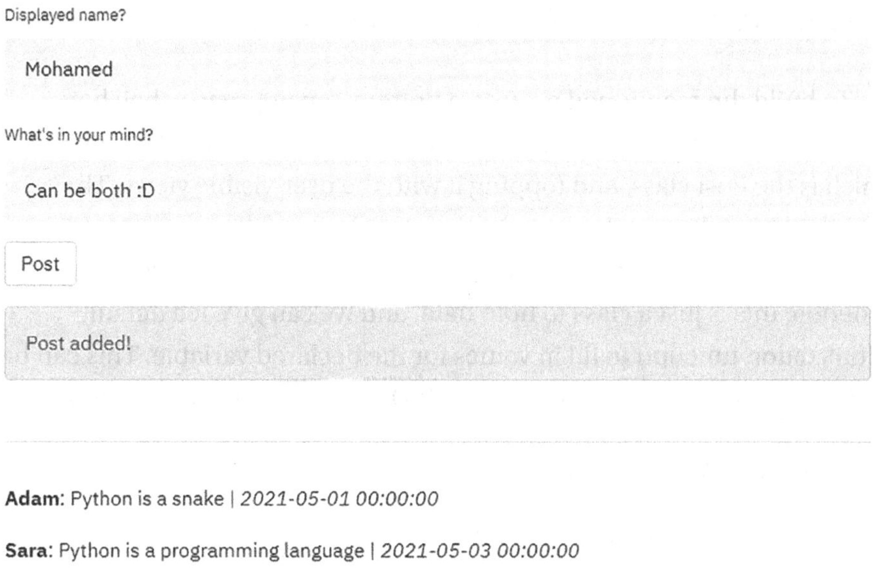

Displayed name?

Mohamed

What's in your mind?

Can be both :D

Post

Post added!

Adam: Python is a snake | *2021-05-01 00:00:00*

Sara: Python is a programming language | *2021-05-03 00:00:00*

Figure 3-15. *Demo social network app*

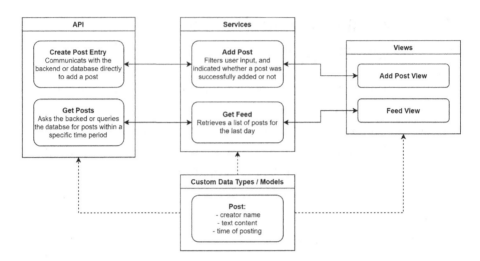

Figure 3-16. *Basic social network Streamlit architecture*

To build the mentioned project, a bottom-top approach shall be followed by starting with the most dependent object of the whole design, which is the Post class, and topping it with the user-visible views. The post shall be a class as shown in Listing 3-14 because it encapsulates related data in one form; in Python, we can use the *dataclasses* decorator to denote this is just a class to hold data, and we can give it a default initialization function to fill in values for the declared variable. This can be seen as the Pythonic alternative for C#'s DTOs (data transfer objects).

Listing 3-14. Models/Post.py

```python
from dataclasses import dataclass
import datetime

@dataclass(init=True)
class Post:
    creator_name: str
    content: str
    posting_date: datetime.datetime
```

Listing 3-15. Models/__init__.py

```python
from .Post import Post
```

Following that, there has to be a data source access mechanism with its only job being to store and write new posts, whether directly on a database or with an external service which can be communicated with HTTP methods or a messaging service, that is, Kafka, RabbitMQ, or AWS's SQS. For this example, we will assume a backend service is already built with two exposed methods, one to add posts and the other to get posts between two timestamps, as shown in Listing 3-16.

Listing 3-16. API.py

```python
from Models import Post
import datetime

class API:
    def __init__(self, config=None):
        self.config = config

    def add_post(self, post: Post):
        # POST HTTP request to backend to add the post
        # Returns true as in post has been added
        return True

    def get_posts(self, start_date: datetime.datetime,
    end_data: datetime.datetime):
        # GET HTTP request to backend to posts within a
        time period
        # Returns a list of Posts
        return [
            Post(
                "Adam", "Python is a snake",
                datetime.datetime(year=2021, month=5, day=1)
            ),
```

```
Post(
    "Sara", "Python is a programming language",
    datetime.datetime(year=2021, month=5, day=3)
)]
```

Once we have our API ready, we can start building an internal service to act the middleware between the visual components and the API, usually referred to as "Services" among seasoned developers.

Listing 3-17. Services/AddPost.py

```
from API import api_instance
from Models import Post

def add_post(post: Post):
    if post is None or len(post.creator_name) == 0
    or len(post.content) == 0:
        return None

    did_add = api_instance.add_post(post)

    return did_add
```

Listing 3-18. Services/GetFeed.py

```
from API import api_instance
import datetime

def get_feed():
    to_date = datetime.datetime.now()
    from_date = to_date - datetime.timedelta(days=1)
    posts = api_instance.get_posts(from_date, to_date)
    return posts
```

Listing 3-19. Services/__init__.py

```python
from .AddPost import add_post
from .GetFeed import get_feed
```

Even though the application is not considered complete due to missing the mostly awaited components that convert it to an interactive web application by users, it can still be used as a stand-alone service by any software as it is structured end to end to serve a clear purpose of adding and getting posts with filtering applied on passing data. Wrapping it up, we will insert our Streamlit visual components in a class-like structure for consistency with the most of the code base so far.

Furthermore, instead of using the service function right away by importing them, we think it is a great opportunity to introduce "*dependency injection*" which is a concept widely used in strongly typed languages such as C# and Java. This mechanism provides the capability of providing different implementations of the same function to be used by the depending class if needed, like when making test cases where making an actual post should be avoidable. Apart from this being a benefit to testable code, this coding pattern is preferred in many frameworks due to its easy readability.

Listing 3-20. FeedView.py

```python
import streamlit as st
from Models import Post
from typing import Callable

class FeedView:
    def __init__(self, get_feed_func: Callable[[], list]):
        posts = get_feed_func()
        for post in posts:
            _PostView(post)
```

```python
class _PostView:
    def __init__(self, post: Post):
        st.write(f"**{post.creator_name}**: {post.content} |
        _{post.posting_date}_")
```

Listing 3-21. AddPostView.py

```python
import datetime
import streamlit as st
from Models import Post
from typing import Callable

class AddPostView:
    def __init__(self, add_post_func: Callable[[Post], bool]):
        user_name_text = st.text_input("Displayed name?")
        post_text = st.text_input("What's in your mind?")
        clicked = st.button("Post")
        if clicked:
            post = Post(
                creator_name=user_name_text,
                content=post_text,
                posting_date=datetime.datetime.now()
            )
            did_add = add_post_func(post)

            if did_add:
                st.success("Post added!")
            else:
                st.error("Error adding post")
```

Listing 3-22. main.py

```python
import streamlit as st
from Views import FeedView, AddPostView
from Services import get_feed, add_post

AddPostView(add_post)
st.write("___")
FeedView(get_feed)
```

3.4.2 Best Practices for Folder Structuring

The example discussed in Section 3.4 can have all the files placed in the project's root folder. Even though this can give us a bug-free application, it can cause entanglements to the code reader if the application continues growing. Hence, we need to structure the files in folders and expose them as modules to be plugged in easily and professionally in other Python scripts. A folder structure such as Figure 3-17 groups similar files together. The *_init_.py* script is included in every subfolder to export the files within it as modules, as shown in Listing 3-23. And the *Views/_init_.py* script as shown in Listing 3-24 exposes an instance of the class instead of the class itself. Note that the underscore before the class instance name is just to rename it in this scope to indicate that this is a private property for this script, giving warnings to developers trying to access it in some IDEs.

Listing 3-23. Views/__init__.py

```python
from .AddPostView import AddPostView
from .FeedView import FeedView
```

Listing 3-24. API/__init__.py

```python
from .API import API as _API

api_instance = _API()
```

It is prudent to note that in Listing 3-23 the imports are from a relative path to a file not absolute. We can know this due to the presence of the "dot" in front of "*.AddPostView*" and "*.FeedView*"; this means using the file with the corresponding name in the local folder of the importing file, instead of searching in the project's root folder.

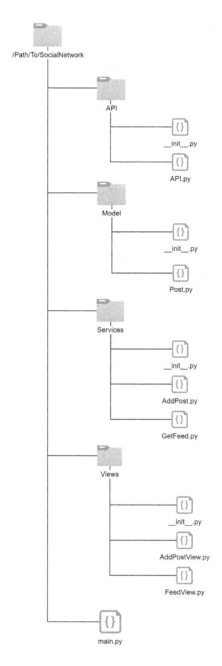

Figure 3-17. *Organized folder structure for Figure 3-16*

3.5 Summary

In this chapter, we provided an overview of how to design the frontend of a Streamlit application. From configuring color schemes and themes to organizing the page with columns, expanders, sidebar, and containers, we covered the methods at the developers' disposal to create their own bespoke user interfaces. Furthermore, we perused over how to create multipage and subpage applications with a modular and scalable system architecture. Finally, we displayed some of the ways that can be used to display dynamic content and visualizations to the user using Streamlit's native placeholder feature. In the next chapter, we will go through the fundamentals of caching big data, data mutation, and rendering a variety of static and interactive data visualizations.

CHAPTER 4

Data Management and Visualization

As with any web application, the management of data is an integral part of the undertaking. Coupled with the rise in big data, we are constantly in need of developing techniques that can manage the sheer magnitude of our data in an efficient and robust manner. In this chapter, we will address some of the key methods used to manage big data. Namely, we will cover encoding large multimedia files and dataframes into bytes data that can then be stored more robustly on database systems or in memory. Subsequently, we will demonstrate the utility of Streamlit's in-house caching capabilities that can be used to cache data, function executions, and objects in order to drastically reduce execution time on reruns of our application. Finally, we will cover techniques to mutate dataframes and tables in our application on demand.

In the second part of this chapter, we will dive into great depths of visualizing data, with a special focus on the Plotly visualization library for Python. We will provide boilerplate scripts that can be used to render basic, statistical, time-series, geospatial charts, and animated data visualizations in Streamlit.

© Mohammad Khorasani, Mohamed Abdou, Javier Hernández Fernández 2022
M. Khorasani et al., *Web Application Development with Streamlit*,
https://doi.org/10.1007/978-1-4842-8111-6_4

4.1 Data Management

The need to wrangle with data is inherent for most if not all web applications. While in this section we will not go into the depths of pre- and postprocessing data, we will however delve into some of the most profound ways of managing data and more specifically big data.

4.1.1 Processing Bytes Data

Depending on your application, you may need to grapple with binary/ bytes data. For instance, you may need to stream multimedia content or store your files on a database system. Luckily, Streamlit attends to a lot of the overhead when it comes to dealing with such data. As discussed in Section A.1, by using the *st.image*, *st.video*, and *st.audio* commands, we are able to natively process not only saved files on disk but also Numpy arrays, URLs, and most importantly bytes data.

While structured databases will be covered in greater depth in Section 5.1, it is worthy to note here that quite literally any bytes data can be saved and retrieved into a PostgreSQL table as long as the column data type is specified as *bytea*. This is particularly handy when working with large objects such as image, video, and audio files that need to be stored as blob (*binary large object*) storage. For such purposes, you will need to encode your data as follows.

Text

String and text can simply be encoded as follows for storage:

```
bytes_data = b'Hello world'

# Or alternatively
text = 'Hello world'
bytes_data = text.encode()
```

Subsequently, encoded string or text may be decoded as follows:

```
bytes_data.decode()
```

The default encoding used in the preceding method will be *UTF-8* unless otherwise specified.

Multimedia

To convert any uploaded image, video, or audio file to bytes data, simply use the following:

```
uploaded_file = st.file_uploader('Please upload a
multimedia file')

if uploaded_file is not None:
bytes_data = uploaded_file.read()
```

Subsequently, you may render the bytes data as an image, video, or audio by using the following commands:

```
# Image
st.image(bytes_data)

# Video
st.video(bytes_data)

# Audio
st.audio(bytes_data)
```

Dataframes

To read and display dataframes, you may use the following method:

```
import pandas as pd

uploaded_file = st.file_uploader('Please upload a CSV file')
```

```
if uploaded_file is not None:
    df = pd.read_csv(uploaded_file)
    st.write(df)
```

Alternatively, to encode dataframes (for storage as BLOB data on databases, for instance), you may use the Python module *StringIO* which stores content such as CSV files on memory as a file-like object, also known as a string-based IO. These objects can then be accessed by other functions and libraries such as Pandas as shown in the following:

```
from io import StringIO
import pandas as pd

uploaded_file = st.file_uploader('Please upload a CSV file')

if uploaded_file is not None:
    stringio = StringIO(uploaded_file.getvalue().decode())
    st.write(pd.read_csv(stringio))
```

Please note that while you may use the preceding method to store Pandas dataframes as a string-based IO, you may however not store the string IO into a database. To store a Pandas dataframe, you are better off saving it as a table using the Pandas command *dataframe.to_sql*, which will be covered in great depth in later sections.

4.1.2 Caching Big Data

Given the sheer magnitude of data exposed to us, it may sometimes be necessary to cache data in volatile storage to access it with reduced latency later on. As discussed in Section 13.1, Streamlit provides us with a native method to cache data, function executions, and objects on memory using the *@st.cache*, *@st.experimental_memo*, and *@st.experimental_singleton* decorators, respectively. You may simply write a function that returns data or an object and precede it with the *@st.cache*, *@st.experimental_memo*, or

@st.experimental_singleton decorator to make use of this feature. The first time you invoke the function, the returned data or object will be cached on memory, and for every subsequent invocation, the return will be from the cache and not the function itself, unless you alter the arguments of the function.

You can utilize Streamlit caching for yourself with Listing 4-1 to benchmark the percentage of runtime saved by recalling your dataframe from the cache. As shown in Figure 4-1, there is a drastic positive effect on the runtime saved especially as you approach dataframes with over 100,000 rows of data. The effect starts to level off at 100,000,000 rows of data with around 70% runtime saved.

Listing 4-1. cache.py

```python
import streamlit as st
import pandas as pd
import numpy as np
import time

@st.cache
def dataframe(rows):
    df = pd.DataFrame(
        np.random.randn(rows, 5),
        columns=('col %d' % i for i in range(5)))
    return df

runtime = pd.DataFrame(data={'Number of rows':[10,100,100
0,10000,100000,1000000, 10000000,100000000], 'First runtime
(s)':None, 'Second runtime (s)':None,'Runtime saved (%)':None})
```

```
for i in range(0,len(runtime)):
    start = time.time()
    dataframe(runtime.loc[i]['Number of rows'])
    stop = time.time()
    runtime.loc[i,'First runtime (s)'] = stop - start

    start = time.time()
    dataframe(runtime.loc[i]['Number of rows'])
    stop = time.time()
    runtime.loc[i,'Second runtime (s)'] = stop - start

    runtime.loc[i,'Runtime saved (%)'] = 100 -
int(100*(runtime.loc[i,'Second runtime (s)']/runtime.
loc[i,'First runtime (s)']))

st.write(runtime)
```

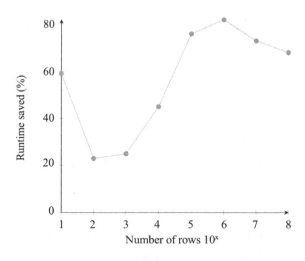

Figure 4-1. *Average percent runtime saved for six trials vs. number of rows while using st.cache*

4.1.3 Mutating Data in Real Time

You may be required to mutate data and specifically dataframes on demand within your application. Whether it is to filter out a time-series dataset based on a given date-time range or to append data to an existing column, the need to mutate data is inherent. To that end, with Streamlit we have the option of mutating data natively or by using third-party toolkits as shown in the following sections.

Native Data Mutation

Streamlit provides an intuitive and native method to add data to existing tables with its *st.add_rows* command. With this method, you can easily append a dataframe to a table created previously and immediately regenerate and view any associated charts in real time using the method shown in Listing 4-2.

Listing 4-2. mutate_data_real_time.py

```python
import streamlit as st
import pandas as pd
import random

def random_data(n):
    y = [random.randint(1, n) for value in range(n)]
    return y

if __name__ == '__main__':
    df1 = pd.DataFrame(data={'y':[1,2]})
    col1, col2 = st.columns([1,3])

    with col1:
        table = st.table(df1)
    with col2:
```

```
chart = st.line_chart(df1)
n = st.number_input('Number of rows to add',0,10,1)

if st.button('Update'):
    y = random_data(n)
    df2 = pd.DataFrame(data={'y':y})
    table.add_rows(df2)
    chart.add_rows(df2)
```

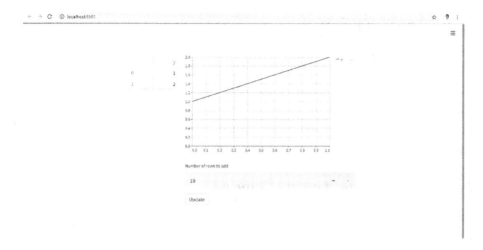

Figure 4-2. *Mutating data in real time using Listing 4-2*

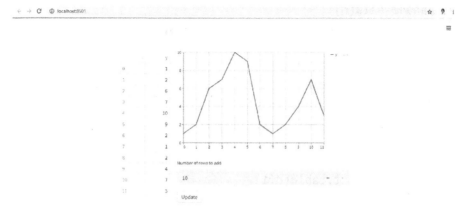

Figure 4-3. *Mutating data in real time using Listing 4-2 (continued)*

4.1.4 Advanced and Interactive Data Mutation

While Streamlit's native method of mutating data allows you to append rows to existing dataframes and charts, it does not however provide other advanced methods of mutating data, such as modifying individual cells, removing data, or filtering. Luckily, a highly versatile and rich third-party component called *streamlit-aggrid* fills that gap. Built on top of the AG Grid library for JavaScript frameworks, streamlit-aggrid displays data in an interactive grid widget, allowing the user to manipulate data with filtering, sorting, selecting, updating, pivoting, aggregating, querying, and a host of other methods. For further information on other features, you may refer to *www.ag-grid.com/*.

To use streamlit-aggrid on your Streamlit application, you must first initiate the widget and configure the features that you require, and then you may insert your Pandas dataframe into it using the *AgGrid()* command. Subsequently, the widget will be rendered, and the return value if invoked will be provided as a *dict*. To access the data within the widget, you must retrieve the *'data'* key of the dictionary, and similarly to access the selected rows, you have to retrieve the *'selected_rows'* key. The data will be returned as a table, whereas the selected rows will be returned as a list of dictionaries.

Specifically, Listing 4-3 will enable you to perform create, read, update, and delete operations on any provided dataset as follows:

- *Create*: To create a new record in the widget, you may simply append an empty row to the end of the dataframe as follows:

```
index = len(df)
df_new['data'].loc[index,:] = 'None'
df_new['data'].to_csv(path,index=False)
st.experimental_rerun()
```

- *Read*: You may read the data by rendering the dataframe as a grid widget. Please note that this step must be performed before any other operation in your script, and the widget must be invoked with a new name that is different from the original dataframe:

```
df = pd.read_csv(path)
df = df.fillna('None')
index = len(df)

gb = GridOptionsBuilder.from_dataframe(df)
gb.configure_side_bar()
gb.configure_default_column(groupable=True, value=True,
enableRowGroup=True, aggFunc="sum",editable=True)
gb.configure_selection(selection_mode="multiple", use_
checkbox=True)
gridOptions = gb.build()

df_new = AgGrid(df,gridOptions=gridOptions,enable_
enterprise_modules=True, update_mode=GridUpdateMode.
MODEL_CHANGED)
```

- *Update*: You can update the value of each individual cell interactively on the widget and immediately save the modified value to disk as follows:

```
if not df.equals(df_new['data']):
    df_new['data'].to_csv(path,index=False)
    st.experimental_rerun()
```

- *Delete*: You may also delete any row whose checkbox has been selected on the widget as follows:

```
if len(df_new['selected_rows']) > 0:
    exclude = pd.DataFrame(df_new['selected_rows'])
    pd.merge(df_new['data'], exclude, how='outer',
    indicator=True).query('_merge == "left_only"').
    drop('_merge', 1).to_csv(path, index=False)
    st.experimental_rerun()
```

In addition, you may choose to delete duplicate rows by using the following method:

```
df_new['data'] = df_new['data'].drop_duplicates()
df_new['data'].to_csv(path,index=False)
st.experimental_rerun()
```

Please note that for our create, update, and delete operations, we are using the *st.experimental_rerun()* command to automatically rerun the script after a modification has made. While this is an experimental feature provided by Streamlit that is still under development, it is necessary to use to render the modified widget without soliciting any further input from the user. Alternatively, you may add a dummy button to rerun the script and effectively update the widget when clicked by the user as shown in the following:

```
if st.button('Update'):
    pass
```

The final rendered widget can be seen in Figure 4-4.

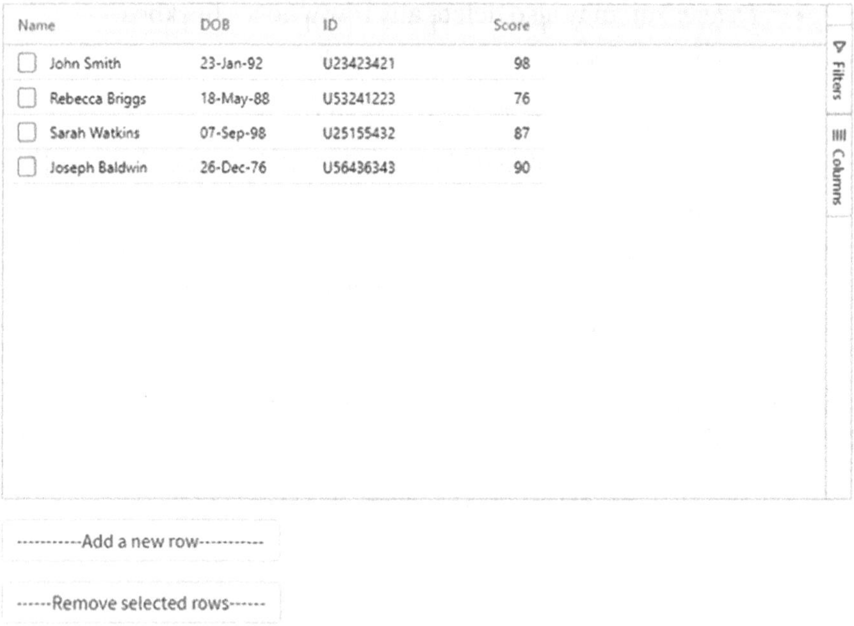

Name	DOB	ID	Score
☐ John Smith	23-Jan-92	U23423421	98
☐ Rebecca Briggs	18-May-88	U53241223	76
☐ Sarah Watkins	07-Sep-98	U25155432	87
☐ Joseph Baldwin	26-Dec-76	U56436343	90

----------Add a new row----------

------Remove selected rows------

Figure 4-4. *Mutating data in real time using Listing 4-3*

In addition to data mutation capabilities, the streamlit-aggrid widget offers a host of filtering and aggregating options. On the right pane of the widget, you can use the *Filters* tab to filter ordinal columns based on entries and numerical columns based on simple mathematical conditions as shown in Figure 4-5. Similarly, you can use the *Columns* tab to aggregate numerical columns as seen in Figure 4-6. Please note that both filtering and aggregation are nonmutable features and may solely be used for visual purposes.

Listing 4-3. crud.py

```python
import streamlit as st
import pandas as pd
from st_aggrid import AgGrid
from st_aggrid.shared import GridUpdateMode
```

```python
from st_aggrid.grid_options_builder import GridOptionsBuilder
def crud(path):
    df = pd.read_csv(path)
    df = df.fillna('None')
    index = len(df)

    # Initiate the streamlit-aggrid widget
    gb = GridOptionsBuilder.from_dataframe(df)
    gb.configure_side_bar()
    gb.configure_default_column(groupable=True, value=True,
    enableRowGroup=True, aggFunc="sum",editable=True)
    gb.configure_selection(selection_mode="multiple",
    use_checkbox=True)
    gridOptions = gb.build()

    # Insert the dataframe into the widget
    df_new = AgGrid(df,gridOptions=gridOptions,enable_
    enterprise_modules=True, update_mode=GridUpdateMode.MODEL_
    CHANGED)

    # Add a new row to the widget
    if st.button('-----------Add a new row-----------'):
        df_new['data'].loc[index,:] = 'None'
        df_new['data'].to_csv(path,index=False)
        st.experimental_rerun()

    # Save the dataframe to disk if the widget has been modified
    if df.equals(df_new['data']) is False:
        df_new['data'].to_csv(path,index=False)
        st.experimental_rerun()
```

```python
    # Remove selected rows from the widget
    if st.button('-----------Remove selected rows-----------'):
        if len(df_new['selected_rows']) > 0:
            exclude = pd.DataFrame(df_new['selected_rows'])
            pd.merge(df_new['data'], exclude, how='outer',
            indicator=True).query('_merge == "left_only"').
            drop('_merge', 1).to_csv(path, index=False)
            st.experimental_rerun()
        else:
            st.warning('Please select at least one row')

    # Check for duplicate rows
    if df_new['data'].duplicated().sum() > 0:
        st.warning('**Number of duplicate rows:** %s' %
        (df_new['data'].duplicated().sum()))
        if st.button('-----------Delete duplicates-----------'):
            df_new['data'] = df_new['data'].drop_duplicates()
            df_new['data'].to_csv(path,index=False)
            st.experimental_rerun()

if __name__ == '__main__':
    st.title('Data')
    crud('data.csv')
```

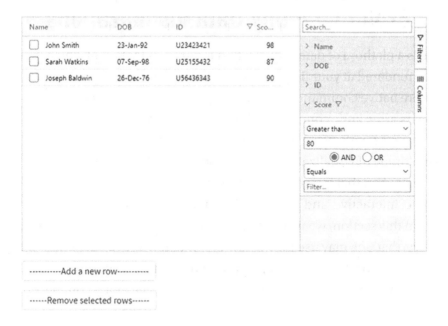

Figure 4-5. *Filtering data with the streamlit-aggrid widget*

Figure 4-6. *Aggregating data with the streamlit-aggrid widget*

4.2 Exploring Plotly Data Visualizations

There is a plethora of data visualization libraries in Python of which many can be rendered at your fingertips in Streamlit. Whether you use one of the more native commands such as *st.vega_lite_chart* or resort to using the Swiss army knife command otherwise known as *st.write*, either way you have at your disposal the ability to visualize aggressively. Among the multitude of visualization libraries, one stands out the most from the crowd. And that is none other than Plotly, arguably one of the most versatile, interactive, and aesthetically ornate visualization stacks out there. In this section, we will showcase some of the most relevant types of charts that one may use for web development. However, the following list will in no way be exhaustive, and should you need to peruse for other charts, you may refer to *https://plotly.com/python/* for a complete list.

4.2.1 Rendering Plotly in Streamlit

As elaborated in Section 13.1, with Streamlit you have at your disposal two native options to display Plotly and other types of charts. Specifically, you may use the *st.write* command, also known as the Swiss army knife of commands, to render the chart by simply writing the Plotly chart object (hereafter invoked as *fig*) as follows:

```
st.write(fig)
```

Alternatively, you may utilize the *st.plotly_chart* command that provides greater functionality when rendering Plotly charts:

```
st.plotly_chart(fig, use_container_width=True,
sharing='streamlit')
```

You may use the *st.plotly_chart* command with the additional arguments of *use_container_width* to specify whether the chart width should be restricted to the encapsulating column width or not, and you may use the *sharing* argument to specify whether the chart should be rendered in Plotly's offline mode (*'streamlit'*) or whether to send the chart to Plotly's chart studio ('private', 'secret', or 'public') for which you will require a Plotly account; for further information, please refer to *plotly.com/chart-studio/*. In addition, you may supply any other keyword argument that is supported by Plotly's *plot()* function.

4.2.2 Basic Charts

In this section, we will cover Plotly line, scatter, bar, and pie charts. Before we proceed any further, we will initially import all of the necessary libraries for this section as listed in the following:

```
import streamlit as st
import numpy as np
import pandas as pd
import plotly.express as px
import plotly.graph_objects as go
```

For the sake of uniformity, we will be using the same randomly generated Pandas dataframe (shown as follows) as our dataset to generate each of the charts:

```
data = np.random.randint(0, 10, size=(40,2))
df = pd.DataFrame(data, columns=['Column 1', 'Column 2'])
```

Line Chart

```
fig = go.Figure()

fig.add_trace(go.Scatter(x=df.index, y=df['Column 1'],
                    mode='lines',
                    name='Column 1'))
```

```
fig.add_trace(go.Scatter(x=df.index, y=df['Column 2'],
                mode='lines',
                name='Column 2'))
```

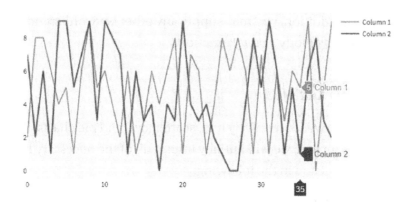

Scatter Chart

```
fig = go.Figure(data=go.Scatter(
    y = df['Column 1'],
    mode='markers',
    marker=dict(
        size=10,
        color=df['Column 2'], # Set color equal to a variable
        colorscale='Viridis', # Select colorscale
        showscale=True
    )
))
```

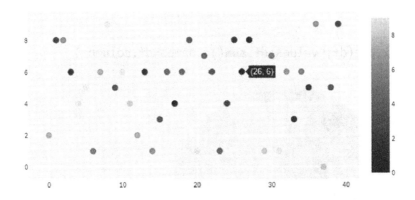

Bar Chart

```
fig = go.Figure(data=[
    go.Bar(name='Column 1', x=df.index, y=df['Column 1']),
    go.Bar(name='Column 2', x=df.index, y=df['Column 2'])
])
```

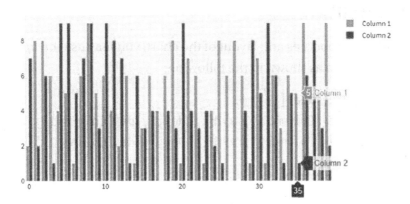

123

Pie Chart

```
fig = px.pie(df, values=df.sum(), names=df.columns)
```

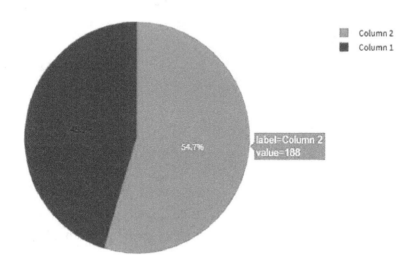

Chart Layout

To update the properties and layout of the chart, you may use the *update_ layout* declaration as shown in the following:

```
fig = go.Figure(data=[
    go.Bar(name='Column 1', x=df.index, y=df['Column 1']),
    go.Bar(name='Column 2', x=df.index, y=df['Column 2'])
])

fig.update_layout(
    title='Column 1 vs. Index',
    xaxis_title='Index',
    yaxis_title='Value',
    legend_title='Columns',
    font=dict(
```

```
        family='Arial',
        size=10,
        color='black'
    )
)
```

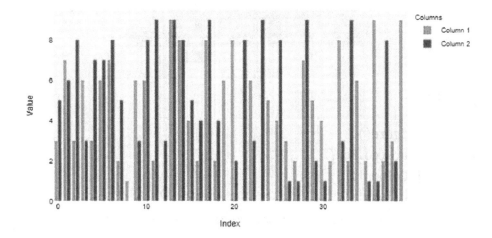

4.2.3 Statistical Charts

In this section, we will generate a Plotly histogram and box plot. The following randomly generated dataframe will be used for both charts:

```
data = np.random.randn(40, 2)
df = pd.DataFrame(data, columns=['Column 1', 'Column 2'])
```

Histogram

```
fig = go.Figure()
fig.add_trace(go.Histogram(name='Column 1', x=df['Column 1']))
fig.add_trace(go.Histogram(name='Column 2', x=df['Column 2']))
fig.update_layout(barmode='overlay')
fig.update_traces(opacity=0.75)
```

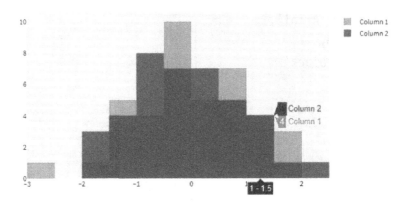

Box Plot

```
fig = go.Figure()
fig.add_trace(go.Box(
    y=df['Column 1'],
    name='Column 1',
    boxmean='sd' # Display mean, median and standard deviation
))
fig.add_trace(go.Box(
    y=df['Column 2'],
    name='Column 2',
    boxmean='sd' # Display mean, median and standard deviation
))
```

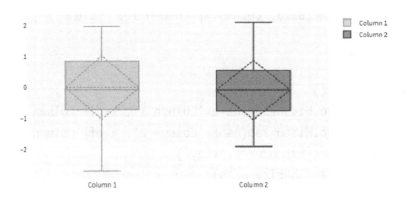

4.2.4 Time-Series Charts

Time-series charts can be generated using the same line chart function used in Section 4.2; the only difference is that the provided index must be in a date-time format. You can use the following function to create a Pandas dataframe with randomly generated values indexed between a range of specified dates:

```
data = np.random.randn(40, 2)
df = pd.DataFrame(data, columns=['Column 1', 'Column 2'])
df.index = pd.date_range(start='1/1/2018', end='2/9/2018',
freq='D')
```

Subsequently, the line chart function can be invoked as follows:

```
fig = px.line(df, x=df.index, y=df.columns)
```

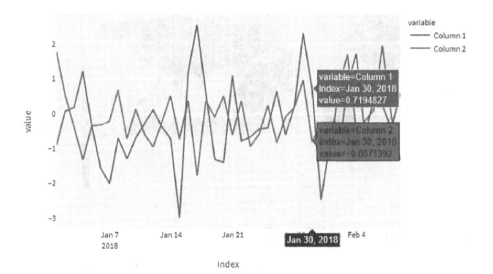

4.2.5 Geospatial Charts

Depending on your application, you may need to render interactive maps with geospatial data. Luckily, Plotly offers geospatial charts with a wealth of features and attributes. In this section, we will cover one type of such charts, namely, the choropleth map, using a dataset of world GDP per capita from 1990 to 2020 [22]:

```
df = pd.read_csv('gdp-per-capita-worldbank.csv').sort_
values(by='Year', ascending=False)
```

```
fig = px.choropleth(df, locations=df['Code'],
    color=df['GDP per capita, PPP (constant 2017
    international $)'],
    hover_name=df['Entity'])
```

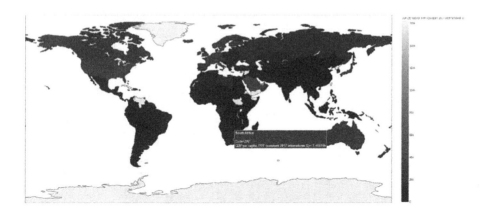

4.2.6 Animated Visualizations

With Plotly, you have the option of incorporating simple animations into your charts. This can be particularly handy when displaying a time-varying value in a time-series dataset. However, you are not restricted to time-series data and may indeed animate other types of numeric data should you wish to do so. In this section, we will animate the same previously used dataset of world GDP per capita from 1990 to 2020 [22] using both an animated bubble map and bar chart as shown in the following.

Animated Bubble Map

```
df = pd.read_csv('gdp-per-capita-worldbank.csv').sort_
values(by=['Year', 'Entity'])

fig = px.scatter_geo(df, locations=df['Code'],
    color=df['GDP per capita, PPP (constant 2017
international $)'],
    hover_name=df['Entity'],
    size=df['GDP per capita, PPP (constant 2017
international $)'],
    animation_frame=df['Year'])
```

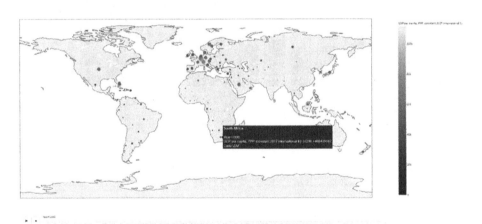

Animated Bar Chart

```
df = pd.read_csv('gdp-per-capita-worldbank.csv').sort_
values(by=['Year', 'Entity'])
df = df[df['GDP per capita, PPP (constant 2017 international
$)'] > 50000]
```

```
fig = px.bar(df, x=df['Entity'],
    y=df['GDP per capita, PPP (constant 2017 international $)'],
    animation_frame=df['Year'])
```

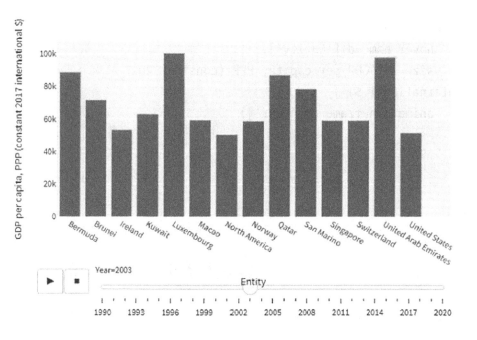

4.3 Summary

In this chapter, we provided an overview of several techniques used to manage big data. Specifically, we learned how to encode multimedia files and dataframes into bytes data to store large quantities of data robustly on databases or in memory. We also observed how Streamlit's caching functions can be utilized to profoundly reduce execution time when our application is rerun. In addition, we covered a native technique and a third-party toolkit that allow us to mutate dataframes and tables within our application. In the latter part of this chapter, we acquired the knowledge to generate various types of charts including basic, statistical, time-series, geospatial, and animated charts in Streamlit using the data visualization library Plotly. Upon completion of this chapter, we should have developed the ability to manage and visualize data of varying scale efficiently and robustly for our web application.

CHAPTER 5

Database Integration

Before we begin to utilize application data and user interaction insights, we need to learn how to store and manage data of varying schemas persistently with the use of robust and distributed database systems in an organized manner. Two types of database systems will be discussed in detail, namely, relational and nonrelational databases. Examples of interfacing with PostgreSQL and MongoDB will be shown to demonstrate the use cases for each. In addition, advanced features such as fuzzy matching and full-text indexing will be exhibited, and boilerplates will be provided to the reader to use as building blocks for their own applications. Finally, the reader will also learn how to seamlessly interface such databases with Streamlit to visualize data and to execute create, read, update, and delete operations on their data. PostgreSQL and pgAdmin installation is required for full understanding in this chapter.

5.1 Relational Databases

Since most of the apps made with Streamlit manipulate data in one way or the other, sometimes that data needs to be stored on disk for later use. In most cases, this data is in a specific format or, in other words, structured. We can make use of this property of the data to use a SQL database to store it.

PostgreSQL will be the tool we will demonstrate such use case with, due to it being free and open source.

5.1.1 Introduction to SQL

Structured Query Language is used to do CRUD operations on data with similar structure. Same structure data refers to different entries (rows) of data with same features (columns). An example of a relational SQL database is a company directory of employee data split into two separate tables, namely, the employees' personal information and their pay grades. Both forms of data can be represented as tables in the DB as shown in Tables 5-1 and 5-2, where there is a one-to-one linkage between both tables indicating that every employee shall have a pay grade. A one-to-one relationship is when every row in one table has a corresponding ID of another table extending the information of the first table with the second.

There are more types of mapping between tables such as one-to-many and many-to-many relationships, but we will not discuss them as it won't give additional value to the purpose of this book. But for the sake of real-life scenario demonstration, we will move forward with one-to-one for some of the examples.

CRUD, which stands for Create, Read, Update, and Delete, refers to the main operations you can do within a database, with SQL commands as follows:

- *Create*: To make a new person entry with pay grade 3

  INSERT INTO Persons VALUES ("Charlie", "01/01/1995", 3);

- *Read*: To retrieve all pay grade data with a base salary level equal to L3

  SELECT * FROM INTO PayGradeLevels WHERE BaseSalary = 'L3';

- *Update*: To update the pay grade of Bob to pay grade 2

  UPDATE Persons SET PayGradeId = 2 WHERE ID = 3;

- *Delete*: To remove pay grade 4 from existence

  DELETE FROM PayGradeLevels WHERE id = 4;

Table 5-1. *Persons table*

ID	Name	DOB	Pay Grade ID
1	Adam	01/01/1990	2
2	Sara	01/01/1980	1
3	Bob	01/01/1970	1
4	Alice	01/01/2000	3

Table 5-2. *Pay grade levels table*

ID	Base Salary	Reimbursements	Bonuses
1	L3	L2	L0
2	L1	L1	L1
3	L3	L3	L3
4	L1	L3	L1

One of the most important keywords that anyone building a database needs to know is the **primary key**; this refers to the *ID* in both Tables 5-1 and 5-2, as this is a unique, always valid, that is, not null, identifier that is used to refer a single row. Moreover, it is indexed, which means it's internally managed by the database in a specific way to further speed up query speeds when filtered with the *ID*. It is worth mentioning that indexing is a feature that can be applied to any column, but not preferred as it grows the disk space usage of that column to up to twice the size.

Indexing helps in quick search of specific values among all rows; hence, it is encouraged to be used in columns which represent IDs.

Another term called foreign key resonates in backend developer ears as an ID used to refer to a row in a different table. This is like the Pay Grade ID column in Table 5-1 which points to the ID column in Table 5-2.

5.1.2 Connecting a PostgreSQL Database to Streamlit

First, we will need to create the database and the tables from the example discussed in Section 5.1 using pgAdmin4, which is a GUI (graphical user interface) program used to interact with and manage PostgreSQL databases. Assuming it is installed and set up, we will create a new database following the steps in Figures 5-1 and 5-2 sequentially.

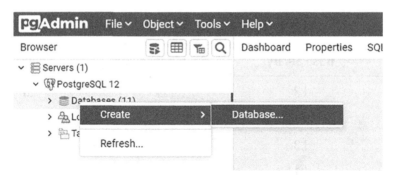

Figure 5-1. *Creating a new PostgreSQL database*

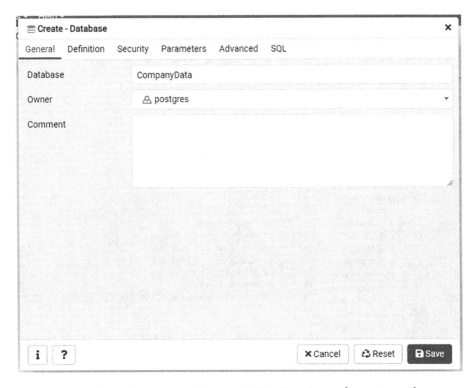

Figure 5-2. *Creating a new PostgreSQL database (continued)*

After our database is ready, we will click the Query Tool in the top-left corner to have run raw SQL commands. As shown in Figure 5-3, we are creating two tables both with primary keys, and one of them has foreign keys. Other features of the columns – also referred to as constraints in the database domains – are specifying a column to be not null and to be autoincrementing. When specifying a column to be not null, it configures the database to reject any insert or updates to a row where this column is set to null or not set at all if the data type's default value is null. *SERIAL* is a unique data type in PostegreSQL that ensures the column is not null and enforces autoincrementing of its integer value.

Figure 5-3. *Running SQL commands from create_tables.sql to create the database tables*

Before proceeding with the integration with Streamlit, we will first add some data into the database using raw SQL as shown in Figure 5-4. Notice how we did not need to set the ID values for both tables as this is being generated on the developer's behalf.

Firstly, we will need to prepare our database access credentials to use in Streamlit. These credentials, including the username and password, can be written as environment variables in a *.env* file, or in a *secrets.yaml* which will then be read and parsed by Streamlit. Ideally, however, they

should be written to the *secrets.toml* file in a folder called *.streamlit* –
which is recommended – as shown in Listing 5-1. This file is then read
by the Streamlit engine and parsed to make the variables within at the
developer's disposal easily. And for this toml file to be parsed correctly,
the database's connection data can be marked as *"db_postrgres,"* which is
also used within Streamlit to get those database connection metadata. As
a reminder, try to always choose strong passwords in the case the database
is public, almost anyone can try brute-forcing the password, gaining access
to the data.

Listing 5-1. .streamlit/secrets.toml

```
[db_postrgres]
host = "127.0.0.1"
port = "5432"
user = "postgres"
password = "admin"
dbname = "CompanyData"
```

```
Query Editor   Query History
1   INSERT INTO paygrades(base_salary, reimbursement, bonuses) VALUES ('L3', 'L2', 'L0');
2   INSERT INTO paygrades(base_salary, reimbursement, bonuses) VALUES ('L1', 'L1', 'L1');
3   INSERT INTO paygrades(base_salary, reimbursement, bonuses) VALUES ('L3', 'L3', 'L3');
4   INSERT INTO paygrades(base_salary, reimbursement, bonuses) VALUES ('L1', 'L3', 'L1');
5
6   INSERT INTO persons(name, date_of_birth, paygrade_id) VALUES ('Adam', '01/01/1990', 2);
7   INSERT INTO persons(name, date_of_birth, paygrade_id) VALUES ('Sara', '01/01/1980', 1);
8   INSERT INTO persons(name, date_of_birth, paygrade_id) VALUES ('Bob', '01/01/1970', 1);
9   INSERT INTO persons(name, date_of_birth, paygrade_id) VALUES ('Alice', '01/01/2000', 3);
```

```
Data Output   Explain   Messages   Notifications
INSERT 0 1

Query returned successfully in 55 msec.
```

Figure 5-4. *Inserting data using inserting_data.sql into the database*

To interface Python with PostgreSQL, we need to use a capable library to do so. For that example, we will use *psycopg2*, but other libraries such as *sqlalchemy* can do the job, and it will be introduced in later chapters.

As discussed in previous chapters, Streamlit reruns the python script upon user actions. This wasn't a big deal before, but it can introduce more overhead as in the current example, a new database connection will be established with every rerun. To avoid that unnecessary call, we can cache the first established connection. Streamlit allows caching function calls out of the box, by using its native function decorator *st.cache*. It can also accept some other parameters, for instance, an expiration date of the cache, which will cause the next function call to reexecute the function body if the cache is invalidated by then. As seen, the fifth line in Listing 5-2 is being applied to save the established connection.

After the new connection is established, we will need a *cursor* to use for querying SQL commands, also known as SQL queries. The cursor needs to be disposed after the query finishes; otherwise, it can retain in memory, and with every new query, the memory can be bloated and cause memory leaks, which is every software developer's nightmare. The developer can choose to close it manually or use a context manager which will close it once its usage scope is exited by the interpreter. Examples of both cases are the functions on lines 14 and 22 with output in Figure 5-5.

Listing 5-2. main.py

```python
import streamlit as st
import psycopg2

@st.cache(allow_output_mutation=True,
          hash_funcs={"_thread.RLock": lambda _: None})
def init_connection():
    return psycopg2.connect(**st.secrets["db_postrgres"])

conn = init_connection()
```

```python
def run_query(query_str):
    cur = conn.cursor()
    cur.execute(query_str)
    data = cur.fetchall()
    cur.close()
    return data

def run_query_with_context_manager(query_str):
    with conn.cursor() as cur:
        cur.execute(query_str)
        return cur.fetchall()

query = st.text_input("Query")

c1, c2 = st.columns(2)

output = None

with c1:
    if st.button("Run with context manager"):
        output = run_query_with_context_manager(query)
with c2:
    if st.button("Run without context manager"):
        output = run_query(query)

st.write(output)
```

5.1.3 Displaying Tables in Streamlit

After querying data from the database, we can display it in text format, or we can use more visually entertaining tools from Streamlit, which will require a modification of the representation of the data.

Among data scientists and developers, it is usually known to parse structured data, whether it is sensor values, identification information, or any repeating data with a structure in the form of a Pandas dataframe. Dataframes are generally Numpy arrays with extra capability such as storing column values and SQL-like querying techniques. That being said, it also shares the same fast vectorization capabilities with normal Numpy arrays, which is essentially a parallelized way to do mathematical computations on an array as a whole instead of doing it one by one.

Streamlit allows printing dataframes right away from a single command in two different *st.table* displays a noninteractive representation of the dataframe as shown in Figure 5-6. And Figure 5-7 displays *st. dataframe*, rendering an interactive representation of the dataframe, where the user can sort any column just by clicking it. As a trade-off, this makes the web application slower as more CPU and/or memory usage is required, since the complexity of the sorting algorithm grows- in an $O(n*log(n))$ manner

Listing 5-3. df_demo.py

```python
import streamlit as st
import pandas as pd

df = pd.DataFrame([["Adam", "01/01/1990", 2],
                   ["Sara", "01/01/1980", 1],
                   ["Bob", "01/01/1970", 1],
                   ["Alice", "01/01/2000", 3]
                   ], columns=["Name", "DOB", "Paygrade ID"])

st.table(df)

st.dataframe(df)
```

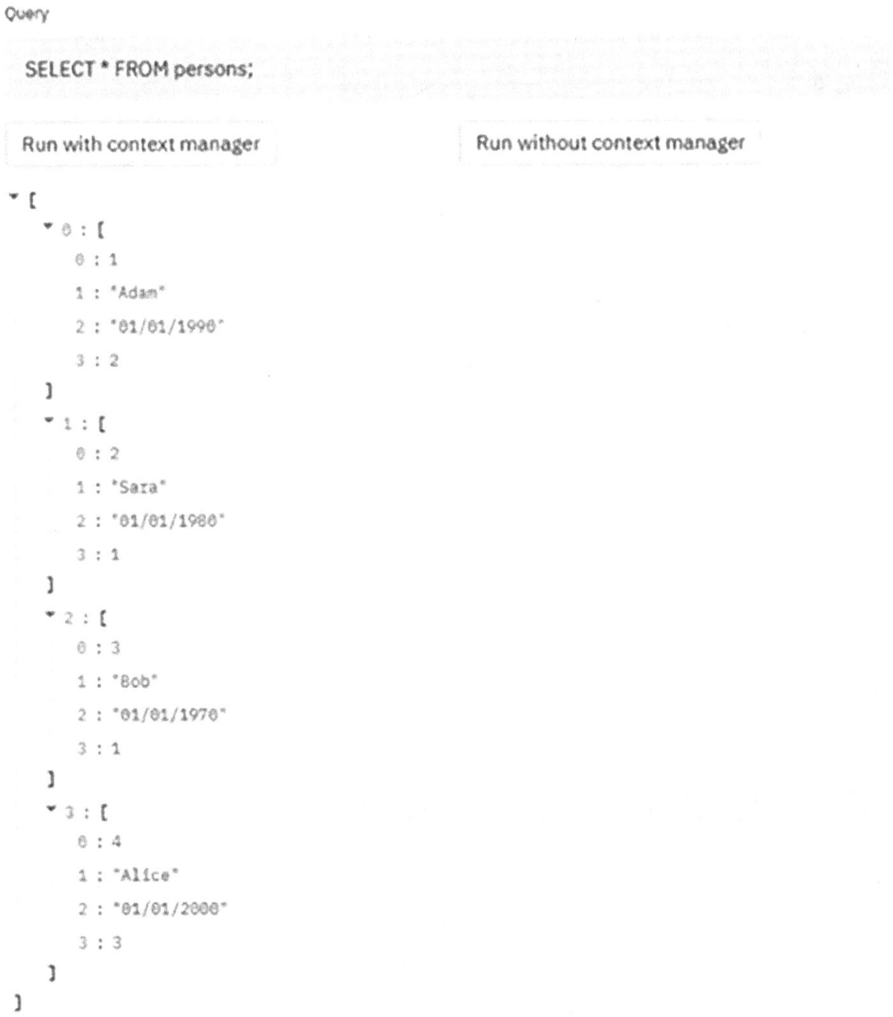

Query

```
SELECT * FROM persons;
```

| Run with context manager | Run without context manager |

```
▼ [
  ▼ 0 : [
      0 : 1
      1 : "Adam"
      2 : "01/01/1990"
      3 : 2
  ]
  ▼ 1 : [
      0 : 2
      1 : "Sara"
      2 : "01/01/1980"
      3 : 1
  ]
  ▼ 2 : [
      0 : 3
      1 : "Bob"
      2 : "01/01/1970"
      3 : 1
  ]
  ▼ 3 : [
      0 : 4
      1 : "Alice"
      2 : "01/01/2000"
      3 : 3
  ]
]
```

Figure 5-5. *Running user SQL commands from Streamlit*

	Name	DOB	Paygrade ID
0	Adam	01/01/1990	2
1	Sara	01/01/1980	1
2	Bob	01/01/1970	1
3	Alice	01/01/2000	3

Figure 5-6. *st.table from Listing 5-3*

	Name	DOB	Paygrade ID
0	Adam	01/01/1990	2
1	Sara	01/01/1980	1
2	Bob	01/01/1970	1
3	Alice	01/01/2000	3

Figure 5-7. *st.dataframe from Listing 5-3*

5.2 Nonrelational Databases

While in most use cases you will be dealing with a structured dataset where the schema, attributes, data types, and metadata will be known beforehand, there are indeed instances where none of these will be known. Imagine that you are trying to create a search engine, where users can input documents with varying lengths, numbers of headers or pictures, and types of media. It is simply impossible to know what sort of schema or table to provision to store such data. In such applications, the utility of a NoSQL database, the likes of MongoDB, is essential to store and manage unstructured data.

5.2.1 Introduction to MongoDB

MongoDB enables you to store data as a JSON *document* with varying attributes and data types into a *collection* with a varying schema. Please note that with MongoDB, a document is analogous to a row, and a collection is analogous to a table in a relational database system. Even if your dataset is structured to begin with, there is no harm in using a NoSQL database system, as you may eventually scale your application enough to end up dealing with an abundance of unstructured data. In addition, if you require features such as full-text indexing where every word in every document in every collection is reverse-indexed, or if you need fuzzy matching in your queries to mitigate the effect of typos, then MongoDB is the place to be.

To provide an overview of MongoDB and how it can be interfaced with Streamlit, in this section we will create a search engine application for restaurants using a publicly available unstructured dataset of restaurant ratings. The goal of the application is to allow the user to search for restaurants based on the type of cuisine and address they want. For the cuisine, a simple one-to-one match with a predefined list of cuisine types will be used to filter the data. However, for the address, full-text indexing will be required to ensure that the address can be matched with n-grams (continuous sequence of words or tokens in a document of text) corresponding to the borough and street address that are located in disparate objects and arrays within the document as shown in Figure 5-8. In addition, fuzzy matching will be needed to guarantee that similar but nonidentical search queries will be matched with a term that is at most two characters different from the record.

5.2.2 Provisioning a Cloud Database

MongoDB can be provisioned both locally and on the cloud; however, to utilize the full-text indexing feature provided by MongoDB's *Atlas Search* service, you will need to host your database on the cloud, as per the following steps:

1. To begin with, you may set up an account and project at *www.mongodb.com/atlas/database*.

2. Provision the free *M0 Sandbox* cluster as shown in Figures 5-9 and 5-10. If necessary, modify the hosted region to ensure minimal latency between your database and server.

3. Once the cluster has been provisioned, you may proceed with whitelisting the IP addresses that you wish to access the database from in the *Network Access* menu item. While it is not recommended, you may whitelist all addresses as shown in Figure 5-11 to access the database from anywhere.

4. Subsequently, you will need to create user credentials to access the database from the *Overview* tab in the *Databases* menu item as shown in Figure 5-12.

```
  _id: ObjectId("5eb3d668b31de5d588f4292a")
v address: Object
    building: "2780"
  v coord: Array
      0: -73.98241999999999
      1: 40.579505
    street: "Stillwell Avenue"
    zipcode: "11224"
  borough: "Brooklyn"
  cuisine: "American"
v grades: Array
  v 0: Object
      date: 2014-06-10T00:00:00.000+00:00
      grade: "A"
      score: 5
  v 1: Object
      date: 2013-06-05T00:00:00.000+00:00
      grade: "A"
      score: 7
  v 2: Object
      date: 2012-04-13T00:00:00.000+00:00
      grade: "A"
      score: 12
  v 3: Object
      date: 2011-10-12T00:00:00.000+00:00
      grade: "A"
      score: 12
  name: "Riviera Caterer"
  restaurant_id: "40356018"
```

Figure 5-8. *A sample document from the restaurants dataset*

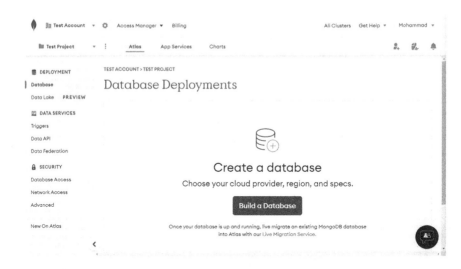

Figure 5-9. *Setting up a MongoDB database*

5. You may then create a connection string by selecting
    the *Connect your application* option in the *Choose
    a connection method* tab and proceeding to select
    the Python driver that is most suitable for your
    application, as shown in Figures 5-13 and 5-14.

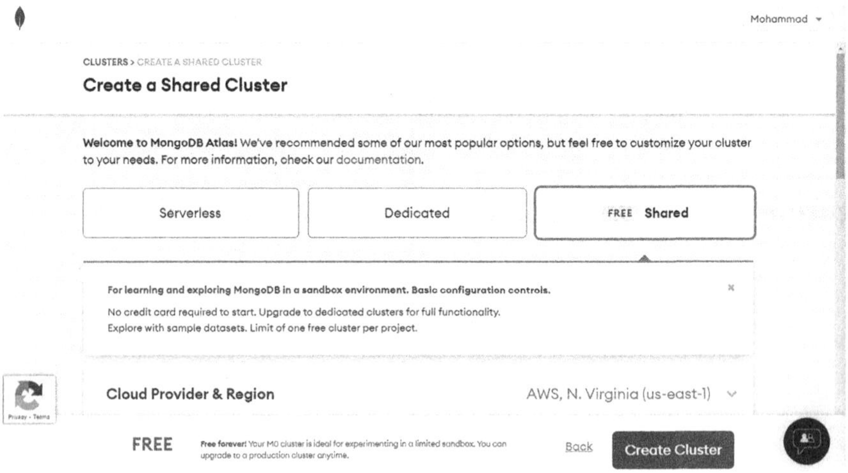

Figure 5-10. *Provisioning a free M0 Sandbox cluster*

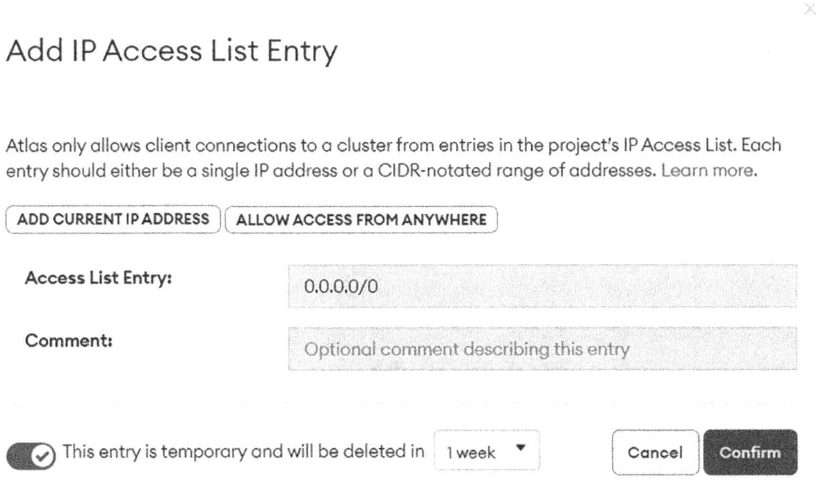

Add IP Access List Entry

Atlas only allows client connections to a cluster from entries in the project's IP Access List. Each entry should either be a single IP address or a CIDR-notated range of addresses. Learn more.

[ADD CURRENT IP ADDRESS]   [ALLOW ACCESS FROM ANYWHERE]

Access List Entry: 0.0.0.0/0

Comment: Optional comment describing this entry

This entry is temporary and will be deleted in 1 week ▼   [Cancel] [Confirm]

Figure 5-11. *Configuring network access to the database*

> 6. Finally, you may upload your own dataset or alternatively load a sample dataset provided by MongoDB in the *Collections* tab of the *Databases* menu item, as shown in Figure 5-15. For this example, we will be using the sample *restaurants* collection from MongoDB's own datasets.

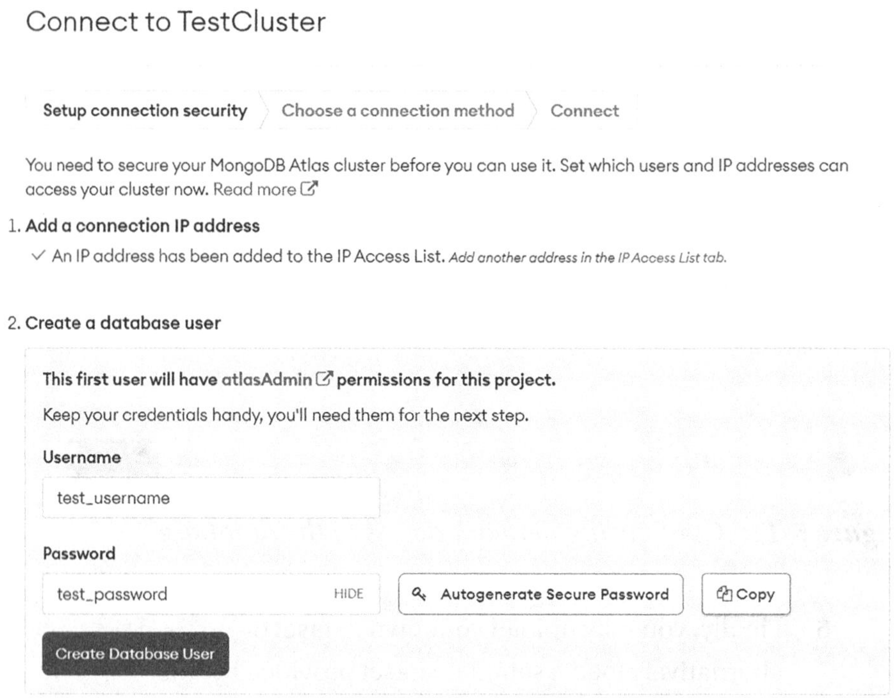

Connect to TestCluster

Setup connection security 〉 Choose a connection method 〉 Connect

You need to secure your MongoDB Atlas cluster before you can use it. Set which users and IP addresses can access your cluster now. Read more ⧉

1. **Add a connection IP address**

    ✓ An IP address has been added to the IP Access List. *Add another address in the IP Access List tab.*

2. **Create a database user**

    This first user will have atlasAdmin ⧉ permissions for this project.

    Keep your credentials handy, you'll need them for the next step.

    Username

    ┌──┐
    │ test_username   │
    └──┘

    Password

    ┌─────────────────────────────┐ ┌──────────────────────────────────┐ ┌──────────┐
    │ test_password   HIDE │ │ ⚷ Autogenerate Secure Password │ │ ⧉ Copy │
    └─────────────────────────────┘ └──────────────────────────────────┘ └──────────┘

    ┌───────────────────────┐
    │ Create Database User │
    └───────────────────────┘

Figure 5-12. *Creating user credentials for the database*

5.2.3 Full-Text Indexing

Full-text indexing indexes every single token, for all the objects in all the documents of a database. It is an extremely powerful form of indexing that allows you to perform accurate queries and retrieve all matching documents, very similar to how search engines work. In MongoDB, you can create a full-text index on a cloud database as follows:

1. To create an index, open the Search tab found in the *Databases* menu item, and click *Create Search Index*, as shown in Figure 5-16.

2. Subsequently, select the *JSON Editor* from the *Configuration Method* tab.

3. Select the database and collection that you want to create the index for, enter a name for the index, and enter the following index, as shown in Figure 5-17:

```
{
  "mappings": {
    "dynamic": true
  }
}
```

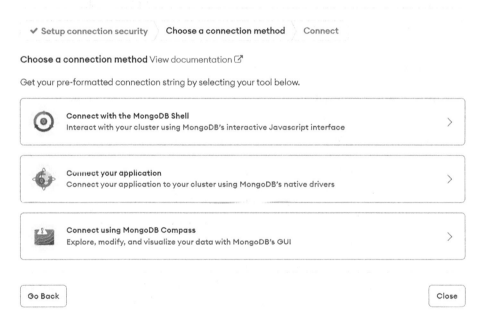

Figure 5-13. *Creating a connection string for the database*

5.2.4 Querying the Database

To query your indexed database in MongoDB, you should initially connect to your database with the connection string acquired in Figure 5-13, by using it to establish a client. It will be handy to invoke the client as a function that is cached with the *@st.cache* command. This will ensure that each time a query is executed, instead of establishing a new client, the one that was previously cached is used, thereby saving a considerable amount of runtime and resources as shown in the following:

```
from pymongo import MongoClient

@st.cache(allow_output_mutation=True, hash_funcs={"_thread.
RLock": lambda _: None})
def create_client():
    return MongoClient('<connection_string>')
```

Subsequently, you will need to create an *Aggregation*, which is simply a multistaged filtering pipeline written in JSON containing all the filters you want to apply to your data in order to query it as follows:

1. **Search using fuzzy matching**

   In this stage, we need to specify the name of the index that we created previously to use for searching the documents. In addition, we need to input the user's *query* with string concatenation; we also need to specify the *path* or in other words the objects to search through in the documents, that is, borough and street address (nested elements and/or objects can be accessed with a period, i.e., *address.street*). Most importantly, however, we need to enable *fuzzy* matching and specify the number of single-character edits needed to match the query

with the token using *maxEdits*, and we also need
to determine the number of characters at the start
of each query that must match the token using
prefixLength:

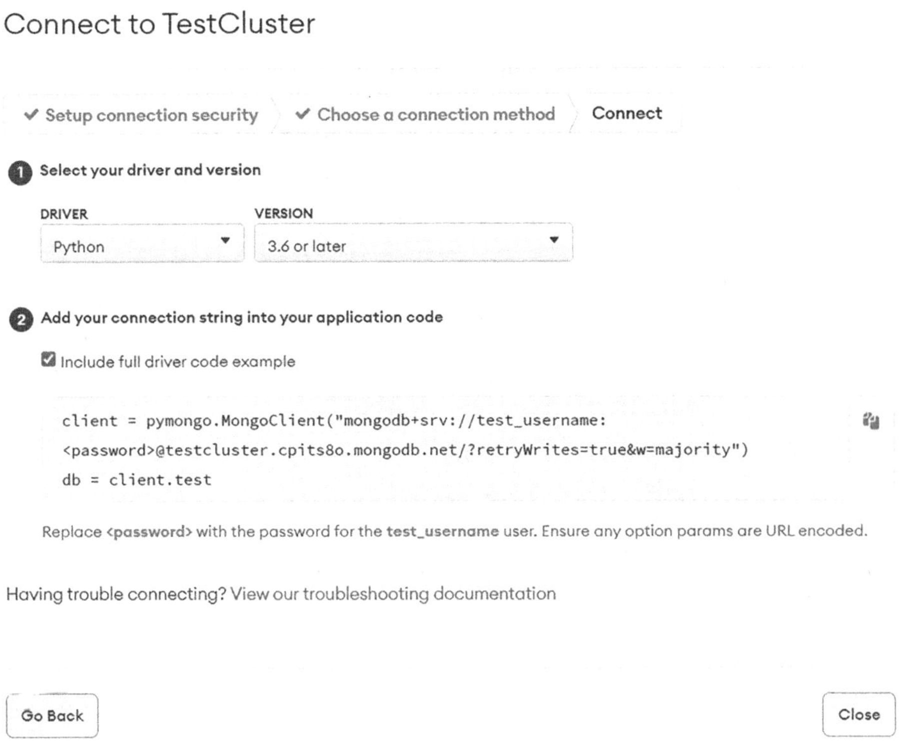

Connect to TestCluster

✔ Setup connection security ❯ ✔ Choose a connection method ❯ **Connect**

① Select your driver and version

DRIVER   VERSION

| Python ▾ | 3.6 or later ▾ |

② Add your connection string into your application code

☑ Include full driver code example

```
client = pymongo.MongoClient("mongodb+srv://test_username:
<password>@testcluster.cpits8o.mongodb.net/?retryWrites=true&w=majority")
db = client.test
```

Replace <password> with the password for the **test_username** user. Ensure any option params are URL encoded.

Having trouble connecting? View our troubleshooting documentation

| Go Back | | Close |

Figure 5-14. *Creating a connection string for the database*
(continued)

```
'$search': {
    'index': 'default',
    'text': {
        'query': '%s' % (address),
        'path': ['borough','address.street'],
        'fuzzy': {
```

```
                    'maxEdits': 2,
                    'prefixLength': 2
            }
        }
    }
```

2. **Project documents with search score**

   At this stage, we will pass only the objects that we
   want from the documents and will also compute the
   relevance score using the *'searchScore'* tag:

```
'$project': {
    'Name': '$name',
    'Cuisine': '$cuisine',
    'Address': '$address.street',
    'Borough': '$borough',
    'Grade': '$grades.grade',
    'Score': {
        '$meta': 'searchScore'
    }
}
```

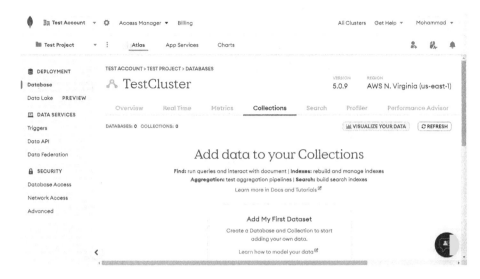

Figure 5-15. *Loading a dataset into the database*

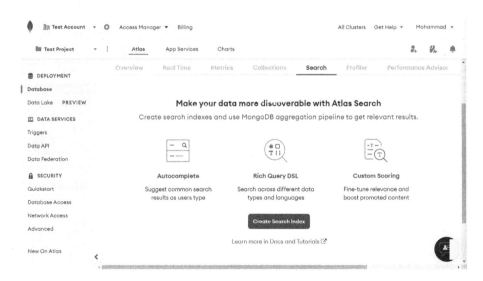

Figure 5-16. *Creating a full-text index for the database*

3. **Filter documents**

Subsequently, we will filter the passed documents with the user entry for the type of cuisine. Please note that unlike fuzzy matching, at this stage queries must be identical to the tokens in the documents for a successful filtering:

```
'$match': {
    'Cuisine': '%s' % (cuisine)
}
```

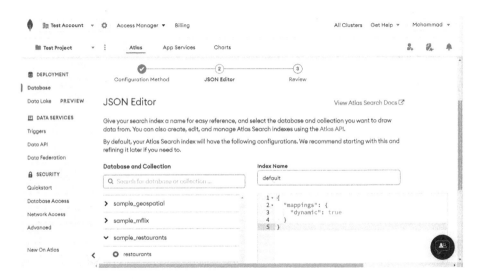

Figure 5-17. *Creating a full-text index for the database (continued)*

4. **Limit results**

Finally, at this stage we will simply limit the number of passed results to the number we require:

```
'$limit': 5
```

For information regarding additional options for the aggregation pipeline, please refer to *https://docs.mongodb.com/manual/reference/aggregation/*.

5.2.5 Displaying Tables in Streamlit

Once the aggregation pipeline is complete and has passed the queried results to Python, you will need to perform postprocessing before you can render the table in Streamlit. Specifically, you will need to convert the returned object from the MongoDB client into a Pandas dataframe and specify the columns you want to keep. In addition, you need to parse any returned lists (such as the restaurant grades) and convert to plain text as shown in the following:

```
df = pd.DataFrame(result)[['Name','Address','Grade','Score']]
df['Grade'] = [','.join(map(str, x)) for x in df['Grade']]
```

You may refer to Listing 5-4 to peruse the complete code for this section. You may also view the associated Streamlit application in Figure 5-18 that displays an example of a fuzzy matched query and the returned table in Streamlit.

Listing 5-4. mongodb.py

```
import streamlit as st
import pandas as pd
from pymongo import MongoClient

@st.cache(allow_output_mutation=True,
    hash_funcs={"_thread.RLock": lambda _: None})

def create_client():
    return MongoClient('<connection_string>')

def query(cuisine,address):

    result = create_client()['sample_restaurants']
    ['restaurants'].aggregate([
        {
```

```
            '$search': {
                'index': 'default',
                'text': {
                    'query': '%s' % (address),
                    'path': ['borough','address.street'],
                    'fuzzy': {
                        'maxEdits': 2,
                        'prefixLength': 2
                    }
                }
            }
        }, {
            '$project': {
                'Name': '$name',
                'Cuisine': '$cuisine',
                'Address': '$address.street',
                'Borough': '$borough',
                'Grade': '$grades.grade',
                'Score': {
                    '$meta': 'searchScore'
                }
            }
        }, {
            '$match': {
                'Cuisine': '%s' % (cuisine)
            }
        }, {
            '$limit': 5
        }
    ])
```

```
    try:
        df = pd.DataFrame(result)[['Name','Address','Grade',
        'Score']]
        df['Grade'] = [','.join(map(str, x)) for x in df['Grade']]
        return df
    except:
        return None

if __name__ == '__main__':
    st.title('Restaurants Explorer')
    cuisine = st.selectbox('Cuisine',['American','Chinese',
    'Delicatessen',
    'Hamburgers','Ice Cream, Gelato, Yogurt, Ices','Irish'])
    address = st.text_input('Address')

    if st.button('Search'):
        if address != ":
            st.write(query(cuisine,address))
        else:
            st.warning('Please enter an address')
```

Figure 5-18. *Output of Listing 5-4*

5.3 Summary

In this chapter, we covered relational and nonrelational databases that are used to store and retrieve structured and unstructured data, respectively. Specifically, we learned how to provision a PostgreSQL database and interface it with a Streamlit application to host and process our structured datasets. Similarly, we learned how to provision a MongoDB cloud database to store unstructured data consisting of collections of documents with varying schemas, objects, and elements. We saw how MongoDB can be used to create a full-text index where every token in each document is indexed for enhanced querying, and we demonstrated how to perform fuzzy matching of query terms with document tokens, thereby mitigating the effects of typos. Finally, we witnessed how to wrap all of these operations from establishing a database client to writing an aggregation pipeline and to postprocessing queried results within a Streamlit application.

CHAPTER 6

Leveraging Backend Servers

In this chapter, we will introduce a more sophisticated and scalable way of designing web applications. Specifically, this chapter will present the process to offload the overhead associated with managing databases from the Streamlit server and onto an independent backend server as it should be in a full-stack environment. To that end, this chapter will walk the developer through the entire process of provisioning a backend server in Python that acts as the middleman between the database and the frontend. And finally, the developer will be acquainted with the workings of a highly modular, versatile, and secure architecture with additional security layers between the application and database.

6.1 The Need for Backend Servers

As part of building a scalable and robust Streamlit application, some of the tasks which are executed within the Streamlit application, are better off being executed in an isolated system that is easy to communicate with. Such environment is referred to as a backend, and it is responsible for managing authentication, authorization, databases, and other gateway connections – all while including managing core business logic which shouldn't be done on the frontend side, that is, Streamlit. Even though

© Mohammad Khorasani, Mohamed Abdou, Javier Hernández Fernández 2022
M. Khorasani et al., *Web Application Development with Streamlit*,
https://doi.org/10.1007/978-1-4842-8111-6_6

Streamlit is a server-side web framework, it's highly recommended to still isolate from other system aspects for modularity as security. As if everything from authentication to database management were run from Streamlit, this can possess multiple security threats, from XSS to SSRF and possibly RCE if not engineered correctly.

Not claiming that a backend-frontend architecture is invulnerable, but having this architecture adds another layer of protection which is made with the API. That needs to be broken or bypassed by malicious actors to reach other protected system aspects. And with modern API designing methodologies, it is attack proof, as it pipelines every request through the same routing mechanism which decreases human error in making a vulnerable code.

6.2 Frontend-Backend Communication

The backend is usually referred to as the server, and the frontend is always known to be the client. Usually, the client triggers a resource or information request upon the user's actions. The request is eventually followed by a response by the server including the solicited data. The request-response communication is how HTTP protocol works. HTTP generally has two major components, headers and a body.

The request or response headers include information about the request itself and payload carried in the body. Some of these information include, but are not limited to, cookies, request identifiers, keys, tokens, data type of the body, host or IP address of the server, and data encoding or compressing mechanisms. For the sake of this book's scope, we will focus on the general aspects of keys, tokens, cookies, and the body's content type. For instance, request body types can be as shown in Table 6-1. Since backends are mainly responsible for sending and receiving information, a good and the most widely used format is JSON.

Table 6-1. *Common content-type header values*

Content-Type Value	Description
text/HTML	Text format but is parseable to HTML to be rendered as a web page
application/JSON	JSON format
application/xml	XML format
image/png	Image binary of type PNG

6.2.1 HTTP Methods

And finally, the last general thing to know about HTTP requests is that they have methods, like what has been discussed previously in Section 5.1. But unlike SQL, the syntax of HTTP methods doesn't require a drastic change in the request's syntax. The main methods are *GET*, *POST*, *PUT*, and *DELETE*, which reference getting, adding, modifying, and deleting a resource, respectively. Adding and modifying resources can have a body to alter the resource upon, but not the deleting and getting as the resource identifiers for them are mostly included in the request URL. Those are the main functions of a RESTful API which is, in a nutshell, an HTTP API gateway to modify resources or data on the server side.

Visiting a website is simply a *GET* request to that URL. Hence, it should have request-specific data in its header, body, and response code. For instance, requesting a page with just its domain name will request its HTTP version by default, but the backend server can propose a redirection to the HTTPS version. An example for that is Google, where if you go to google.com it will redirect to `https://google.com`; you can check this by inspecting the page's network traffic or by using Curl. Curl is a tool made to make HTTP requests from the terminal or CMD. It allows you to check

163

out the response body, headers, and status code. It can also give support to understanding some of the backend server's commands to the frontend, such as following a redirect. Figure 6-1 shows the possibility to do the mentioned actions in the CMD by running curl -i -L google.com; -i is used to display response headers and -L to follow redirects if any.

```
C:\>curl -i -L google.com
HTTP/1.1 301 Moved Permanently
Location: http://www.google.com/
Content-Type: text/html; charset=UTF-8
Date: Sun, 07 Nov 2021 07:43:52 GMT
Expires: Tue, 07 Dec 2021 07:43:52 GMT
Cache-Control: public, max-age=2592000
Server: gws
Content-Length: 219
X-XSS-Protection: 0
X-Frame-Options: SAMEORIGIN

HTTP/1.1 200 OK
Date: Sun, 07 Nov 2021 07:43:53 GMT
Expires: -1
Cache-Control: private, max-age=0
Content Type: text/html; charset=ISO 8859 1
P3P: CP="This is not a P3P policy! See g.co/p3phelp for more info."
Server: gws
X-XSS-Protection: 0
X-Frame-Options: SAMEORIGIN
Set-Cookie: 1P_JAR=2021-11-07-07; expires=Tue, 07-Dec-2021 07:43:53 GMT; path=/; domain=.google.com; Secure
Set-Cookie: NID=511=jJl8pfDOZBQFbJ33BeiBUmWUg3HK1GU8IMqtqFAJApLNKL3CJ9XC45Ob6gmxLYr2sxKuxKGeX5pkH473f-gYiHimMpXbfFFvOrs
/; domain=.google.com; HttpOnly
Accept Ranges: none
Vary: Accept-Encoding
Transfer-Encoding: chunked
```

Figure 6-1. Getting google.com and watching response headers and redirection

6.3 Working with JSON Files

JSON documents can be used to represent and parse data with. Essentially, they can contain a list/array or a key/value pair similar to dictionaries in Python. They can also include other primitive data types such as integers, floats, strings, and boolean. With such simple data types, a complex structural representation of any data can be represented. A sample JSON representing one of the previously introduced examples is as shown in Listing 6-1.

Listing 6-1. sample_json.json

```json
[
    {
        "Name": "Adam",
        "DOB": "01/01/1990",
        "Paygrade ID": "2"
    },
    {
        "Name": "Sara",
        "DOB": "01/01/1980",
        "Paygrade ID": "1"
    },
    {
        "Name": "Bob",
        "DOB": "01/01/1970",
        "Paygrade ID": "1"
    },
    {
        "Name": "Alice",
        "DOB": "01/01/2000",
        "Paygrade ID": "3"
    }
]
```

6.4 Provisioning a Backend Server

To stick with the Python theme of the book, we will build a Pythonic backend server. Looking to the potential options for such requirements, we can mainly find Flask and Django good for the job. Both can be used as frontend application servers as both can serve HTML for browsers to render, but Django is built with that task in mind due to the presence of a web template engine called *Jinja*. But Flask is flexible and configurable to the developer's need, plus it being lighter in weight. To get started, install it with Pip.

6.4.1 API Building

A backend will run a single or multiple methods or functions upon a request to the server. Those methods and functions depend on the URL and can be configured to also take the headers in consideration. A simple example for that is like Listing 6-2, which will serve the user the page in Figure 6-2 if *http://<SERVER-HOST>/server_status* was requested, and *404 Not Found* otherwise.

Listing 6-2. flask_sample.py

```python
from flask import Flask

app = Flask(__name__)

@app.route('/server_status')
def welcome_controller():
    return {
        "message": "Welcome to your Flask Server",
        "status": "up",
        "random": 1 + 1
    }

    app.run()
```

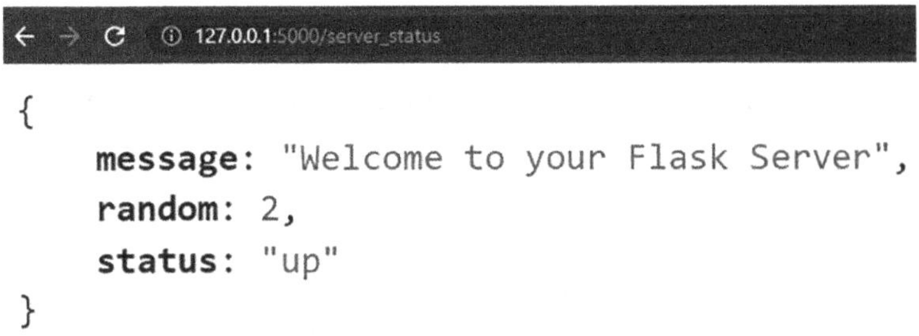

```
{
    message: "Welcome to your Flask Server",
    random: 2,
    status: "up"
}
```

Figure 6-2. *Page returned when the /server_status route is requested for the server with Listing 6-2*

To trigger a specific function call when a route is requested, a function decorator needs to be added before it with the route name. It is not necessary to have static routes, they can also be dynamic, by specifying a specific string format which will be mapped by Flask to that function. For instance, */text/1* and */text/3* map to */text/<id>*. Calling a specific method depending on the HTTP method can also be configured through the same function decorator by adding an extra parameter as follows:

```
@app.route('/text/<id>', methods=['GET', 'PUT'])
```

Following up with the Employee and Pay Grade example from before, we will reuse the same database for this example but using *SQLAlchemy* instead of *psycopg2*, to make use of the **ORM** which represents SQL commands with Python class objects. To start, we would first need to represent our tables as classes and a Base class which the other two classes will inherit SQL properties from. These properties include parameterization of SQL queries which prevent SQLI. The classes in Listings 6-4 and 6-5 shall point to already existing tables in the database, and the *_tablename_* property shall be the table name.

Listing 6-3. Base.py

```python
from sqlalchemy.ext.declarative import declarative_base

Base = declarative_base()
```

Listing 6-4. PayGrades.py

```python
from sqlalchemy import Column, Integer, String
from .Base import Base

class PayGrades(Base):
    __tablename__ = 'paygrades'
    id = Column(Integer, primary_key=True)

    base_salary = Column(String)
    reimbursement = Column(String, default=True)
    bonuses = Column(String)

    def to_dict(self):
        return {
            "id": self.id,
            "base_salary": self.base_salary,
            "reimbursement": self.reimbursement,
            "bonuses": self.bonuses
        }
```

Listing 6-5. Employees.py

```python
from sqlalchemy import Column, Integer, String
from .Base import Base

class Employees(Base):
    __tablename__ = 'persons'
    id = Column(Integer, primary_key=True)
```

```python
    name = Column(String)
    date_of_birth = Column(String, default=True)
    paygrade_id = Column(Integer, unique=True, index=True)

    def to_dict(self):
        return {
            "id": self.id,
            "name": self.name,
            "date_of_birth": self.date_of_birth,
            "paygrade_id": self.paygrade_id
        }
```

Subsequently we can support adding and getting employee data over HTTP requests using Flask as shown in Listing 6-6. This backend server includes two routes, the first is to query all employees using the database connection made with SQLAlchemy, and the second is to insert or add a new employee to the employees table with the user-supplied properties sent in the HTTP body as a JSON document.

Listing 6-6. main.py

```python
from flask import Flask, request
from DataBase import Connection
from DataBase import Employees

app = Flask(__name__)

@app.route('/employees')
def get_all_employees():
    with connection.use_session() as session:
        employees = session.query(Employees).all()
        employees = [employee.to_dict() for employee in employees]
        return {"data": employees}
```

```
@app.route('/employee', methods=["POST"])
def add_employee():
    body = request.json
    with connection.use_session() as session:
        session.add(Employees(**body))
        session.commit()
    return {"message": "New employee added successfully"}

connection = Connection("postgresql://
postgres:admin@127.0.0.1:5432/CompanyData")
app.run()
```

6.4.2 API Testing

In this example, the user will be a human interfacing with the backend
using an API testing platform such as Postman as shown in Figures 6-3
and 6-4. In a later section, Streamlit will be the user of this server directly
without the need for an API testing platform.

Figure 6-3. *Adding a new employee*

Wrapping this section up, we need to point out that we didn't set any headers, including the content type for the "POST/*employee*" route which uses a JSON payload, because Postman took care of that behind the scenes. And Flask took care of also adding the JSON content type to the response as Python's lists and dictionaries are easily parseable to JSON as mentioned before.

Figure 6-4. *Getting all employees*

6.5 Multithreading and Multiprocessing Requests

Once an application scales or when one of its initial requirements is to do heavy multiple independent computations of processes, a lot of power is wasted whether on the backend's Flask side or Streamlit's side. This is due to not harnessing the power of the CPUs which gets even stronger over time. Modern CPU strength is not due to them being quicker with faster clock cycles, but with the more cores it packs. Streamlit and Flask are single-threaded, single-processed applications by default. And to speed them up, we can try either or both of *multiprocessing* and *multithreading*, which introduces true parallelization to our application. The usage of both approaches shall be controlled by the developer to run a function a multiple number of times which then will be executed in parallel by the CPU. An example of using both techniques in Streamlit is Listing 6-7.

Listing 6-7. streamlit_main.py

```python
import streamlit as st
from multiprocessing import Pool, cpu_count
import threading
import time

def func(iterations, id):
    i = 0
    for i in range(iterations):
        i += 1
    print("Finished job id =", id)

if __name__ == "__main__":
    pool = Pool(cpu_count())

    st.title("Speed You Code!")

    jobs_count = 5
    iterations = 10 ** 3
    c1, c2 = st.columns(2)

    with c1:
        if st.button("multiprocess"):
            inputs = [(iterations, i) for i in
            range(jobs_count)]
            t11 = time.time()
            pool.starmap(func, inputs)
```

```
            t21 = time.time()
            st.write(f"Finished after {t21 - t11} seconds")
    with c2:
        if st.button("multithread"):
            threads = [threading.Thread(target=func,
            args=(iterations, i)) for i in range(10)]

            t12 = time.time()
            for thread in threads:
                thread.start()
            for thread in threads:
                thread.join()
            t22 = time.time()
            st.write(f"Finished after {t22 - t12} seconds")
```

Speed up Your Code!

multiprocess   multithread

Finished after 0.028998374938964844 seconds

Figure 6-5. *Output of Listing 6-7*

Notice that in Listing 6-7, the first code to be executed is after line 13 which is required for the whole example to work error-free due to Streamlit knowing that this code block shall be executed only once, which means the processing pool won't be initialized again in reruns. Similar precaution shall be taken even in Flask applications.

The main difference between multiprocessing and multithreading is that multithreading reuses the already existing memory space and spawns new threads within the same process, which is a faster operation than spawning totally new processes which adds an overhead of CPU context switching. Moreover, every new process in the multiprocessing

pool requires an entirely new memory space. In addition, each
processes' inputs need to be copied or cloned, thereby introducing a
memory-greedy application. It may seem that multithreading is the better
option, however, that is not true due to the fact that multiprocessing is
more CPU efficient when executing hefty tasks as the CPU scheduler
allocates more time to those processes. Figure 6-6 shows the correlation
between execution time and the job iteration count in 10x^ from
Listing 6-7.

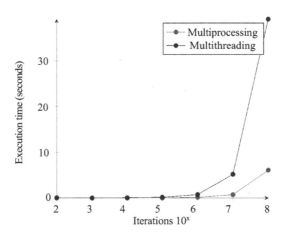

Figure 6-6. *Multiprocessing vs. multithreading for five jobs with
increasing iteration count*

6.6 Connecting Streamlit
to a Backend Server

Once we have an optimized the backend server with multiprocessing and/
or multithreading, we are ready to connect our Streamlit application to it.
For this, we will need to use an HTTP client library to communicate with
the backend API. Listing 6-8 uses the popular requests library to do the job
with the output shown in Figure 6-7.

Listing 6-8. streamlit_api.py

```python
import streamlit as st
import requests
import datetime

url = "http://127.0.0.1:5000"
def add_employee(name, dob, paygrade):
    data = {
        "name": name,
        "date_of_birth": dob,
        "paygrade_id": paygrade
    }
    response = requests.post(url + "/employee", json=data)
    if response.status_code == 200:
        return True
    return False

def get_employees():
    response = requests.get(url + "/employees")
    return response.json()['data']

form = st.form("new_employee")
name = form.text_input("Name")
dob = str(form.date_input("DOB", min_value=datetime.
datetime(year=1920, day=1, month=1)))
paygrade = form.number_input("paygrade", step=1)

if form.form_submit_button("Add new Employee"):
    if add_employee(name, dob, paygrade):
        st.success("Employee Added")
    else:
        st.error("Error adding employee")
```

```
st.write("___")

employees = get_employees()
st.table(employees)
```

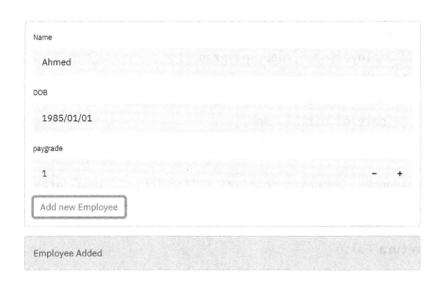

Figure 6-7. *Output of Listing 6-8*

6.7 Summary

In this chapter, we learned that backend servers are the backbone of every expanding web application, as they add layers of obscurity and security to the frontend. In addition to that, we dived deep into HTTP communication, which is the language of APIs, and how it is structured. As a step toward having efficient and organized API communication, JSON was introduced and explained as it is the most widely used data formatting in APIs. As we have the building blocks of an API ready, we then introduced Flask as a Python backend framework to make a well-structured backend to serve data from a local database by exposing specific endpoints. And to top it off, we showcased ways to speed up Python code execution whether in Streamlit or the backend server, by leveraging multiprocessing and multithreading with a comparison between each one's performance and use cases.

CHAPTER 7

Implementing Session State

In order to develop more advanced Streamlit applications, it is vital to establish session-specific data that can be utilized to deliver a more enhanced experience to the user. Specifically, the application will need to preserve the user's data and entries using what is referred to as session states. These states can be set and accessed on demand whenever necessary, and they will persist whenever the user triggers a rerun of the Streamlit application or navigates from one page to another. In addition, we will establish the means to store state across multiple sessions with the use of cookies that can store data on the user's browser to be accessed when they restart the associated Streamlit application. Finally, we will learn how to record and visualize rich insights of how users are interacting with our application, to provide analytics to both the developer and product owner alike.

7.1 Implementing Session State Natively

Since Streamlit version 0.84.1, a native way to store and manage session-specific data including but not limited to variables, widgets, text, images, and objects has been introduced. The values of session states are stored in a dictionary format, where every value is assigned to a unique key to be

© Mohammad Khorasani, Mohamed Abdou, Javier Hernández Fernández 2022
M. Khorasani et al., *Web Application Development with Streamlit*,
https://doi.org/10.1007/978-1-4842-8111-6_7

indexed with. Previously without this feature, all variables would be reset whenever the user triggered Streamlit to rerun the script by interacting with the application. Similarly, widgets would also be reset to their default value when the user navigated from one page to another. However, with session state, users can receive an enhanced and more personalized experience by being able to access variables or entries that were made previously on other pages within the application. For instance, users can enter their username and password once and continue to navigate through the application without being prompted to reenter their credentials again until they log out. In a nutshell, session states enable us to develop far more complex applications which will be discussed extensively in subsequent chapters.

The way to set and get session state data can be implemented as shown in Listing 7-1 with the associated output in Figure 7-1. Please note that the first two key-value entries (*KeyInput1* and *KeyInput2*) are present even though they haven't been created by the user. Those keys are present to store the state of the user-modified components, which are the defined text input components. This means that the developer also has the capability of modifying the values of any component as long as it has a unique key set with its definition. Another caveat is that each session state must be invoked before it can be read; otherwise, you will be presented with an error. To avoid this, ensure that you always initialize the state with a null or fault value.

Listing 7-1. session_state.py

```python
import streamlit as st

def get_state_value(key):
    return st.session_state.get(key)

def set_state_value(key, value):
    st.session_state[key] = value
```

```
st.title("Session State Management")
c1, c2, c3 = st.columns(3)

with c1:
    st.subheader("All")
    st.write(st.session_state)
with c2:
    st.subheader("Set Key")
    key = st.text_input("Key", key="KeyInput1")
    value = st.text_input("Value")

    if st.button("Set"):
        st.session_state[key] = value
        st.success("Success")
with c3:
    st.subheader("Get Key")
    key = st.text_input("Key", key="KeyInput2")

    if st.button("Get"):
        st.write(st.session_state.get(key))
```

Figure 7-1. *Session state data display and manipulation*

7.1.1 Building an Application with Session State

To demonstrate the utility of session states, in the following example we will create a trivial multipage application where the user can use states to store the key of the selected page, an uploaded dataframe, and the value of a slider widget. As shown in Listing 7-2, in our main page we first initialize the state of our page selection, and then we use buttons to change the state to the key of the requested page. Subsequently, the associated function of the selected page is invoked directly from the session state to render the page.

In Page One of the application shown in Listing 7-3, we will use session states to store an uploaded dataframe and the value of a slider that is used to filter the number of rows shown in the dataframe. The user can navigate back and forth between the pages and still be able to access a previously uploaded dataframe with the same number of rows set on the slider as shown in Figure 7-2.

Listing 7-2. main_page.py

```python
import streamlit as st
from page_1 import func_page_1

def main():
    # Initializing session state for page selection
    if 'page_state' not in st.session_state:
        st.session_state['page_state'] = 'Main Page'

    # Writing page selection to session state
    st.sidebar.subheader('Page selection')
    if st.sidebar.button('Main Page'):
        st.session_state['page_state'] = 'Main Page'
    if st.sidebar.button('Page One'):
        st.session_state['page_state'] = 'Page 1'
```

```python
    pages_main = {
        'Main Page': main_page,
        'Page 1': run_page_1
    }

    # Run selected page
    pages_main[st.session_state['page_state']]()

def main_page():
    st.title('Main Page')

def run_page_1():
    func_page_1()

if __name__ == '__main__':
    main()
```

Listing 7-3. page_1.py

```python
import streamlit as st
import pandas as pd

def func_page_1():
    st.title('Page One')

    # Initializing session states for dataframe and slider
    if 'df' not in st.session_state:
        st.session_state['df'] = None
    if 'rows' not in st.session_state:
        st.session_state['rows'] = None

    file = st.file_uploader('Upload file')

    # Writing dataframe to session state
    if file is not None:
        df = pd.read_csv(file)
        st.session_state['df'] = df
```

```
if st.session_state['df'] is not None:
    # Creating slider widget with default value from
    session state
    rows = st.slider('Rows to display',value=st.session_
    state['rows'], min_value=1,max_value=len(st.session_
    state['df']))

    # Writing slider value to session state
    st.session_state['rows'] = rows

    # Rendering dataframe from session state
    st.write(st.session_state['df'].iloc[:st.session_
    state['rows']])
```

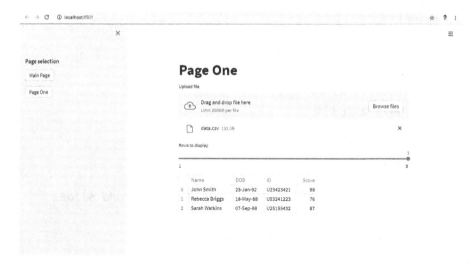

Figure 7-2. *Output of Listings 7-2 and 7-3*

7.2 Introducing Session IDs

Session IDs are unique identifiers of a new connection to Streamlit's HTML serving WebSocket. A new WebSocket connection is established if a new browser page is opened even if another connection is established. But both are treated independently by the server. These WebSocket connections are used to transfer data from the server to the client's browser and vice versa.

Those unique identifiers can be used to provide the end user with a personalized experience. And to do so, the server needs to map users' progress and updates to their corresponding identifiers. This mapping can be done natively in an effortless way using Streamlit's native API. In Listing 7-4, we show how to get the current session's ID or all the active session IDs, with the output shown in Figure 7-3, which shows two web pages both at *http://localhost:8501/*.

Listing 7-4. session_id_demo.py

```python
import streamlit as st
from streamlit.scriptrunner.script_run_context import get_
script_run_ctx
from streamlit.server.server import Server

all_sessions = Server.get_current()._session_info_by_id

session_id = get_script_run_ctx().session_id
session_number = list(all_sessions.keys()).
index(session_id) + 1

st.title("Session ID #"+str(session_number))
st.header("Id of this session is: " + session_id)
st.subheader("All sessions ("+str(len(all_sessions))+") :")
st.write(all_sessions)
```

Figure 7-3. *Two different browser windows with different session IDs*

7.3 Implementing Session State Persistently

Streamlit's native method to store session state will more than suffice for most if not all applications. However, it may be necessary to store session state on an accessible database to retrieve later on or, in other words, store session state persistently. This can be especially useful for generating user insights and traffic metrics for your application.

For the example shown in Listing 7-5, we will be making use of PostgreSQL to store and retrieve a variable and a dataframe while our user navigates through the pages of the application as shown in Figures 7-4 and 7-5. Specifically, the entered name and uploaded dataset will be written to the database in tables named with the unique session ID, as shown in Figure 7-6, and read/rendered with the previous value each time the user refers back to Page Two, as long as the user is still within the same session. Once the application is refreshed and a new session ID generated, the user will no longer have access to the variables; however, the database administrator can access the historical states in the database should they need to do so. Given that Streamlit reruns the script with every user interaction, without session state both the name and dataframe would be reset each time the script is run; however, with this implementation, we can save the data persistently and access it in the associated database on demand.

Figure 7-4. *Output of Listing 7-5*

Figure 7-5. *Output of Listing 7-5 (continued)*

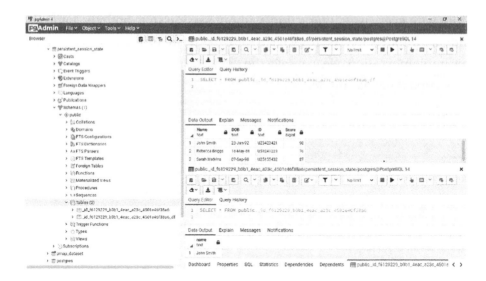

Figure 7-6. *Associated PostgreSQL database for Listing 7-5 (continued)*

This method is scalable and can be extended to as many variables, and even files (in the form of byte strings) if required, using the four read and write functions shown as follows:

```
# Read session variables
read_state('column name', database_engine, session_ID)
```

```
# Read session dataframes
read_state_df(database_engine, session_ID)
```

```
# Write and overwrite session variables
write_state('column name', value, database_engine, session_ID)
```

```
# Write and overwrite session dataframes
write_state_df(dataframe, database_engine, session_ID)
```

Listing 7-5. persistent_session_state.py

```python
import streamlit as st
import pandas as pd
import psycopg2
from sqlalchemy import create_engine
from streamlit.scriptrunner.script_run_context import
get_script_run_ctx

def get_session_id():
    session_id = get_script_run_ctx().session_id
    session_id = session_id.replace('-','_')
    session_id = '_id_' + session_id
    return session_id

def read_state(column,engine,session_id):
    state_var = engine.execute("SELECT %s FROM %s" %
    (column,session_id))
    state_var = state_var.first()[0]
    return state_var

def read_state_df(engine,session_id):
    try:
        return pd.read_sql_table(session_id,engine)
    except:
        return pd.DataFrame([])

def write_state(column,value,engine,session_id):
    engine.execute("UPDATE %s SET %s='%s'" % (session_id,
    column,value))

def write_state_df(df,engine,session_id):
    df.to_sql('%s' % (session_id),engine,index=False,
    if_exists='replace')
```

```python
def page_one(engine,session_id):
    st.title('Hello world')

def page_two(engine,session_id):

    name = st.text_input('Name',read_
    state('name',engine,session_id))
    write_state('name',name,engine,session_id)

    file = st.file_uploader('Upload dataset')

    if file is not None:
        df = pd.read_csv(file)
        write_state_df(df,engine,session_id + '_df')

    if read_state_df(engine,session_id + '_df').empty is False:
        df = read_state_df(engine,session_id + '_df')
        df = df[df['Name'] == name]
        st.write(df)

if __name__ == '__main__':
    # Creating PostgreSQL engine
    engine = create_engine('postgresql://<username>:<password>
    @localhost:<port>' '/<database>')

    # Getting session ID
    session_id = get_session_id()

    # Creating session state tables
    engine.execute("CREATE TABLE IF NOT EXISTS %s (name text)"
    % (session_id))
    len_table = engine.execute("SELECT COUNT(*) FROM %s"
    % (session_id));
    len_table = len_table.first()[0]
```

```python
if len_table == 0:
    engine.execute("INSERT INTO %s (name) VALUES (")"
    % (session_id));

# Creating page selector
pages = {
    'Page One': page_one,
    'Page Two': page_two
    }

page_selection = st.sidebar.selectbox('Select page',
['Page One','Page Two'])
pages[page_selection](engine,session_id)
```

7.4 User Insights

Having the ability to record user interactions with a web application can in many instances be quite critical. The developer or product owner must have at their disposal rich and accurate data of how many users are visiting their website, at what times, and how exactly they are engaging with it in order to better tailor and refine their product or service. Imagine you have an ecommerce web application that has been curated impeccably, but is failing to convert leads into sales, and you cannot figure out why. Perhaps, there is a bug with your interface or backend that is inhibiting the user's actions, or maybe your server is overloaded and is failing to cater to the traffic. Regardless, you will need to diagnose where exactly in your pipeline the problem is located to rectify it, and this is where user insights come into play.

While Google Analytics can deliver rich insights including but not limited to numbers of visits, user demographics, time spent on various pages, and a lot more at the server level, it will not readily be able to record interactions at the application level. Consequently, you are required to develop your own means of recording user insights for the application, and this can be done in several ways. The simplest of which, as shown in Listing 7-6, allows you to read the timestamp each time the user engages with a subsection of your code, such as clicking a button or uploading a dataset as shown in Figure 7-7, and record it in a PostgreSQL database as seen in Figure 7-8. Similarly, the number of rows of the uploaded dataset can also be recorded. Each insight is stored in a separate column in a table whose primary key is the unique session ID. Once the application has been restarted, a new row with a different session ID will be created. By inserting the following *update* function, you can record any value at any step in your program:

```
update_row(column,new_value,session_id,mutable,engine)
```

Figure 7-7. *Output of Listing 7-6*

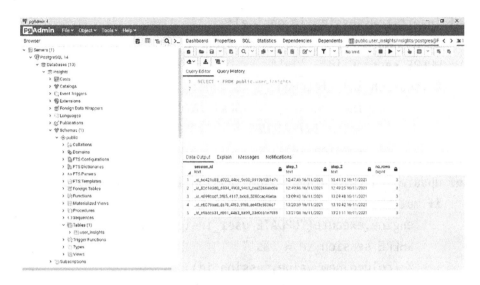

Figure 7-8. *Associated PostgreSQL database for Listing 7-6*

Please note that insights can be overwritten multiple times by setting the *mutable* argument to True or left as False if you want to record a value only the first time it was generated.

Listing 7-6. record_user_insights.py

```python
import streamlit as st
from streamlit.scriptrunner.script_run_context import get_
script_run_ctx
from datetime import datetime
import pandas as pd
import psycopg2
from sqlalchemy import create_engine

def get_session_id():
    session_id = get_script_run_ctx().session_id
    session_id = session_id.replace('-','_')
    session_id = '_id_' + session_id
    return session_id
```

193

```python
def insert_row(session_id,engine):
    if engine.execute("SELECT session_id FROM user_insights
    WHERE session_id = '%s'"
    % (session_id)).fetchone() is None:
            engine.execute("""INSERT INTO user_insights
            (session_id) VALUES ('%s')"""
            % (session_id))

def update_row(column,new_value,session_id,mutable,engine):
    if mutable:
        engine.execute("UPDATE user_insights SET %s = '%s'
        WHERE session_id = '%s'"
        % (column,new_value,session_id))
    elif engine.execute("SELECT %s FROM user_insights WHERE
    session_id = '%s'"
    % (column,session_id)).first()[0] is None:
        engine.execute("UPDATE user_insights SET %s = '%s'
        WHERE session_id = '%s'"
        % (column,new_value,session_id))

if __name__ == '__main__':
    # Creating PostgreSQL engine
    engine = create_engine('postgresql://<username>:<password>@
    localhost:'
 '<port>/<database>')

    # Getting session ID
    session_id = get_session_id()

    # Creating session state tables
    engine.execute("'CREATE TABLE IF NOT EXISTS user_insights
    (session_id text, step_1 text, step_2 text, no_rows bigint)"')

    insert_row(session_id,engine)
```

```
st.title('Hello world')

st.subheader('Step 1')
if st.button('Click'):
    st.write('Some content')
    update_row('step_1',datetime.now().strftime("%H:%M:%S
    %d/%m/%Y"),session_id,
True,engine)

st.subheader('Step 2')
file = st.file_uploader('Upload data')

if file is not None:
    df = pd.read_csv(file)
    st.write(df)
    update_row('step_2',datetime.now().strftime("%H:%M:%S
    %d/%m/%Y"),session_id, False,engine)
    update_row('no_rows',len(df),session_id,True,engine)
```

7.4.1 Visualizing User Insights

Now that we have established how to read insights from a Streamlit application and record them on a PostgreSQL database, the next step will be to visualize the data on demand. Initially, to extract the data we can run Listing 7-7 to import the insights table into a Pandas dataframe and save it locally on disk as an Excel spreadsheet if you wish to render your own customized charts. Otherwise, we can visualize the data with Listing 7-8, where we import the Excel spreadsheet generated earlier into a Pandas dataframe, convert the timestamps into hourly and daily values, sum the number of rows that are within the same hour or day, and finally visualize them with Plotly charts as shown in Figure 7-9. In addition, we can filter the data by using a *st.selectbox* to select the column from the insights table to visualize.

Listing 7-7. read_user_insights.py

```python
import pandas as pd
import psycopg2
from sqlalchemy import create_engine

def read_data(name,engine):
    try:
        return pd.read_sql_table(name,engine)
    except:
        return pd.DataFrame([])

if __name__ == '__main__':
    # Creating PostgreSQL engine
    engine = create_engine('postgresql://<username>:<password>@
    localhost:'
 '<port>/<database>')
    df = read_data('user_insights',engine)
    df.to_excel('C:/Users/.../user_insights.xlsx',index=False)
```

Listing 7-8. plot_user_insights.py

```python
import streamlit as st
import pandas as pd
import plotly.express as px

st.set_page_config(layout='wide')
st.title('User Insights')

df = pd.read_excel('C:/Users/.../user_insights.xlsx')
column_selection = st.selectbox('Select column',df.
columns[1:-2])
df = df[column_selection]
df = pd.to_datetime(df,format='%H:%M:%S %d/%m/%Y')

df_1h = df.copy()
```

```
df_1d = df.copy()

col1, col2 = st.columns(2)

with col1:
    st.subheader('Hourly chart')
    df_1h = df_1h.dt.strftime('%Y-%m-%d %I%p')
    df_1h = pd.DataFrame(df_1h.value_counts())
    df_1h.index = pd.DatetimeIndex(df_1h.index)
    df_1h = df_1h.sort_index()
    fig = px.bar(df_1h, x=df_1h.index, y=df_1h[column_selection])
    st.write(fig)

with col2:
    st.subheader('Daily chart')
    df_1d = df_1d.dt.strftime('%Y-%m-%d')
    df_1d = pd.DataFrame(df_1d.value_counts())
    df_1d.index = pd.DatetimeIndex(df_1d.index)
    df_1d = df_1d.sort_index()
    fig = px.line(df_1d, x=df_1d.index, y=df_1d[column_selection])
    st.write(fig)
```

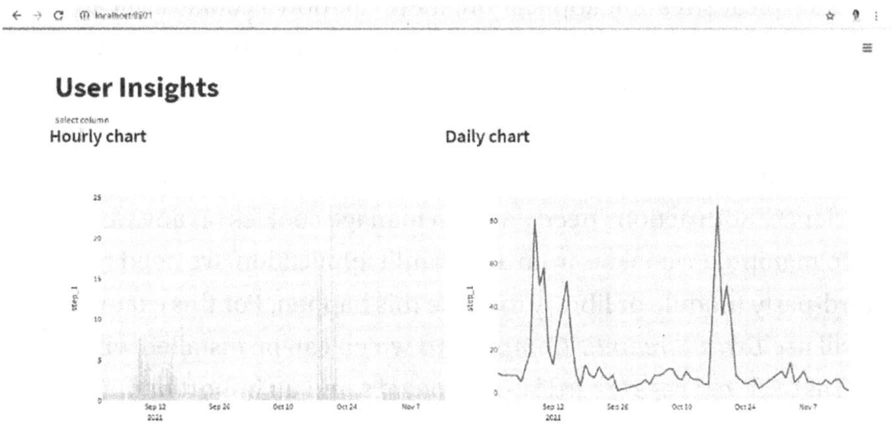

Figure 7-9. *Output of Listing 7-8*

7.5 Cookie Management

We have discussed how to store and manage data within a session using native and workaround approaches. However, what might be missing is the ability to manage data between sessions. For instance, storing a counter of how many times a button has been clicked or even more usefully not prompting the user to log in each and every time they open a new session. To do so, we require the utility of cookies.

Cookies can be used to track a user's actions across many websites or store their personal information such as authentication tokens. Cookies are stored and managed on the user's end, specifically, in their browser. This means the server doesn't know about its content by default. In order to check out the cookies on any web application, we can simply open developer tools from the browser and head to the console tab. Then type 'document.cookie', and then the cookies will be displayed as shown in Figure 7-10.

```
> document.cookie
< 'ajs_user_id=%22666c29e8-0a66-5f62-bdf5-b9ceaf8a6414%22; ajs_anonymous_id=%22648586…
```

Figure 7-10. *A web page cookie*

In a typical Streamlit application, more unknown cookies will appear apart from the one in Figure 7-10; those might be for advertisement tracking or other purposes. Which might require the developer to remove them depending on the cookie policy they adopt. Or in other cases, the developer might want to add other cookies to enhance the application experience. Both actions need a way to manage cookies on any web app.

To manipulate cookies from a Streamlit application, we need to use a third-party module or library to make this happen. For this example, we will use *Extra-Streamlit-Components* which can be installed with pip install extra-streamlit-components and an import naming convention as *stx*, where the *X* denotes the extra capabilities that can be provided on a vanilla Streamlit application. Within this library, there is a module called *Cookie Manager* which will be our tool for such task. Listing 7-9 builds a simple Streamlit application with the capability of setting, getting, and deleting cookies. The controls are even customizable based on the developer needs. For instance, an expiration date can be set to any new cookie added which will autodelete itself after the set date is reached. Figures 7-11 and 7-12 show adding and getting an example authentication token, respectively.

Listing 7-9. cookie_management.py

```python
import streamlit as st
import extra_streamlit_components as stx

st.title("Cookie Management Demo")
st.subheader("_Featuring Cookie Manager from Extra-Streamlit-
Components_")

cookie_manager = stx.CookieManager()

st.subheader("All Cookies:")
cookies = cookie_manager.get_all()
st.write(cookies)

c1, c2, c3 = st.columns(3)
with c1:
    st.subheader("Get Cookie:")
    cookie = st.text_input("Cookie", key="0")
    clicked = st.button("Get")
    if clicked:
        value = cookie_manager.get(cookie)
        st.write(value)
with c2:
    st.subheader("Set Cookie:")
```

```
        cookie = st.text_input("Cookie", key="1")
        val = st.text_input("Value")
        if st.button("Add"):
            cookie_manager.set(cookie, val)
with c3:
    st.subheader("Delete Cookie:")
    cookie = st.text_input("Cookie", key="2")
    if st.button("Delete"):
        cookie_manager.delete(cookie)
```

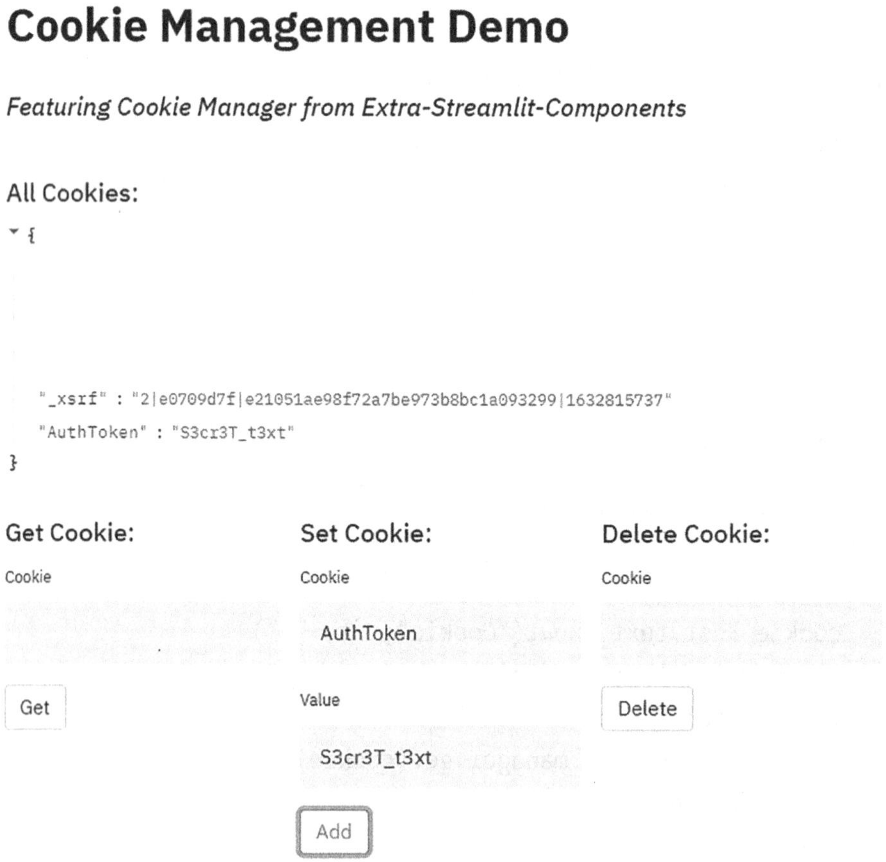

Cookie Management Demo

Featuring Cookie Manager from Extra-Streamlit-Components

All Cookies:

▾ {

   "_xsrf" : "2|e0709d7f|e21051ae98f72a7be973b8bc1a093299|1632815737"

   "AuthToken" : "S3cr3T_t3xt"

}

Get Cookie: **Set Cookie:**   **Delete Cookie:**

Cookie   Cookie   Cookie

                    AuthToken

Get   Value   Delete

                    S3cr3T_t3xt

                  Add

Figure 7-11. *Adding an AuthToken cookie*

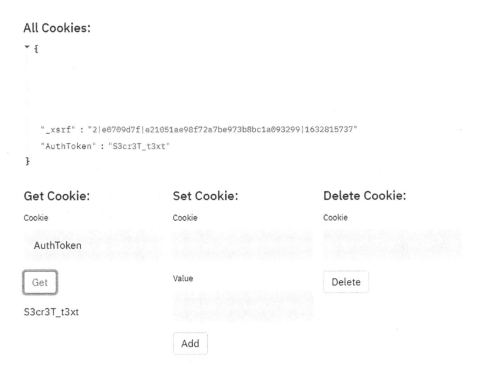

Cookie Management Demo

Featuring Cookie Manager from Extra-Streamlit-Components

All Cookies:

▼ {

"_xsrf" : "2|e0709d7f|e21051ae98f72a7be973b8bc1a093299|1632815737"
"AuthToken" : "S3cr3T_t3xt"
}

Get Cookie: **Set Cookie:**   **Delete Cookie:**

Cookie   Cookie   Cookie

AuthToken

Get   Value   Delete

S3cr3T_t3xt

                       Add

Figure 7-12. *Getting an AuthToken cookie*

Please note that the All Cookies section in Figures 7-11 and 7-12 is displayed in a well-structured JSON format but has some redacted cookies for privacy concern purposes. Good to note that there is not a visual aspect to this Streamlit application from the newly introduced module as it is classified as a service, hence the name *Cookie Manager*. However, this doesn't mean all other Streamlit-compatible libraries share the same behavior, as they can contain a visual aspect to them.

7.6 Summary

In this chapter, we were introduced to storing and accessing session states with Streamlit natively. The use of session state can be essential in many cases and will be utilized extensively to develop advanced applications in subsequent chapters. In addition, the reader was acquainted with session IDs that are unique identifiers associated with every new instance of a Streamlit application and shown how they can be used to store session state in a persistent manner on a PostgreSQL database and also how they can be utilized to record and visualize user insights. Finally, the reader was shown how to store and retrieve cookies on a browser, which is required to store session state across multiple sessions of a Streamlit application on the same browser. This is necessary for instances such as when the user wants to automatically log in without re-entring their credentials .

CHAPTER 8

Authentication and Application Security

After acquainting ourselves with the necessary building blocks of a well-structured Streamlit web application, we require an additional feature to deploy a production-ready application, namely, a secure user authentication service. Once all users requesting access to the application are authenticated, we can guarantee a secure user experience whereby private data is safe and any unwelcome or malicious requests are formidably denied. In this chapter, we will learn how to establish user accounts, verify user actions, and implement other housekeeping measures that are expected of any well-versed software engineer.

8.1 Developing User Accounts

In this chapter, we will build on the example from Chapters 5 and 6, by introducing HR admins who get to see and add employees and their pay grades. Assume there are admins responsible to do those actions, and the company keeps changing and assigning new admins. In this case, we need our application to support making more admin accounts and authorize them.

© Mohammad Khorasani, Mohamed Abdou, Javier Hernández Fernández 2022
M. Khorasani et al., *Web Application Development with Streamlit*,
https://doi.org/10.1007/978-1-4842-8111-6_8

Now those actions need authorized people to execute them, so we mainly need three main additions: adding an admin table in our database, allowing admin account creations, and authorizing users with admin accounts to use the rest of the service.

8.1.1 Hashing

To add a new table to the database, we will need to follow a step similar to what was done previously and as shown in Figure 8-1. Notice that we are storing mainly two pieces of information per admin, username and password hash. The hash or a nonguessable representation of the password is stored instead of the password itself. By doing this, we are protecting our users' privacy and credentials in case of a data breach. As if this happens, the attacker will have to spend billions of years to brute-force all hashes to find a single user's actual password. So what hashing mainly does is a one-way transformation of data that is not reversible.

Figure 8-1. *Creating a new table to store admin credentials, using the contents of Flask/create_admins_table.sql*

After creating the new table, we will need to create a corresponding Python class to make an ORM for SQLAlchemy as shown in Listing 8-1. Hashing a password can be done in multiple ways, a few of which can be MD5, SHA256, SHA512, and others. However, the most commonly used algorithm by modern systems is Bcrypt. Infact Bcrypt is used by default to protect users' passwords in Linux environments. Before explaining how Bcrypt works, we first need to know what methods are used to make a hash more secure.

As mentioned before, hashing transforms data. So, for instance, the text

`Password123`

maps to

`42f749ade7f9e195bf475f37a44cafcb`

using MD5. However, a slight modification to the original plain text would make a bigger difference in the hashed output as such:

`MD5(Password1239) -> abd7fdbb048a611ea0a0937265765404`

8.1.2 Salting

Including extra bytes in the password, also known as adding a salt, gives a totally different hash. This helps in password reusability cases by users across different websites, and one has been breached. By doing so, attackers won't know whether the same user uses the same password among multiple domains. And it will give them a harder time to break the hash. However, this trick will not be useful if the attacker knows the hashing salt and how it is applied. Hence, Bcrypt falls under the spotlight by introducing a cryptographic way to store randomly generated salts within the hash. This makes it possible to check if a Bcrypt hash is generated from a plain text, using an abstracted Bcrypt library's function, as shown in Listing 8-2.

Listing 8-1. Flask/DataBase/Models/Admins.py

```python
from sqlalchemy import Column, Integer, String
from .Base import Base

class Admins(Base):
    __tablename__ = 'admins'
    id = Column(Integer, primary_key=True)

    username = Column(String)
    password_hash = Column(String, default=True)

    def to_dict(self):
        return {
            "id": self.id,
            "username": self.username,
            "password_hash": self.password_hash
        }
```

Listing 8-2. Flask/DataBase/Services/HashingService.py

```python
import bcrypt

class HashingService:
    def __init__(self, bcrypt_gen_salt: int = 12):
        self.gen_salt = bcrypt_gen_salt

    def hash_bcrypt(self, plain_text: bytes) -> bytes:
        return bcrypt.hashpw(plain_text, bcrypt.gensalt(self.
        gen_salt))

    def check_bcrypt(self, plain_text: bytes, hashed_password:
    bytes) -> bool:
```

```
try:
    return bcrypt.checkpw(plain_text, hashed_password)
except:
    return False
```

8.2 Verifying User Credentials

Now after we have the needed service and storage support to manage passwords, we can proceed with the backend refactoring to support authentication for every route. This means we need to intercept every request to the server and decide whether it is authenticated or not. In other words, we need to have an independent piece of software to sit between the client's request and the access controller; this is usually referred to as *middleware* among backend developers. The authentication process has to be checking for a specific identifier of the request that the server can trust; such identifier is referred to as "authentication token," or "token" for short. This token shall be issued by the server, and it shall be verified.

Tokens are mainly either of the two: custom session IDs or JWTs. For this example, we will proceed with JWTs as it doesn't require the server to store it, which makes it stateless. JWTs consist of three main parts encoded in base64 and separated by a period. The first part contains information about the payload signing mechanism, the second holds the raw payload, and lastly the third contains a password-protected signature of the payload using the same hashing mechanisms in the first part. This can be seen in more detail in Figure 8-2 from *jwt.io*.

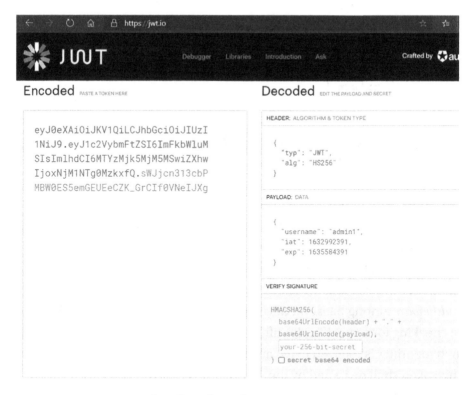

Figure 8-2. *JSON Web Token (JWT) content*

So on a new request, we will check the headers for a token. The token's payload will be signed, and the signature will be compared against the passed token's signature; if they match, we have confirmed that the token is issued by the server. And for more security purposes, to avoid attackers stealing other people's legit tokens, we shall have an expiration date *(30 days from issuing by default)*, which will require the user to log in again upon expiration. Since this will contain many logic parts, it is best to isolate it as a whole service to manage tokens as shown in Listing 8-3.

Listing 8-3. Flask/DataBase/Services/JWTService.py

```python
from jwt import PyJWT
from time import time
from typing import Union

class JWTService:
    expires_in_seconds = 2592000
    signing_algorithm = "HS256"

    def __init__(self, signing_key: str, expires_in_seconds:
    int = 2592000):
        self.signing_key = signing_key
        self.expires_in_seconds = expires_in_seconds

    def generate(self,
                data: dict,
                expires_in_seconds: int = expires_in_seconds)
                -> Union[str, None]:
        try:
            instance = PyJWT()

            curr_unix_epoch = int(time())
            data['iat'] = curr_unix_epoch

            if isinstance(expires_in_seconds, int):
                data['exp'] = curr_unix_epoch + expires_in_seconds

            token = instance.encode(
                payload=data,
                key=self.signing_key,
                algorithm=self.signing_algorithm)

            if type(token) == bytes:
                token = token.decode('utf8') # Needed for some
                versions of PyJWT
```

```python
            return token
        except BaseException as _:
            return None

    def is_valid(self, token: str, verify_time: bool = True)
    -> bool:
        try:
            payload = self.get_payload(token)

            if payload is None:
                return False

            if verify_time and 'exp' in payload and
            payload['exp'] < int(time()):
                return False

            return True
        except:
            return False

    def get_payload(self, token: str):
        try:
            instance = PyJWT()
            payload = instance.decode(
                jwt=token,
                key=self.signing_key,
                algorithms=[self.signing_algorithm])
            return payload
        except Exception as e:
            return None
```

Since we have a way to issue and validate any token, we can integrate it with our middleware class in Listing 8-4, which has a function responsible to check if the requested route shall be authenticated or not.

If authentication is needed, it will check if the JWT passed is valid. If it is
not, it will return a famous 401 error which is the status code equivalent
to "Not Authorized"; otherwise, a None is returned which means proceed
to the next step in the backend's code, which will be the controller in our
case. And as seen on line 8, we are declaring login and sign-up routes –
which will be introduced later – don't need to be authenticated, because
after a successful login, a token will be supplied. The same for signing up,
but another layer of protection will be introduced later, to avoid abuse by
externals making new accounts without control and supervision.

Listing 8-4. Flask/DataBase/Middleware.py

```python
from flask import Request
from Services.JWTService import JWTService
from werkzeug import exceptions

class Middleware:
    def __init__(self, jwt_service: JWTService):
        self.unauthenticated_route_names = {"/api/auth/login",
        "/api/auth/sing_up"}
        self.jwt_service = jwt_service

    def auth(self, request: Request):
        is_route_unauthenticated = request.path in self.
        unauthenticated_route_names

        if is_route_unauthenticated:
            return None

        if "token" in request.headers:
            token = request.headers['token']
            is_valid = self.jwt_service.is_valid(token)
            if is_valid:
                return None
```

```
        else:
            return exceptions.Unauthorized()

    return exceptions.Unauthorized()
```

Finally, we need to initialize the previously made services and make three more routes for logging in, signing up, and checking login status. We need the last route to allow the frontend to make the decision whether to display the login page or not. So the server's main file shall look like Listing 8-5. We can notice that secrets and keys are read from an external YAML file and then parsed. One of those secrets is to make sure only who knows it can make new accounts as shown in Figures 8-3 and 8-4 using Postman.

Listing 8-5. Flask/flask_main.py

```
from flask import Flask, request
from DataBase import Connection, Employees, Admins
from Services import JWTService, HashingService
from Middleware import Middleware
from werkzeug import exceptions
import yaml

app = Flask(__name__)

with open("secrets.yaml") as f:
    yaml_dict = yaml.safe_load(f)
    sing_up_key = yaml_dict['sing_up_key']
    jwt_secret = yaml_dict['jwt_secret']

jwt_service = JWTService(jwt_secret)
middleware = Middleware(jwt_service)
hashing_service = HashingService()

app.before_request(lambda: middleware.auth(request))

@app.route('/api/employees')
def get_all_employees():
```

```python
    with connection.use_session() as session:
        employees = session.query(Employees).all()
        employees = [employee.to_dict() for employee in
        employees]
        return {"data": employees}

@app.route('/api/employee', methods=["POST"])
def add_employee():
    body = request.json
    with connection.use_session() as session:
        session.add(Employees(**body))
        session.commit()
    return {"message": "New employee added successfully"}

@app.route('/api/auth/login', methods=["POST"])
def log_in():
    username, password = request.json['username'], request.
    json['password']
    with connection.use_session() as session:
        admin_account = session.query(Admins).filter(
            Admins.username == username).first()
        if admin_account is None:
            # Username doesn't exist. But don't inform the
            client with that as
            # they can use it to bruteforce valid usernames
            return exceptions.Unauthorized(
                description="Incorrect username/password
                combination")

        # Checking if such hash can be generated from that password
        is_password_correct = hashing_service.check_bcrypt(
            password.encode("utf8"), admin_account.password_
            hash.encode("utf8"))
```

```python
    if not is_password_correct:
        return exceptions.Unauthorized(
            description="Incorrect username/password
            combination")

    token_payload = {"username": username}
    token = jwt_service.generate(token_payload)

    if token is None:
        return exceptions.InternalServerError(description="
        Login failed")

    return {"token": token}

@app.route('/api/auth/sing_up', methods=["POST"])
def sign_up():
    username, password = request.json['username'], request.
    json['password']
    if request.headers.get("sing_up_key") != "sing_up_key":
        exceptions.Unauthorized(description="Incorrect Key")

    with connection.use_session() as session:
        password_hash = hashing_service.hash_bcrypt(
            password.encode("utf-8")).decode("utf-8")
        admin = Admins(username=username, password_
        hash=password_hash)
        session.add(admin)
        session.commit()
        return {"message": "Admin account created successfully"}

@app.route('/api/auth/is_logged_in')
```

```
def is_logged_in():
    # If this controller is reached this means the
    # Auth middleware recognizes the passed token
    return {"message": "Token is valid"}

connection = Connection("postgresql://
postgres:admin@127.0.0.1:5432/CompanyData")
app.run()
```

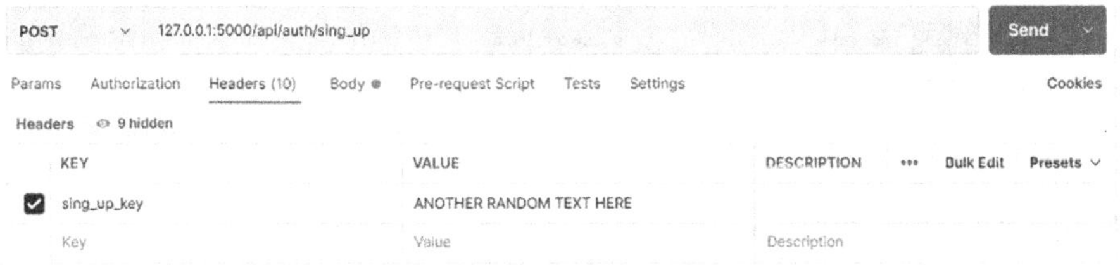

Figure 8-3. *Creating an admin account step 1: adding a sign-up key*

Figure 8-4. *Creating an admin account step 2: setting the new account's credentials*

After creating the account, we can manually check the database if the new credentials are present. This can be verified in Figure 8-5, where the username is as supplied and the other column is a valid Bcrypt hash for the supplied password.

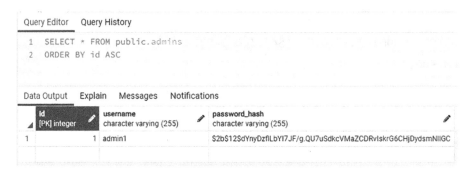

Figure 8-5. *Created account details in the database*

Now as we have admin accounts ready, we can test logging in with Postman before moving on to the next steps. By inserting the same username and password used in signing up, in a JSON format to a POST of the responsible route, we get a token back as seen in Figure 8-6.

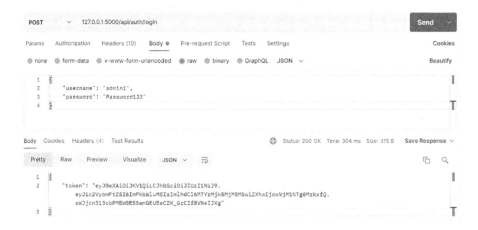

Figure 8-6. *Logging in with Postman using credentials from Figure 8-4*

Taking this to the next phase of development on Streamlit's side, we will first refactor Listing 8-6 to support initialization with an authentication token. Then use this token as part of every request, except the one used for logging in as it is not needed. Good to note that the *is logged in* function is implemented for a quick check of the current token's validity if supplied.

Listing 8-6. Streamlit/API.py

```python
import requests

class API:
    def __init__(self, base_url: str, token: str):
        self.base_url = base_url
        self.base_headers = {"token": token}

    def add_employee(self, name, dob, paygrade):
        try:
            data = {
                "name": name,
                "date_of_birth": dob,
                "paygrade_id": paygrade
            }
            response = requests.post(self.base_url + "/employee",
            json=data, headers=self.base_headers)
            if response.status_code == 200:
                return True
        except:
            return False

    def get_employees(self):
        try:
            response = requests.get(self.base_url + "/employees",
            headers=self.base_headers)
            return response.json()['data']
```

```python
        except:
            return None

    def login(self, username, password):
        try:
            response = requests.post(self.base_url + "/auth/
            login", json={
                "username": username,
                "password": password
            })
            body = response.json()
            token = body.get("token") if type(body) == dict
            else None

            return token
        except:
            return None

    def is_logged_in(self):
        return requests.get(self.base_url + "/auth/is_logged_
        in", headers=self.base_headers).status_code == 200
```

Having our API adapted to authentication tokens as shown in Listing 8-7, we can take it to the actual frontend side by implementing cookie support to store the authentication tokens and use it wherever needed as shown in Listing 8-8. Whenever the Streamlit renders, it will check the local cookies and look for authentication tokens; if the token is valid, it will display the management portal as shown in Figure 8-8 with a customized welcome message. Otherwise, it will prompt for an obligatory login, which can be seen in Figure 8-7.

Listing 8-7. Streamlit/API.py

```python
import requests

class API:
    def __init__(self, base_url: str, token: str):
        self.base_url = base_url
        self.base_headers = {"token": token}

    def add_employee(self, name, dob, paygrade):
        try:
            data = {
                "name": name,
                "date_of_birth": dob,
                "paygrade_id": paygrade
            }
            response = requests.post(self.base_url +
            "/employee", json=data, headers=self.base_headers)
            if response.status_code == 200:
                return True
        except:
            return False

    def get_employees(self):
        try:
            response = requests.get(self.base_url +
            "/employees", headers=self.base_headers)
            return response.json()['data']
        except:
            return None

    def login(self, username, password):
        try:
            response = requests.post(self.base_url + "/auth/
            login", json={
```

```
            "username": username,
            "password": password
        })
        body = response.json()
        token = body.get("token") if type(body) == dict
        else None

        return token
    except:
        return None

def is_logged_in(self):
    return requests.get(self.base_url + "/auth/is_logged_
    in", headers=self.base_headers).status_code == 200
```

Listing 8-8. Streamlit/streamlit_main.py

```
import streamlit as st
from Views import AddEmployee, DisplayEmployees, Login
from API import API
import extra_streamlit_components as stx
import base64, json

cookie_manager = stx.CookieManager()
cookies = cookie_manager.get_all()
authentication_token = cookies.get("token")\
    if type(cookies) == dict else cookies

api = API("http://127.0.0.1:5000/api", authentication_token)

def get_username_from_token(auth_token):
    b64 = str(auth_token).split(".")[1]
    b64 = b64 + "=" * (4 - (len(b64) % 4))
```

```
    data = base64.b64decode(b64).decode("utf8")
    username = json.loads(data)['username']
    return username

def manage_login(username, password):
    token = api.login(username, password)
    cookie_manager.set("token", token)
    return token is not None

st.title("Company Management Portal")

if api.is_logged_in():
    st.subheader(f"_Welcome "
                 f"**{get_username_from_
                 token(authentication_token)}**_")
    st.write("_____")
    AddEmployee(api.add_employee)
    st.write("___")
    DisplayEmployees(api.get_employees)
else:
    Login(manage_login)
```

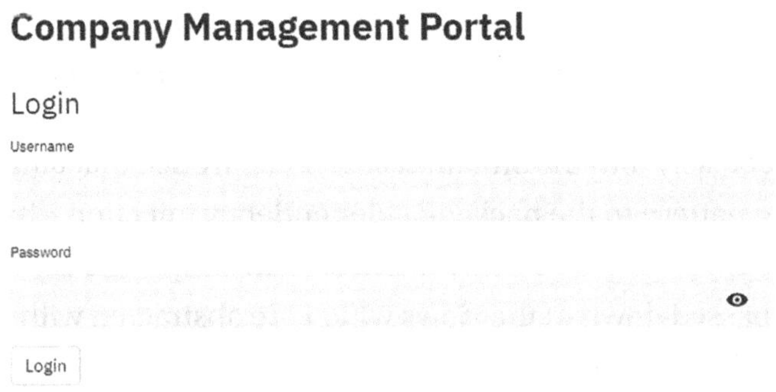

Figure 8-7. *Login page*

Company Management Portal

Welcome admin1

Add a new employee

Name

DOB

2021/10/03

paygrade

0   —   +

Add new Employee

Current Employees

	date_of_birth	id	name	paygrade_id
0	01/01/1990	1	Adam	2
1	01/01/1980	2	Sara	1
2	01/01/1970	3	Bob	1
3	01/01/2000	4	Alice	3

Figure 8-8. *Adding and viewing the list of authenticated employees*

Looking closely into the Streamlit side code, we see that almost the same coding pattern to the backend – dependency injection – has been used. This makes the code coherent end to end. Simply the actions of the API are passed down to the views which are abstracted with a class as shown in Listings 8-9, 8-10, and 8-11.

Listing 8-9. Streamlit/Views/AddEmployee.py

```python
import streamlit as st
from typing import Callable
import datetime

class AddEmployee:
    def __init__(self, on_submit: Callable[[str, str, int], bool]):
        st.header("Add a new employee")

        form = st.form("new_employee")
        name = form.text_input("Name")
        dob = str(form.date_input("DOB",
                    min_value=datetime.datetime(year=1920,
                    day=1, month=1)))
        paygrade = form.number_input("paygrade", step=1)

        if form.form_submit_button("Add new Employee"):
            success = on_submit(name, dob, paygrade)
            if success:
                st.success("New employee added")
            else:
                st.error("Employee not added")
```

Listing 8-10. Streamlit/Views/DisplayEmployees.py

```python
import streamlit as st
from typing import Callable

class DisplayEmployees:
    def __init__(self, get_employees: Callable[[], list]):
        st.header("Current Employees")

        employees = get_employees()
```

```python
    if employees is None:
        st.error("Error getting employees")
    else:
        st.table(employees)
```

Listing 8-11. Streamlit/Views/Login.py

```python
import streamlit as st
from typing import Callable

class Login:
    def __init__(self, on_login: Callable[[str, str], bool]):
        st.header("Login")
        username = st.text_input("Username")
        password = st.text_input("Password",type="password")

        if st.button("Login"):
            success = on_login(username, password)
            if success:
                st.success("Login successful")
            else:
                st.error("Incorrect username and password
                combination")
```

8.3 Secrets Management

As we have already discussed how to keep a Streamlit application's secret credentials safe from an external's reach, we now will introduce another way to be used in Flask and that can also be applied in a Streamlit context. Basically, we need a file to add the secrets in. This means the JWT signing key and the signing up header key need to be stored somewhere on disk and then loaded into our application's memory usage. Secrets and keys can be stored in different ways, but one of the most user-friendly ways is using YAML files, as shown in Listing 8-12, which are then parsed and converted to a Python dictionary.

Listing 8-12. Flask/secrets.yaml

```
jwt_secret: "A RANDOM TEXT HERE"
sing_up_key: "ANOTHER RANDOM TEXT HERE"
```

8.4 Anti-SQL Injection Measures with SQLAlchemy

As a final code implemented protection, we aim to protect the backend's SQL queries by preventing a nonintended action to happen. First, we need to identify what a SQL injection is. It is mostly when a user-controlled text changes the SQL command behavior. For instance, assume we want to support searching for employees starting with a string of character to be input by the end user; it will result in a final query as such: SELECT * FROM Employees WHERE name = 'input%'. This poses a threat if the input was OR 1=1 -- as it would result in a final query of SELECT * FROM Employees WHERE name = '%' OR 1=1 -- which orders the database to select all employees, instead of treating the input as the search string.

To overcome this problem, we need to use parameterization which is a technique to isolate the original SQL command from the changing variables. So, for the example from before, it would rather look something like SELECT * FROM Employees WHERE name = '@name%' where *@name* is a SQL variable initialized before submitting the query. As a developer, this might be an overhead toward a more secure SQL. Thus, we use libraries and/or packages to do this on our behalf. For this scenario, we are using SQLAlchemy, which is a library that can connect to many types of databases and change SQL command formats depending on the architecture, origin, and version, all by following an intuitive API that is documented in docs.sqlalchemy.org.

8.5 Configuring Gitignore Variables

Having all files tracked with a version control system like Git is a must for big projects, as it adds more simplicity in managing what files are important and their modification history. However, not all files must be tracked, and some will pose security threats if tracked, as the code base can be accessed by anyone if it is public, or broken into if it is private. This makes the secrets managed under threat; hence, it is widely agreed among software developers to not track the secrets file and store the actual secrets in a security vault, which is accessible using multiple methods of authentication.

As this adds one more layer of security over the application's secrets, it gives a direct hit to code readability and understanding if an unaware developer started working on the code. This can be fixed by adding another file with the following naming conventions: Flask/secrets.***example***.yaml which will host similar content to what is shown in Listing 8-12 albeit with a replacement of the actual key values with something vague yet understandable, as shown in Listing 8-13. Subsequently, we can remove the original secrets file from Git by updating the .gitignore file as shown in Listing 8-14. If needed, any file and folder in or under the same folder as .gitignore can be set to be ignored or excluded depending on the syntax.

Listing 8-13. Flask/secrets.example.yaml

```
# Copy the content of this file to secrets.yaml
# and replace its contents with the correct values
jwt_secret: "<INSERT TEXT>"
sing_up_key: "<INSERT TEXT HERE>"
```

Listing 8-14. Flask/.gitignore

```
secrets.yaml
```

8.6 Summary

As part of making any web application public, you are required to manage resources served, by verifying each and every user's authorization level. In this chapter, we have explained how to create and manage user accounts and how to utilize them for authentication. We introduced essential application security mechanisms such as generating JSON Web Tokens, hashing passwords, and embedding secure signatures into cookies. In addition, this chapter showcased techniques to obstruct SQL injection attacks to prevent unauthorized access to databases. Finally, we observed how application keys and secrets can be secured during deployment, and also how they can be excluded from being committed toa version control framework such as Git.

CHAPTER 9

Deploying Locally and to the Cloud

As you approach the end of the development phase with your Streamlit application, it is time for it to see the light for the first time. In other words, you are ready to deploy the application and unleash your goodness to the world at large. To that end, you will need a machine to serve your application continuously, robustly, and resiliently. And while you can transform your local machine into a server of sorts, you are better off deploying the application to the mighty cloud, with the likes of Amazon Web Services, Microsoft Azure, Google Cloud Platform, and last but not least Streamlit itself.

In this chapter, we will walk through the steps required to forward your local application to the Web and more importantly how to deploy your application on remote servers with Linux containers, Windows Server, and with Streamlit's dedicated cloud service *Streamlit Cloud*. Upon completion of this chapter, you will have acquired the technical know-how to serve your users both within a local network and across the World Wide Web.

© Mohammad Khorasani, Mohamed Abdou, Javier Hernández Fernández 2022
M. Khorasani et al., *Web Application Development with Streamlit*,
https://doi.org/10.1007/978-1-4842-8111-6_9

9.1 Exposing Streamlit to the World Wide Web

After making an application with Streamlit, you get to see it in action by visiting the loopback address from the browser as such: http://127.0.0.1:8501. In addition to that, you can also share it locally with people and devices on your local network which usually assigns your IP address which starts with 192.168.*, 172.(16-31).*, or 10.*. Then you can access your running Streamlit application from any device on the same network by prepending your IP address with http and appending 8501 or the listening port of Streamlit. However, there is no straightforward way to temporarily showcase your Streamlit application to anyone, anywhere, without having to lease a static public IP from your ISP or rent a cloud computer from a big tech. Here, we will showcase free, easy-to-configure methods to present your application globally at no extra cost.

9.1.1 Port Forwarding over a Network Gateway

Nowadays, almost every household contains a broadband device, which is technically the gateway to the Internet. However, the household's network and devices are not exposed to the Internet; rather, their Internet requests are routed through the broadband device. The broadband uses NAT to map private to public IPs. But the opposite way doesn't work by default, unless configured to do so. With most broadbands, a web server is exposed to control multiple things on the network. Usually, the very first IP of the network is the broadband's. Pasting this IP in the browser will serve a web page to configure the routing rules and other things as seen in Figure 9-1. It might not look the same with everybody, but all mostly have a method to configure *port forwarding* and *port mapping*. In that page, we want to map an internal IP with a port to one of the broadband's public ports. Ideally, we want to map Streamlit's default 8501 port to the default HTTP's port 80.

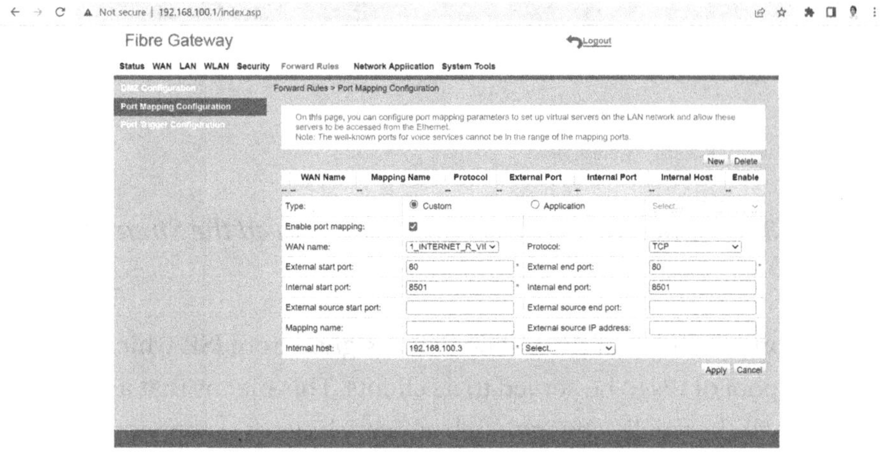

Figure 9-1. *Broadband's configuration website*

The next step is to know the gateway's public IP. A simple method to know it is just by googling it, as seen in Figure 9-2. Essentially, any website you visit can see your public IP, which then can be echoed to you for your reference. Now if we paste the same IP in the browser's search bar, we will be presented by our Streamlit application as shown in Figure 9-3.

Figure 9-2. *Host's public IP address*

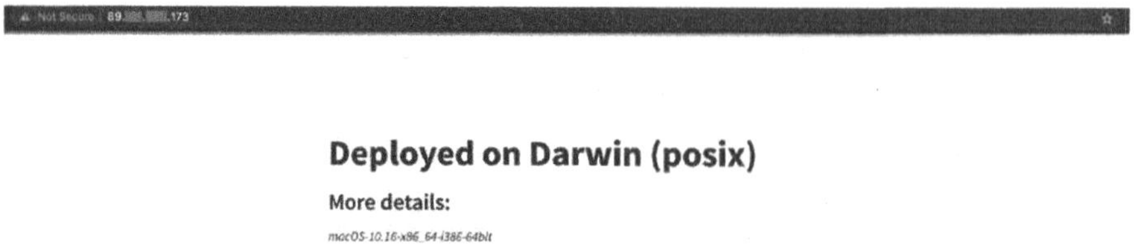

Deployed on Darwin (posix)

More details:

macOS-10.16-x86_64-i386-64bit

Figure 9-3. *Visiting the public IP and being served the Streamlit application*

It is worth noting that the public IP is assigned from ISP, which rotates through a pool of IPs to be served to its clients. This means that anyone's public IP will eventually change, such as every hour or on network reentry. This will happen unless you request a static IP from the ISP, which guarantees the broadband is allocated the IP address requested, even if your network is unavailable.

9.1.2 HTTP Tunneling Using NGROK

The concept of tunneling is like establishing a VPN connection between two devices, even if they are further apart and not in the same network. Ngrok utilizes tunneling to allow private network devices to be accessed by the public network for a short period of time (usually two hours) by allocating a temporary subdomain on their servers that access your service to expose and serve it on your behalf. In a nutshell, a Streamlit application running on `http://127.0.0.1:8501` can be accessed by a specific ngrok URL with the following format:

`http://<random-uuid-here>.ngrok.io`

Once the tunnel command is initiated by the Ngrok user, the connection is established and the Ngrok URL is provided. The user can then share it with anyone to access their local Streamlit application for the next few hours. After installing Ngrok on your computer, you can process it by typing the following into the CMD or terminal:

```
ngrok http <port_to_tunnel_to>
```

where the *<port_to_tunnel_to>* block can be replaced with *8501* for tunneling to the running Streamlit application. Listing 9-1 shows a simple Streamlit application using an iframe to display the user's public IP address. After running ngrok on 8501 in the CMD, the user gets presented with the allocated subdomain as seen in Figure 9-4. The location of the subdomain is the United States as mentioned by ngrok; however, once a public IP website is visited, it doesn't show the United States as the origin according to Figure 9-5. The IP shown is the original user's ID which is in Qatar even though the ngrok tunneled through the United States; this is because it is not a VPN but a network, and the request to that page is done through the Streamlit host machine.

Listing 9-1. main.py

```python
import os
import platform
import streamlit as st

st.title(f"Deployed on {platform.system()} ({os.name})")

st.subheader("More details:")
st.write(f"_{platform.platform()}_")
```

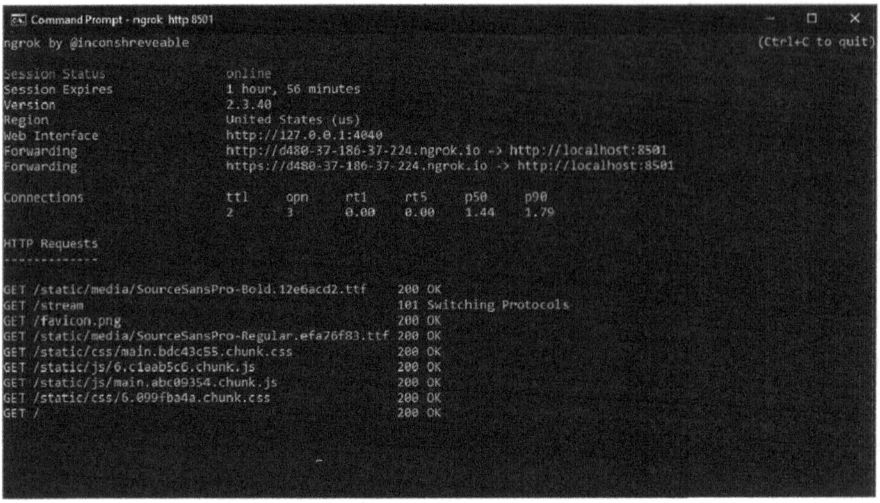

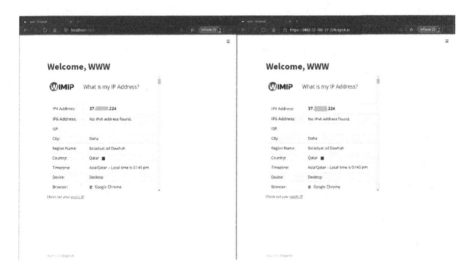

Figure 9-4. *Ngrok dashboard after tunneling to port 8501*

Figure 9-5. *Two browser windows, one being served locally and the other by ngrok, and both showing the same client IP*

9.2 Deployment to Streamlit Cloud

Deploying a web application on the cloud can be somewhat of a demanding undertaking, contingent on who your cloud service provider is. Some like Heroku have made it as trivial as connecting your GitHub repository, installing your build packs, configuring the application, and then launching. Others require you to orchestrate the entire process including setting up the virtual machine, creating containers, port forwarding, load balancing, and routing requests yourself. Regardless, deployment to the cloud solicits at least a minimum understanding of cloud computing concepts; after all, this is why we have DevOps engineers.

Streamlit however is democratizing this one last frontier and making deployment quite literally a one-click process. With *Streamlit Cloud*, you can simply connect your GitHub repository and then click deploy. Streamlit will then provision the application with all of its required dependencies for you and will update it each time you push a new version of your source code. No additional intervention is required by the developer whatsoever. Furthermore, if you require more than one private application, additional computing resources, or enterprise-grade features, you may upgrade to Streamlit's premium packages.

9.2.1 One-Click Deployment

Before you proceed to deploy your first application to Streamlit Cloud, you should open a GitHub account and push your script to a repository. Subsequently, you can follow these steps to deploy:

1. Navigate to *share.streamlit.io*, log in with your GitHub account, and click *New app* as shown in Figure 9-6.

Figure 9-6. *Deploying an application to Streamlit Cloud (1)*

2. Select the repository, branch, and file where your source code is located. Then click *Deploy!* as shown in Figure 9-7.

Figure 9-7. *Deploying an application to Streamlit Cloud (2)*

3. Sit back and relax while Streamlit Cloud provisions your application, shown in Figure 9-8.

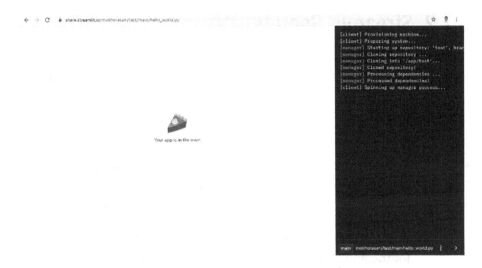

Figure 9-8. *Deploying an application to Streamlit Cloud (3)*

4. And there you have it, your first application
   deployed to Streamlit Cloud, shown in Figure 9-9.

Figure 9-9. *Deploying an application to Streamlit Cloud (4)*

9.2.2 Streamlit Secrets

Another benefit associated with using Streamlit Cloud is that you can securely store private data on Streamlit's servers and readily access them in your application. This feature is exceptionally useful for storing user credentials, database connection strings, API keys, and other passwords, without having to enter them in plain text form in your code (which you should never do under any circumstances). Instead, you can execute the following steps to store and access private data with Streamlit's *Secrets Management.*

1. Navigate to *share.streamlit.io* and open the settings for the application you want to add secrets to, as shown in Figure 9-10.

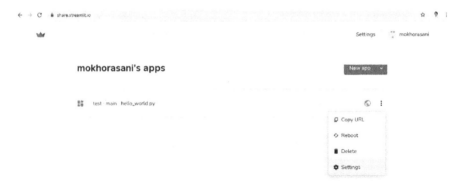

Figure 9-10. *Adding secrets to Streamlit Cloud's Secrets Management (1)*

2. Add your secrets in the form of a TOML file, as shown in Figure 9-11.

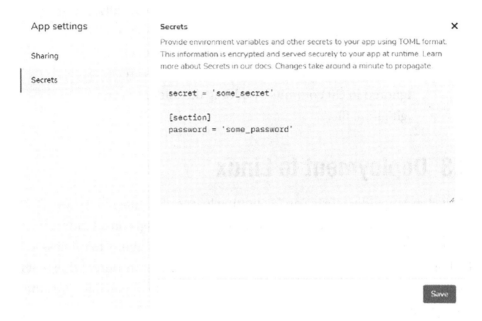

Figure 9-11. *Adding secrets to Streamlit Cloud's Secrets Management (2)*

3. Access your secrets in your script using the *st. secrets* command, as shown in the following and in Figure 9-12:

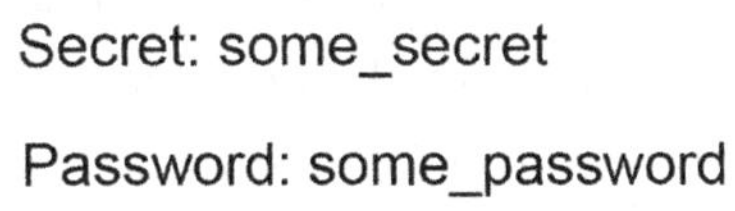

Secret: some_secret

Password: some_password

Figure 9-12. *Using secrets in a Streamlit Cloud application*

```
import streamlit as st
st.write('**Secret:**',st.secrets['secret'])
st.write('**Password:**',st.secrets['section']['password'])
```

4. If you wish to replicate Secrets Management locally
    on your own server, you can simply add the same
    TOML file as *secrets.toml* in the *.streamlit* folder
    in your root directory. Ensure that such files are
    ignored in Git commits by adding the folder to your
    .gitignore file.

9.3 Deployment to Linux

Most cloud providers thrive on facilitating leases of virtual machines
to corporations and individuals to run services and apps on a Linux
environment. The beauty of Linux revolves around its ability to process at
higher speeds and make better utilization of computer resources due to its
use of fewer kernel layers. All those factors contribute in making Linux the
go-to option for cloud machines.

9.3.1 Native Deployment on a Linux Machine

Having access to a Linux machine, whether with GUI or terminal access,
you can run Streamlit in a nonblocking way. To do so, you have to make
the command run in the background by using & after the command as
shown in Listing 9-2. Then untie it from the terminal by using the `disown`
in order to prevent the process being killed after the terminal being closed,
but by still displaying standard input and output as shown in Figure 9-13.
Output of Listing 9-1 can be seen in Figure 9-14.

Figure 9-13. *Running Listing 9-2 in the terminal*

Figure 9-14. *Output of Listing 9-1, showing the operating system being Linux*

At the point of closing the application, we need to find its PID first with

ps -aux | grep "streamlit run"

Then gather the leftmost number and, as shown in Figure 9-15, stop
the process with

kill <PID>

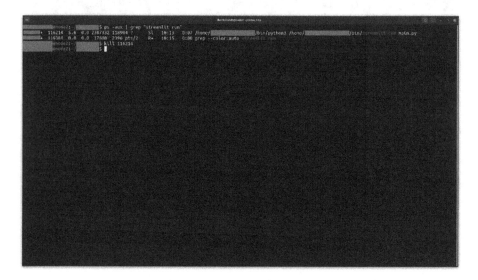

Figure 9-15. *Searching for the background Streamlit process ID and
running the* kill *command against it*

Listing 9-2. run.sh, with main.py being Listing 9-1

streamlit run main.py &

disown

9.3.2 Deployment with Linux Docker Containers

To avoid the hassle of running your Streamlit application in a specific way, and for other security reasons, you can use a Docker container to run it. Docker allows you to host an application in any OS environment with its own variables, applications, and services. All while having the ability to control computer resources it has access to. Moreover, if the application was compromised by a malicious actor, most likely they won't be able to escape the Docker container to further compromise the machine it is running on, only if configured correctly.

Knowing why deployment of any service in a containerized environment is beneficial, we can proceed by creating Docker's main file, which is shown in Listing 9-3. Assuming Docker is already installed, this file essentially initiates a Linux environment with a Python 3.8 installed by default and then makes a new folder to place your Streamlit/Python files in. After that, it copies your (should be existing) requirements.txt file, as shown in Listing 9-4, to Docker's working directory, which will then be installed. Once Streamlit is installed, we order the Docker container to allow access to its 8501 port from the outside Docker scope; this is the port which Streamlit will run on by default. And finally, Streamlit files are copied to the working directory and run.

Listing 9-3. Dockerfile

```
FROM python:3.8
WORKDIR /app
COPY requirements.txt ./requirements.txt
RUN pip install -r requirements.txt
EXPOSE 8501
COPY . /app
ENTRYPOINT ["streamlit", "run"]
CMD ["main.py"]
```

Listing 9-4. requirements.txt

```
streamlit==1.2.0 # Latest version as of writing this book
```

Having our files ready, we need to build a custom Docker image out of our work like in Figure 9-16 by running Listing 9-5 in the project's root folder, where the Dockerfile shall exist.

Listing 9-5. Building a Docker image

```
docker build -t <CUSTOM_IMAGE_NAME>:latest .
```

Figure 9-16. *Building image and verifying its existence*

Running the image is done by executing the code shown in Listing 9-6; the -d option is to detach the process from the command line, similar to the disown command in Linux. Figure 9-17 shows how the process does not detached and therefore stops reusing the same command-line window. Now we have a running container overriding the current machine's port 8501 with its own, which means the Streamlit application can be visited from localhost as seen in Figure 9-18.

Listing 9-6. Making a container out of a Docker image

```
docker run -d -p 8501:8501 <CUSTOM_IMAGE_NAME>:latest
```

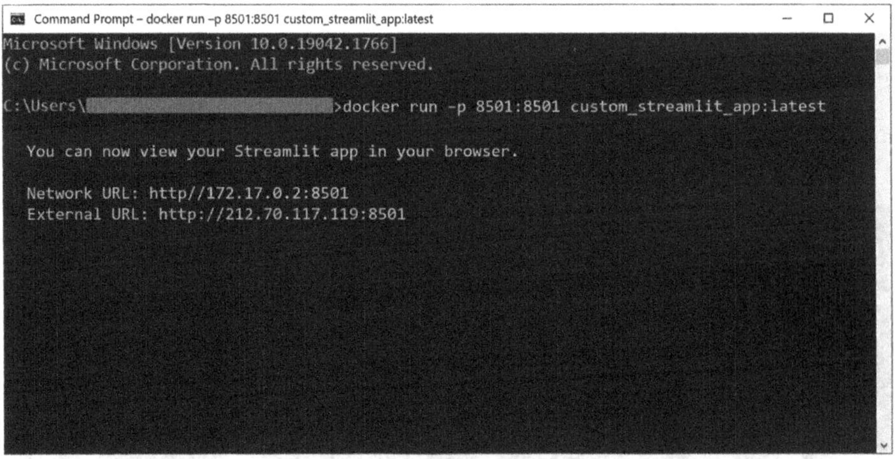

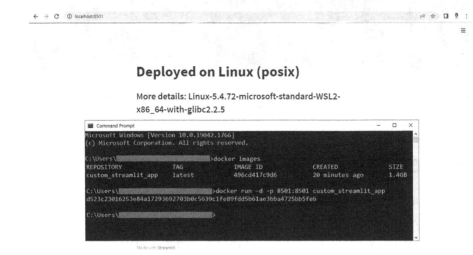

Figure 9-17. *Running the Docker image*

Figure 9-18. *Streamlit application running from a Docker container*

Finally, we can destroy the container, without affecting the image, by running Listing 9-8. First, we need to know the container ID by running Listing 9-7, then apply the stopping action as seen in Figure 9-19.

Listing 9-7. Displaying all running Docker container metadata

```
docker ps
```

Listing 9-8. Stopping a specific Docker container

```
docker stop <CONTAINER_ID>
```

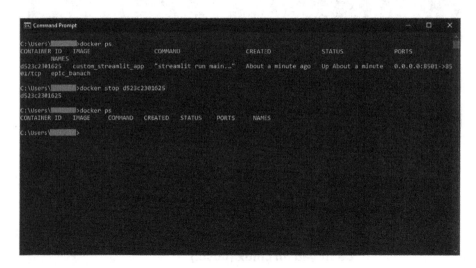

Figure 9-19. *Checking active containers and closing a specific container*

9.4 Deployment to Windows Server

Given the affinity of the corporate world with Microsoft, if you are going to deploy your Streamlit application on a corporate server, chances are you will be using Windows Server. Luckily, the process to provision your application is rather simple and straightforward, and while this section is dedicated to Windows Server, it is by no means exclusive to it either; you may in fact follow the same steps to deploy on a normal Windows operating system as well. Before we proceed however, we are going to make several assumptions that may or may not be true, namely, that your corporate server is located remotely and that you only have local intranet access to it with no Internet connectivity. Consequently, you will require additional steps to overcome these two assumptions that will be explained in the following sections.

9.4.1 Establishing a Remote Desktop Connection

As mentioned earlier, your server may be located remotely, and your most likely means of connecting to it will be through the Remote Desktop Protocol or RDP for short. RDP provides you with a graphical user interface to connect to the remote server over a network connection. The Microsoft client for RDP is *Remote Desktop Connection*, as shown in Figure 9-20. Please proceed by entering the IP address of the remote server in the *Computer* field and the associated domain (if required) appended to the username in the *User name* field as *domain/username*. Subsequently, click connect and you will be prompted to enter your password to log in to the server.

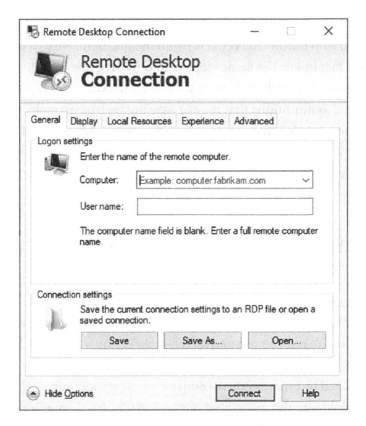

Figure 9-20. *Establishing a RDP connection to the remote server*

Since your remote server might not have access to the Internet, you may also use RDP to transfer files from your local disk to the server by selecting the *Drives* checkbox in the *Local Resources* tab as shown in Figure 9-21. With this feature, you also have the option of providing access to other local resources such as I/O devices and peripherals on the server should you require.

Figure 9-21. *Transferring local resources to the remote server*

9.4.2 Opening TCP/IP Ports

Before you proceed any further, you need to ensure that all the relevant inbound and outbound TCP/IP ports of the server are open, so that the Streamlit application can be forwarded across the local network:

1. Open *Windows Defender Firewall with Additional Security.*

2. Select *Inbound Rules* or *Outbound Rules* in the left pane.

3. Click *New Rule* in the right pane to open the *New Rule Wizard* window.

4. Select the *Port* option and then click next as shown in Figure 9-22.

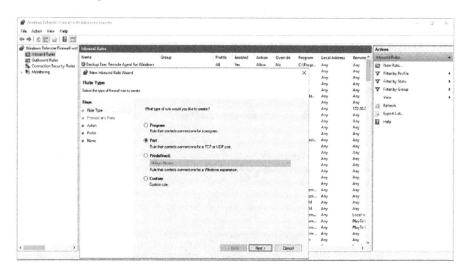

Figure 9-22. *Opening TCP/IP ports (1)*

5. Select *TCP* and enter the port number that your Streamlit application will be served on, for example, 8501, as shown in Figure 9-23.

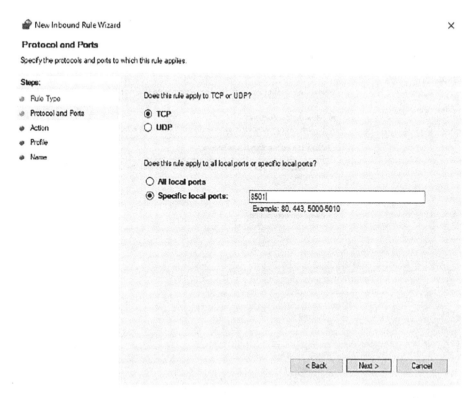

Figure 9-23. *Opening TCP/IP ports (2)*

6.   Select *Allow the connection* to serve the port to all
      users, or alternatively select *Allow the connection
      if it is secure* to serve the port to specific users, as
      shown in Figure 9-24.

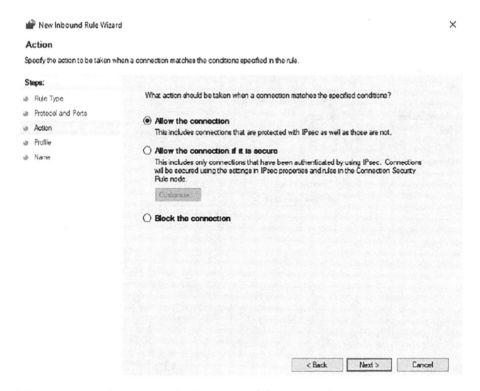

Figure 9-24. *Opening TCP/IP ports (3)*

7. Subsequently, select *Domain* and *Private* to serve
   the port to secure networks, as shown in Figure 9-25.

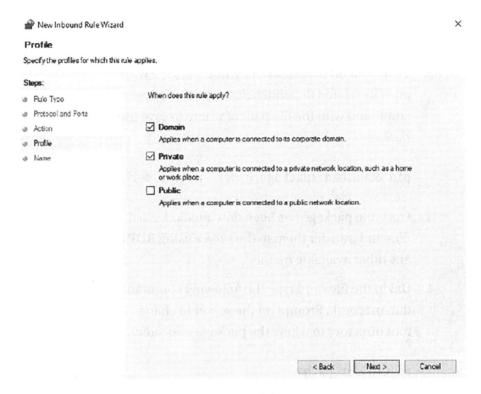

Figure 9-25. *Opening TCP/IP ports (4)*

8. Finally, enter a name for your rule and follow the
    same steps to open the same port for inbound/
    outbound communication.

9.4.3 Anaconda Offline Package Installation

As your server may not have Internet access, you will not have the ability of
installing Python packages and their dependencies using Pip as you would
normally. Instead, you must carry out an offline installation by following
these steps:

1. Open the Anaconda Prompt on a computer with access to the Internet.

2. To download the required Python package with all of its related dependencies, type the following command with the file path of where to save the package:

    ```
    pip download <package name> -d "<folder path>"
    ```

3. Once the package has been downloaded, zip the files and transfer them to the server using RDP or any other available method.

4. Unzip the files and type the following command into the Anaconda Prompt on the server to change the root directory to where the package is located:

    ```
    cd <folder path>
    ```

5. Enter the following command into the Anaconda Prompt to initiate an offline installation of the required package:

    ```
    pip install <package name> -f ./ --no-index
    ```

9.4.4 Adding Anaconda to System Path

In order to run your Streamlit application as an executable batch file (explained in the following section), it is first necessary to add Anaconda or any other Python interpreter of your choice to the system path in Windows with the following steps:

1. Determine the location of Anaconda.exe by typing the following command into the Anaconda Prompt:

   `where anaconda`

2. Open the Windows search bar and launch *Edit the system environment variables*.

3. Once the *System Properties* window opens, click the *Advanced* tab and select *Environment Variables*.

4. Subsequently, highlight *Path* and click *Edit* to add the path for Anaconda, as shown in Figure 9-26.

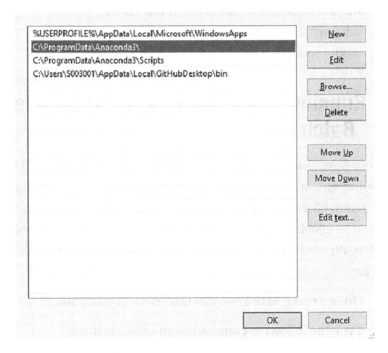

Figure 9-26. *Adding Anaconda to the system path*

5. If the necessary paths do not already exist, add the path that was found in step 1 by entering the following two:

```
C:\...\Anaconda3\
```

and

```
C:\...\Anaconda3\Scripts\
```

6. To ensure that Anaconda has been successfully added to the system path, open the Windows Command Prompt and type *anaconda*. If Anaconda has not been added, an error will be raised; otherwise, you will be able to use any Anaconda command, for example, *conda list*.

9.4.5 Running Application as an Executable Batch File

To run your Streamlit application as a Windows service (explained in the following section), you will first need to create an executable batch file for it. Batch files are in effect analogous to *.exe* files. They can be run by double-clicking the file, similar to how you would run any other application. Please follow the steps to create a batch file for your Streamlit application:

1. Open a notepad or any other text editor of your choice.

2. Type the following commands on separate lines:

```
call activate <environment name>
cd <folder path>
streamlit run <script name.py>
pause
```

3. Save the script as a batch file by adding the *.bat* extension to the end of the filename.

4. Run the batch file to ensure that the application is being launched as expected.

9.4.6 Running Application As a Persistent Windows Service

The final part of preparing for deployment on Windows Server is to run your Streamlit application persistently as a Windows service. While you can still serve it as you would normally with any Streamlit application, there are however several benefits to running it as a Windows service as listed in the following:

- Your application will be run in the background without opening a console.

- The application will not be attached to a RDP session, thereby ensuring that it will continue to run even when RDP is terminated.

- You can schedule your application to run on Windows startup or on any other trigger.

To configure your application as a persistent Windows service, please follow these steps:

1. Open *Windows Task Scheduler* and click *Create Task* on the right pane, as shown in Figure 9-27.

Figure 9-27. *Running application as a persistent Windows service (1)*

2. Enter a name for the task, then select the *Run whether user is logged on or not* and *Run with highest privileges* options, as shown in Figure 9-28.

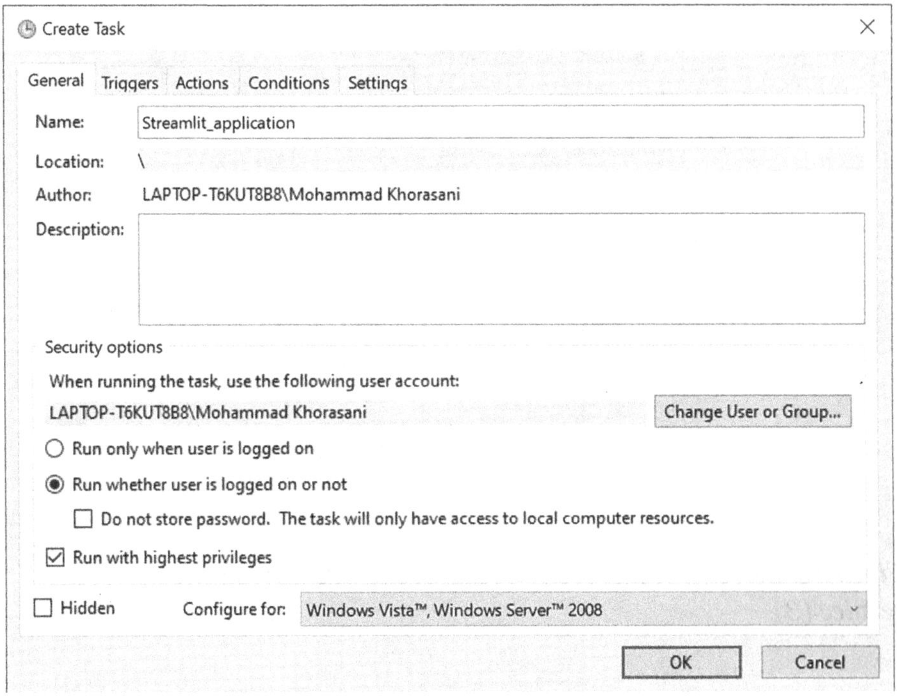

Figure 9-28. *Running application as a persistent Windows service (2)*

3. Navigate to the *Actions* tab and select *Start a program* from the action menu, then browse to the location of the batch file you created for your Streamlit application (explained in the previous section), as shown in Figure 9-29.

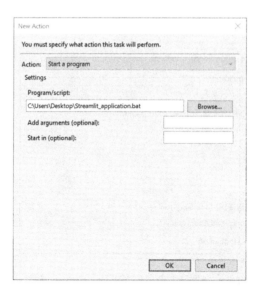

Figure 9-29. *Running application as a persistent Windows service (3)*

4. Open the *Task Scheduler Library* on the left pane,
    select your created task in the list, and select *Run* on
    the right pane, as shown in Figure 9-30.

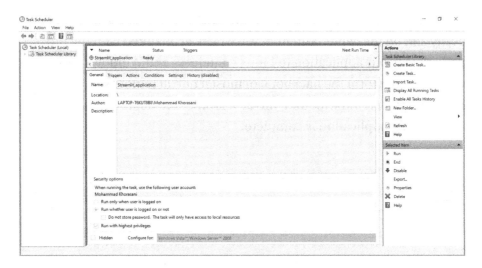

Figure 9-30. *Running application as a persistent Windows service (4)*

5. To ensure that your Windows service task has been configured successfully, terminate the RDP session, open the browser on another device on the local network, and navigate to the network URL of your Streamlit application to check whether the application is running.

9.5 Summary

In this chapter, we learned how to expose our Streamlit application to the Internet by port forwarding over a network gateway, as well as utilizing HTTP tunneling with ngrok to that end. Subsequently, we were introduced to Streamlit's in-house cloud platform *Streamlit Cloud*, with which the skills gap for deployment is largely covered. Now any developer can simply connect their GitHub repository and deploy their application with one click, quite literally. In addition, we saw how we can integrate private data securely into our applications using Streamlit's *Secrets Management*, both locally and on the cloud. And finally, we were acquainted with the process for deploying our application to Linux containers and Windows Server, which together form the backbone of most if not all remote servers located across the globe. And with that, the development to deployment life cycle of a Streamlit application is complete.

## CHAPTER 10

Building Streamlit Components

Streamlit regularly extends its features to incorporate additional capabilities that can be utilized by developers in a few short lines of code. At some point however, developers will need to take matters into their own hands and build something tailored to address their own specific user requirements. Whether this is to modify the user interface or to offer a bespoke experience to the user, Streamlit allows the developer to create custom components on demand. Furthermore, Streamlit supports using ReactJS as a wingman to build components that can be used as a live web server or built using deployment-ready code. In this chapter, we will walk through the steps required to make new Streamlit components, to use them in a Pythonic context, and to share them with the general public.

10.1 Introduction to Streamlit Custom Components

Fundamentally, Streamlit is a backend server, serving web page changes to client browsers using DG. HTML and JavaScript can be generated by any web frameworks. Hence, Streamlit can help serving components from any web application framework. Web application frameworks can be quite advanced like ReactJS, where the developer codes in JSX but builds the

© Mohammad Khorasani, Mohamed Abdou, Javier Hernández Fernández 2022
M. Khorasani et al., *Web Application Development with Streamlit*,
https://doi.org/10.1007/978-1-4842-8111-6_10

application to give out a combination of files that can be served statically from disk. In a production environment, it is highly advised to have static files served from disk as illustrated in Figure 10-1. However, Streamlit still allows including components that are hosted locally, but as a trade-off, this component imported in the Streamlit application will share different features from the Streamlit app. For instance, if you print the current URL from the custom component, it will not give out the same URL which the Streamlit application is hosted on.

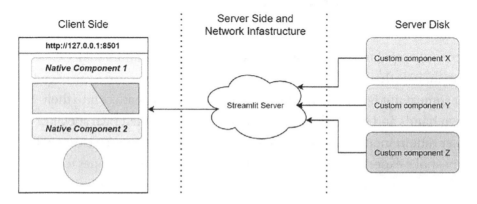

Figure 10-1. *How custom components are served through Streamlit*

10.2 Using ReactJS to Create Streamlit Custom Components

In this section, we will showcase how to make a ReactJS-based component to be used in Streamlit. Along with that, we will also demonstrate how to share data bidirectionally between Streamlit and the component. This can be used to send initial values, user action triggers, or even styling themes and colors to the custom component.

10.2.1 Making a ReactJS Component

Initially, Node and npm needs to be installed from *NodeJS.org*. Then, we will use Streamlit's official template for making custom components from *GitHub*. In this subsection, we will quickly cover making a ReactJS component.

In this example we will produce a rating stars widget as shown in Figure 10-2 in ReactJS and build upon it in the following subsections. The developer community of ReactJS is considerably larger than that of other frameworks, making it worthwhile to invest time in creating such components. .

Figure 10-2. *Interactive rating star view from Material UI*

Copying the content of `component-template/template/my_component` to our working directory will set up a ReactJS application with a one file module, which is in `src/MyComponent.tsx`, and that is the file that needs to be modified in order to achieve our goal of making a rating star component. Modifying the file will result in Listing 10-1

Listing 10-1. stars_demo/rating_stars/frontend/src/CleanedTemplate.tsx

```
import {
    Streamlit,
    StreamlitComponentBase,
    withStreamlitConnection,
} from "streamlit-component-lib"
import React, { ReactNode } from "react"
```

```typescript
interface State {}

class MyComponent extends StreamlitComponentBase<State> {
  public state = {}

  public render = (): ReactNode => {

    return (
     <div></div>
    )
  }
}

export default withStreamlitConnection(MyComponent)
```

Use the following command to install the Material UI library:

```
npm i @mui/material
```

Then run the following command to install other packages in the package.json file:

```
npm i
```

After running both commands, make sure to change the name in package.json to be your component's reference name in Streamlit down the road as shown in Listing 10-2.

Listing 10-2. Updated Package.json

```json
{
   "name": "rating_star",
   "version": "0.1.0",
   "private": true,
   "dependencies": {
```

```
    "@mui/material": "^5.0.6",
    "..."
  },
  "scripts": ...,
  "eslintConfig": ...,
  "browserslist": ...,
  "homepage": "."
}
```

Having the necessary packages ready, and with a little JavaScript/
TypeScript knowledge, or with a little bit of Googling, we can start making
our first ReactJS module to be used as a custom Streamlit component. We
have to modify Listing 10-1 to display the rating stars as documented in
Material UI's site. As an end result, the new file content will be as shown in
Listing 10-3 which should reside in frontend/src/. And don't forget to
change the file to be run in the index.tsx.

Listing 10-3. Initial version of RatingStar.tsx

```
import {
    Streamlit,
    StreamlitComponentBase,
    withStreamlitConnection,
} from "streamlit-component-lib"
import React, { ReactNode } from "react"
import { Rating } from '@mui/material';

interface State {}

class RatingStar extends StreamlitComponentBase<State> {
  public state = {}
```

```
public render = (): ReactNode => {

  return (
    <Rating size="large" defaultValue={3} />
  )
 }
}

export default withStreamlitConnection(RatingStar)
```

10.2.2 Using a ReactJS Component in Streamlit

To get the React application ready, run the following command. If errors
popped up mentioning a missing package, install it using the command
mentioned before.

```
npm start
```

Now, on Streamlit's side, we will use the already running ReactJS
application as a component, by leveraging Streamlit's API to include
external components. But first, we need to populate the __init__.py
as shown in Listing 10-4.

Listing 10-4. Initial version of __init__.py

```
import os
import streamlit.components.v1 as components

IS_RELEASE = False

if IS_RELEASE:
   absolute_path = os.path.dirname(os.path.abspath(__file__))
   build_path = os.path.join(absolute_path, "frontend/build")
   _component_func = components.declare_component("rating_
   stars", path=build_path)
```

```
else:
  _component_func = components.declare_component("rating_
  stars", url="http://localhost:3001")

def rating_stars():
  _component_func()
```

The previous code snippet uses a live component running locally on port 3001, which in our case needs to be the ReactJS app. Then it exposes a function to be used by any other Python source to be run as a Streamlit module. Executing Listing 10-5 with Streamlit's CLI tool, will result in what is shown in Figure 10-3.

Listing 10-5. Initial version of main.py

```
import streamlit as st
from rating_stars import rating_stars

st.title("Rating stars demo!")
rating_stars()
```

Rating stars demo!

Figure 10-3. *First custom component!*

That being made, we were able to display a live ReactJS application in a Streamlit context, but if we become more creative and make more custom components, it will be a hassle to go to the folder of each and run it as a ReactJS application before running the Streamlit application. Maybe even run out of ports as each custom component has its own unique local URL. Hence, we can overcome this issue by building the ReactJS application into static files, after it is been developed, by running

```
npm run build
```

Now a new folder called build will appear in the frontend folder, containing the necessary JavaScript, CSS, and HTML files to be used by Streamlit to load it into an application. Once that is done and it is fixed to run the built version of a component, we need to change the IS_RELEASE to True, forcing Streamlit to load the new custom component from the frontend/build/ folder. And that is exactly what is being conveyed by Figure 10-1.

10.2.3 Sending Data to the Custom Component

At this point, we can just display ReactJS applications in a Streamlit context, albeit without a communication mechanism between the front and back ends. Now, we will showcase how to send data from Streamlit to ReactJS, when the transferable data is dynamic, giving us the capability of sending information from Streamlit with every rerender to the ReactJS application.

As a step toward making our rating star custom component more useful, we will add the support of setting the total star count and how many of them are selected, all from Streamlit's Python code. First, we need to understand that Streamlit converts Python's passed parameter of _component_func to ReactJS's properties. So, our goal is to refactor the component's __init__.py file to allow the new parameters as shown in Listing 10-6 and read them from RatingStar.tsx and then place them in the view's properties like Listing 10-7.

Listing 10-6. Second version of __init__.py

```
import os
import streamlit.components.v1 as components

IS_RELEASE = False

if IS_RELEASE:
    absolute_path = os.path.dirname(os.path.abspath(__file__))
    build_path = os.path.join(absolute_path, "frontend/build")
    _component_func = components.declare_component("rating_
    stars", path=build_path)
else:
    _component_func = components.declare_component("rating_
    stars", url="http://localhost:3001")

def rating_stars(stars_count: int, selected: int):
    _component_func(stars_count=stars_count, selected=selected)
```

Listing 10-7. Second version of RatingStar.tsx

```
import {
    Streamlit,
    StreamlitComponentBase,
    withStreamlitConnection,
} from "streamlit-component-lib"
import React, { ReactNode } from "react"
import { Rating } from "@mui/material"

interface State {}

class RatingStar extends StreamlitComponentBase<State> {
    public state = {}

    public render = (): ReactNode => {
        const {selected, stars_count} = this.props.args
```

```
    return <Rating size="large" defaultValue={selected}
    max={stars_count}/>
  }
}
```

export **default** withStreamlitConnection(RatingStar)

Bringing this new update to action, we will make the Streamlit application as shown in Listing 10-8 to showcase native and custom components side by side. Figure 10-4 shows the homogeneity between our newly made configurable component and out-of-the-box components by Streamlit.

Listing 10-8. Second version of main.py

```
import streamlit as st
from rating_stars import rating_stars

st.title("Rating stars demo!")

total_stars = st.slider(label="Total Stars", min_
value=0, max_value=20, value=10, step=1) selected_stars =
st.slider(label="Selected Stars", min_value=0, max_value=total_
stars, step=1) rating_stars(total_stars, selected_stars)
```

Figure 10-4. Using native and custom components

10.2.4 Receiving Data from the Custom Component

After playing around with the sliders to set our custom rating component, we can notice how our Streamlit application's view is bloated with extra widgets that are used to set another view's behavior, when we already could have set the number of selected stars by hovering the mouse to and clicking any star. However, this will require the Streamlit application to know what value is selected, and here comes a way to get data from custom components in Streamlit.

Streamlit didn't only make an API to include a ReactJS application in its context but also communicate bidirectionally with it. Sending data out of ReactJS can be made using a library already included in the template's `package.json`. Using this library, we can trigger many ReactJS component-specific actions, but we will only shed the light on the function `Streamlit. setComponentValue`, which makes the component's return value in a Streamlit's Python context the same as what is fed to its first parameter. Knowing this, we will add it to the callback of the rating view in ReactJS as shown in Listing 10-9. Then accordingly change the component's `__init__.py` content to be as shown in Listing 10-10 to forward the return value back to our ran Streamlit file.

Listing 10-9. Final version of RatingStar.tsx

```
import {
    Streamlit,
    StreamlitComponentBase,
    withStreamlitConnection,
} from "streamlit-component-lib"
import React, { ReactNode } from "react"
import { Rating } from "@mui/material"

interface State {}
```

```
class RatingStar extends StreamlitComponentBase<State> {
  public state = {}

  public render = (): ReactNode => {
    const { selected, stars_count } = this.props.args

    return (
     <Rating
       size="large"
       defaultValue={1}
       max={stars_count}
       onChange={(_, stars_count) => Streamlit.
       setComponentValue(stars_count)}
     />
    )
  }
}

export default withStreamlitConnection(RatingStar)
```

Listing 10-10. Final version of __init__.py

```
import os
import streamlit.components.v1 as components

IS_RELEASE = False

if IS_RELEASE:
    absolute_path = os.path.dirname(os.path.abspath(__file__))
    build_path = os.path.join(absolute_path, "frontend/build")
    _component_func = components.declare_component("rating_
    stars", path=build_path)
else:
    _component_func = components.declare_component("rating_
    stars", url="http://localhost:3001")
```

```
def rating_stars(stars_count: int):
  stars_selected = _component_func(stars_count=stars_count)
  if stars_selected is None:
    stars_selected = 0
  return stars_selected
```

Now in our main Streamlit file, we remove the slider for the selected star count and then replace it with the output of the custom component. And finally, we display on our application the number of stars selected, as shown in Listing 10-11, with the output shown in Figure 10-5.

Listing 10-11. main.py, Streamlit file to be run

```
import streamlit as st
from rating_stars import rating_stars

st.title("Rating stars demo!")

total_stars = st.slider(label="Total Stars", min_value=0,
max_value=20, value=10, step=1) selected_stars = rating_
stars(total_stars)

st.write(str(selected_stars) + " star(s) have been selected")
```

Figure 10-5. *Result of communicating back and forth with a custom Streamlit component*

10.3 Publishing Components As Pip Packages

Once you finally make your first custom component, you will want to share it with your friends or dedicate it to the open source developer community like many do. Sending a zip file of the source code or uploading the component to a version control service like GitHub might not be a scalable option to reach unlimited number of developers with ease, as this adds more overhead for them to get it running.

A more developer-friendly yet professional approach to share Python packages specifically is to compress them in a pip wheel format, which then can be easily installed in the interpreter by running

```
pip install <PIP_PACKAGE_NAME>.whl
```

Following up with the continuous example in this chapter, we don't need to install any new package to make this possible as Python supports wheel building out of the box. The goal is to package the `rating_stars/` folder in a file which then can be installed and referenced from any script like it is a local package.

Building a pip file is as simple as running the following command:

```
python setup.py sdist bdist_wheel
```

Before making the pip wheel, make sure to build the ReactJS part of the custom component, as it will not be run live on the user end; rather, it should be a seamless plug-and-play experience using that new component. After navigating to the `rating_stars/frontend/`, run

```
npm run build
```

However, the wheel builder needs more information about the exact folder to package and other miscellaneous metadata such as version number and description. No need to mention the folder to be packaged, as Python looks for all "Python Packages" in the current folder, and for a folder to be considered as a Python package, it needs to have an __init__. py file, which we already have. However, by default the wheel builder doesn't include non-Python files and folders if they don't have a single Python file. This is an issue in our case as our component relies on the ReactJS build folder which contains all static web files necessary for it to run. To overcome this issue, a new file as shown in Listing 10-12 needs to be added in the project's root folder with its content to force inclusion of the build folder and its content.

Listing 10-12. MANIFEST.in

```
recursive-include rating_stars/frontend/build *
```

As we now have half of the requirements to make a pip wheel, we can tackle the final part by making a file called setup.py with the content shown in Listing 10-13 in the same folder as the MANIFEST.in. The setup file can include the version number of your custom component, description, and other information such as its pip download name if uploaded to pypi.org.

Listing 10-13. setup.py

```python
import setuptools

setuptools.setup(
    name="rating_stars",
    version="0.1",
    author="YOUR-NAME",
    author_email="YOU-EMAIL@DOMAIN.com",
    description="INSERT-DESCRIPTION-HERE",
    long_description="INSERT-LONGER-DESCRIPTION-HERE",
    packages=setuptools.find_packages(),
    include_package_data=True,
```

```
    classifiers=[
       "Programming Language :: Python :: 3",
       "License :: OSI Approved :: MIT License",
       "Operating System :: OS Independent",
    ],
    keywords=['Python', 'Streamlit', 'React', 'JavaScript',
    'Custom'],
    python_requires=">=3.6",
    install_requires=[
       "streamlit >= 0.86",
    ],
)
```

After finally running the Python package command, we can find three new folders appearing in the project's root folder as seen in Figure 10-6. We are interested in the `rating_stars-0.1-py3-none-any.whl` file in the second folder; this file can be sent to anyone and installed easily as long as the package requirements are met.

Other created folders can have some benefits as well. For instance, the `dist/` folder can be used by twine, which is the package and tool used to upload pip wheels to the global pip repository. If interested in sharing your package with the general public, sign up to pypi.org and then run the following command:

```
python -m twine upload dist/* --verbose
```

after building the wheel to upload it.

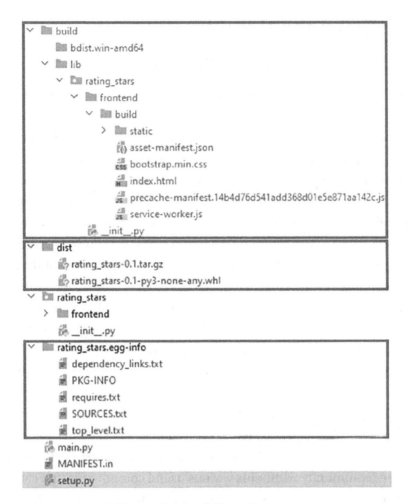

Figure 10-6. *New folders after building the custom component*

10.4 Component in Focus: Extra-Streamlit-Components

Streamlit as a framework is constantly evolving, which means it may not offer certain bespoke features that you may need for a production-ready web application. Features such as application routing and having custom URLs for multiple views or saving user-related data on the browser side. Apart from our usability requirements, sometimes it may just be necessary to offer a unique look and feel for the application or to add a widget which is not natively supported by Streamlit. Previously, we learned how to make a simple custom component; however, with components the sky is truly the limit, and in this chapter, we will showcase *Extra-Streamlit-Components (STX)*, an open source collection of intricate Streamlit components and services. In addition, we will explain how every subcomponent is built from the Streamlit and ReactJS perspective, and hopefully creative developers will be inspired enough to unleash components of their own.

10.4.1 Stepper Bar

This is inspired by Material UI's Stepper. As mentioned before, ReactJS's developer community withholds various useful components that can be imported into the Streamlit world without a big hassle. And this stepper bar can actually be useful in the context of most Streamlit application, as it allows moving through sequential steps in a specific order to do something which is mostly data science related. It is a simple component as it returns the index of the stage the user has arrived to, as seen in Figures 10-7, 10-8, and 10-9. You, as a developer, are not bound to only three phases; rather, you can supply a list of all tab names, and the return value will be the selected list item index as might be shown in Listing 10-15. Numbering and animations are already taken care of.

Phase #0

Figure 10-7. *Stepper bar phase 3*

Phase #1

Figure 10-8. *Stepper bar phase 3*

Phase #2

Figure 10-9. *Stepper bar phase 3*

The ReactJS side of this component requires installing the stepper package through *npm*, then importing it in the source file as shown in Listing 10-14. This file is responsible in detecting user clicks and returning the equivalent level index, as well as managing each step's theme depending on where the user currently is.

Listing 10-14. StepperBar/frontend/src/StepperBar.jsx

```
import {
  Streamlit,
  StreamlitComponentBase,
  withStreamlitConnection,
} from "streamlit-component-lib"
import React from "react"

import { withStyles, createStyles } from "@material-ui/
core/styles"
import Stepper from "@material-ui/core/Stepper"
import Step from "@material-ui/core/Step"
import StepLabel from "@material-ui/core/StepLabel"

const styles = createStyles((theme) => ({
  root: {
    width: "100%",
    backgroundColor: "transparent",
  },
  icon: {
    color: "grey",
    cursor: "pointer",
    "&$activeIcon": {
      color: "#f63366",
     },
    "&$completedIcon": {
      color: "#f63366",
    },
  },

  activeIcon: {},
  completedIcon: {},
}))
```

```
class StepperBar extends StreamlitComponentBase {
  state = { activeStep: 0, steps: [] }

  componentDidMount() {
    this.setState((prev, state) => ({
      steps: this.props.args.steps,
      activeStep: this.props.args.default,
    }))
  }
  onClick = (index) => {
    const { activeStep } = this.state

    if (index == activeStep + 1) {
      this.setState(
        (prev, state) => ({
          activeStep: activeStep + 1,
        }),
        () => Streamlit.setComponentValue(this.state.
        activeStep)
      )
    } else if (index < activeStep) {
      this.setState(
        (prev, state) => ({
          activeStep: index,
        }),
        () => Streamlit.setComponentValue(this.state.
        activeStep)
      )
    }
  }
```

```
getLabelStyle = (index) => {
  const { activeStep } = this.state
  const style = {}
  if (index == activeStep) {
      style.color = "#f63366"
      style.fontStyle = "italic"
    } else if (index < activeStep) {
      style.color = "#f63366"
      style.fontWeight = "bold"
    } else {
      style.color = "grey"
    }
    return style
}

render = () => {
  let { classes } = this.props

  const { activeStep } = this.state
  const steps = this.state.steps

  return (
    <div className={classes.root}>
      <Stepper
        activeStep={activeStep}
        alternativeLabel
        className={classes.root}
      >
        {steps.map((label, index) => (
         <Step key={label} onClick={() => this.
         onClick(index)}>
           <StepLabel
```

```
            StepIconProps={{
              classes: {
                cursor: "pointer",
                root: classes.icon,
                active: classes.activeIcon,
                completed: classes.completedIcon,
              },
            }}
          >
            <p style={this.getLabelStyle(index)}>{label}</p>
          </StepLabel>
        </Step>
      ))}
    </Stepper>
  </div>
  )
 }
}

export default withStreamlitConnection(withStyles(styles)
(StepperBar))
```

Listing 10-15. StepperBar/__init__.py

```python
import os
import streamlit.components.v1 as components
from streamlit.components.v1.components import CustomComponent
from typing import List

from extra_streamlit_components import IS_RELEASE

if IS_RELEASE:
    absolute_path = os.path.dirname(os.path.abspath(__file__))
    build_path = os.path.join(absolute_path, "frontend/build")
```

```
_component_func = components.declare_component("stepper_
bar", path=build_path)
else:
    _component_func = components.declare_component("stepper_
bar", url="http://localhost:3001")

def stepper_bar(steps: List[str]) -> CustomComponent:
    component_value = _component_func(steps=steps, default=0)
    return component_value
```

10.4.2 Bouncing Image

This component offers zooming animations for an image with a bouncing effect. It can be used in loading moments or splash screen. This might not be a frequently used component, but when it does, the animation duration, control switch, and dimensions are needed for it to work based on different requirements as seen in Listing 10-16. The ReactJS aspect of it is a little more complex than thePythonic aspect, as it needs to manage animation cycles and return back the status which requires setting state and reporting widget state back to Streamlit every cycle. Even though JavaScript is not the main focus of this book, Listing 10-17 is relatively simple to understand. However, the final result shall look something like Figure 10-10.

Listing 10-16. BouncingImage/__init__.py

```
import os
import streamlit.components.v1 as components

from extra_streamlit_components import IS_RELEASE

if IS_RELEASE:
    absolute_path = os.path.dirname(os.path.abspath(__file__))
    build_path = os.path.join(absolute_path, "frontend/build")
```

```
_component_func = components.declare_component("bouncing_
image", path=build_path)
```
else:
```
_component_func = components.declare_component("bouncing_
image", url="http://localhost:3001")
```

def bouncing_image(image_source: **str**, animate: **bool**, animation_
time: **int**, height: **float**, width: **float**):
```
_component_func(image=image_source, animate=animate,
animation_time=animation_time, height=height, width=width)
```

Listing 10-17. BouncingImage/frontend/src/BouncingImage.jsx

```jsx
import {
   Streamlit,
   StreamlitComponentBase,
   withStreamlitConnection,
} from "streamlit-component-lib"
import React from "react"

import { withStyles, createStyles } from "@material-ui/
core/styles"
import Grow from "@material-ui/core/Grow"
import CardMedia from "@material-ui/core/CardMedia"

const styles = createStyles((theme) => ({
   root: {
     height: 180,
   },
   container: {
     display: "flex",
   },
```

```
  paper: {
    margin: 1,
  },
  svg: {
    width: 100,
    height: 100,
  },
  polygon: {
    fill: "white",
    stroke: "red",
    strokeWidth: 1,
  },
}))

class BouncingImage extends StreamlitComponentBase {
  state = {
    animationTimeRoundTrip: 1750,
    isAnimating: true,
    keepAnimating: false,
  }

  constructor(props) {
    super(props)
  }

  componentDidMount() {
    const { animation_time, animate } = this.props.args

    Streamlit.setComponentValue(animate)
    this.setState(
      () => ({
        animationTimeRoundTrip: animation_time,
        keepAnimating: animate,
      }),
```

```
    () =>
      setInterval(
        () =>
          this.state.keepAnimating &&
          this.setState(
            () => ({
              isAnimating:
                !this.state.isAnimating && this.state.
                keepAnimating,
            }),
            () => Streamlit.setComponentValue(this.state.
            keepAnimating)
          ),
        this.state.animationTimeRoundTrip / 2
      )
  )
}

render = () => {
  const isAnimating = this.state.isAnimating
  let {
    classes,
    args: { image, height, width },
  } = this.props

  return (
    <div className={classes.root}>
      <div className={classes.container}>
        <Grow
          in={isAnimating}
          style={{ transformOrigin: "0 0 0" }}
          {...(isAnimating
```

```
                ? { timeout: this.state.
                animationTimeRoundTrip / 2 }
                : {})}
        >
          <CardMedia image={image} style={{ height, width }} />
        </Grow>
      </div>
      </div>
    )
    }
  }

export default withStreamlitConnection(withStyles(styles)
(BouncingImage))
```

Bouncing Image

Figure 10-10. *Bouncing image demo (a snapshot from the zoom animation)*

10.4.3 Tab Bar

Instead of making a Streamlit column widget to host multiple buttons which will act as a tab bar, you can just use this custom component. It provides a way to encapsulate the title, description, and ID of each button in a UI-organized way as it provides a horizontal scroll view if the tabs – side-to-side length – exceeded the window's width.

Figures 10-11 and 10-12 show the behavior of the tab button once it is clicked and the output of the component in Streamlit. Creating those tabs requires passing a list of specific Python objects as shown in Listing 10-19 which will then be parsed to JSON and be processed by the TypeScript ReactJS component in Listing 10-18.

Listing 10-18. TabBar/frontend/src/TabBar.tsx

```
import {
   Streamlit,
   StreamlitComponentBase,
   withStreamlitConnection,
} from "streamlit-component-lib"
import React, { ComponentProps, ReactNode } from "react"
import ScrollMenu from "react-horizontal-scrolling-menu"

interface State {
   numClicks: number
   selectedId: number
}

interface MenuItem {
   id: number
   title: string
   description: string
}

class TabBar extends StreamlitComponentBase<State> {
public state = { numClicks: 0, selectedId: 1, list: [] }

   constructor(props: ComponentProps<any>) {
     super(props)
     this.state.list = this.props.args["data"]
     this.state.selectedId = this.props.args["selectedId"]
   }
```

```
MenuItem = ({ item, selectedId }: { item: MenuItem;
selectedId: number }) => {

  return (
    <div className={'menu-item ${selectedId == item.id ?
    "active" : ""}'}>
      <div>{item.title}</div>
      <div style={{ fontWeight: "normal", fontStyle:
      "italic" }}>
        {item.description}
      </div>
    </div>
  )
}

Menu(list: Array<MenuItem>, selectedId: number) {
  return list.map((item) => (
    <this.MenuItem item={item} selectedId={selectedId}
    key={item.id} />
  ))
}
Arrow = ({ text, className }: { text: string; className:
string }) => {
  return <div className={className}>{text}</div>
}

ArrowLeft = this.Arrow({ text: "<", className: "arrow-prev" })
ArrowRight = this.Arrow({ text: ">", className: "arrow-next" })

public render = (): ReactNode => {
  return (
    <div>
```

```
        <ScrollMenu
            alignCenter={false}
            data={this.Menu(this.state.list, this.state.
            selectedId)}
            wheel={true}
            scrollToSelected={true}
            selected={'${this.state.selectedId}'}
            onSelect={this.onSelect}
        />
        <hr
            style={{
              borderColor: "var(--streamlit-primary-color)",
            }}
        />
      </div>
    )
  }

  onSelect = (id: any) => {
    this.setState(
      (state, props) => {
        return { selectedId: id }
      },
      () => Streamlit.setComponentValue(id)
    )
  }
}

export default withStreamlitConnection(TabBar)
```

Listing 10-19. TabBar/__init__.py

```python
import os
import streamlit.components.v1 as components
from dataclasses import dataclass
from typing import List
from extra_streamlit_components import IS_RELEASE

if IS_RELEASE:
    absolute_path = os.path.dirname(os.path.abspath(__file__))
    build_path = os.path.join(absolute_path, "frontend/build")
    _component_func = components.declare_component("tab_bar",
    path=build_path)
else:
    _component_func = components.declare_component("tab_bar",
    url="http://localhost:3001")

@dataclass(frozen=True, order=True, unsafe_hash=True)
class TabBarItemData:
    id: int
    title: str
    description: str

    def to_dict(self):
        return {"id": self.id, "title": self.title,
        "description": self.description}

def tab_bar(data: List[TabBarItemData], default=None, return_
type=str, key=None):
    data = list(map(lambda item: item.to_dict(), data))
    component_value = _component_func(data=data,
    selectedId=default, key=key, default=default)
```

```
try:
    if return_type == str:
        return str(component_value)
    elif return_type == int:
        return int(component_value)
    elif return_type == float:
        return float(component_value)
except:
        return component_value
```

Tab Bar

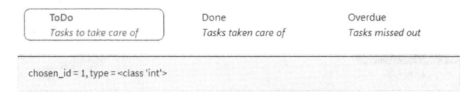

Figure 10-11. *Tab bar with first element selected*

Tab Bar

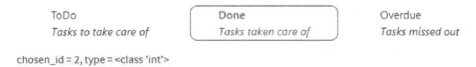

Figure 10-12. *Tab bar with first element selected*

10.4.4 Cookie Manager

This has been introduced before in the previous chapter; however, it was treated as a black box which can just save data we think of on the client browser side. The Cookie Manager is not only a custom component but

295

also a Python service, as it relies on data managing in a Pythonic context with CRUD operations on a ReactJS-based component. If you are a web developer, you might already know that setting cookies is not a big deal, as you are writing code to be executed on the client side. Fortunately, in Streamlit we can write both server-side and client-side code in the same script. Knowing that we can make React custom component which will then be executed on the browser, we can set it up to control cookies on the client's end, as shown in Figure 10-13.

Figure 10-13. *Using Streamlit to control client-side data*

Leveraging the knowledge from the material introduced in this chapter, we can set up a bidirectional communication between Streamlit's server end and the custom ReactJS component running on the client's browser. By doing so, we can command our component to gather, delete, or add cookies on the browser and even listen to the return value, if any. Starting with the ReactJS side in Listing 10-20, we first read the expected arguments such as the operation needed and then the data to act on, then based on what is asked we take actions against the cookies using the npm's package `universal-cookie`, and finally we send back a response about the status of the operation.

On Python's end, Listing 10-21 just encapsulates the whole communication method with the browser's component. Also, it stores all the cookies in memory for that user once initialized, in order to save more network traffic time. However, if the class's constructor is not cached once first initialized, it will have no added value as it will be executed every time Streamlit reruns. That is why it is advised to use the snippet in Listing 10-22 when using the Cookie Manager. Figure 10-14 shows a demo of this custom component.

Listing 10-20. CookieManager/frontend/src/CookieManager.tsx

```tsx
import {
  Streamlit,
  ComponentProps,
  withStreamlitConnection,
} from "streamlit-component-lib"
import React, { useEffect, useState } from "react"

import Cookies from "universal-cookie"

let last_output = null
const cookies = new Cookies()

const CookieManager = (props: ComponentProps) => {
  const setCookie = (cookie, value, expires_at) => {
    cookies.set(cookie, value, {
      path: "/",
      samesite: "strict",
      expires: new Date(expires_at),
    })
    return true
  }

  const getCookie = (cookie) => {
    const value = cookies.get(cookie)
    return value
  }
```

```javascript
const deleteCookie = (cookie) => {
  cookies.remove(cookie, { path: "/", samesite: "strict" })
  return true
}

const getAllCookies = () => {
  return cookies.getAll()
}

const { args } = props

const method = args["method"]
const cookie = args["cookie"]
const value = args["value"]
const expires_at = args["expires_at"]

let output = null

switch (method) {
  case "set":
    output = setCookie(cookie, value, expires_at)
    break
  case "get":
    output = getCookie(cookie)
    break
  case "getAll":
    output = getAllCookies()
    break
  case "delete":
    output = deleteCookie(cookie)
    break
  default:
    break
}
```

```javascript
  if (output && JSON.stringify(last_output) != JSON.
  stringify(output)) {
    last_output = output
    Streamlit.setComponentValue(output)
    Streamlit.setComponentReady()
  }

  useEffect(() => Streamlit.setFrameHeight())
      return <div></div>
}

export default withStreamlitConnection(CookieManager)
```

Listing 10-21. CookieManager/__init__.py

```python
import os

import streamlit.components.v1 as components
import datetime

from extra_streamlit_components import IS_RELEASE

if IS_RELEASE:
    absolute_path = os.path.dirname(os.path.abspath(__file__))
    build_path = os.path.join(absolute_path, "frontend/build")
    _component_func = components.declare_component("cookie_
    manager", path=build_path)
else:
    _component_func = components.declare_component("cookie_manager",
        url="http://localhost:3001")

class CookieManager:
    def __init__(self, key="init"):
        self.cookie_manager = _component_func
        self.cookies = self.cookie_manager(method="getAll",
        key=key, default={})
```

299

```python
def get(self, cookie: str):
    return self.cookies.get(cookie)

def set(self, cookie, val,
    expires_at=datetime.datetime.now() + datetime.
    timedelta(days=1), key="set"):
    if cookie is None or cookie == "":
        return
    expires_at = expires_at.isoformat()
    did_add = self.cookie_manager(method="set",
    cookie=cookie, value=val, expires_at=expires_at, key=key,
    default=False)
    if did_add:
        self.cookies[cookie] = val

def delete(self, cookie, key="delete"):
    if cookie is None or cookie == "":
        return
    did_add = self.cookie_manager(method="delete",
    cookie=cookie, key=key, default=False)
    if did_add:
        del self.cookies[cookie]

def get_all(self, key="get_all"):
    self.cookies = self.cookie_manager(method="getAll",
    key=key, default={})
    return self.cookies
```

Listing 10-22. How to initialize and use Cookie Manager

```
@st.cache(allow_output_mutation=True)
def get_manager():
    return stx.CookieManager()

cookie_manager = get_manager()
```

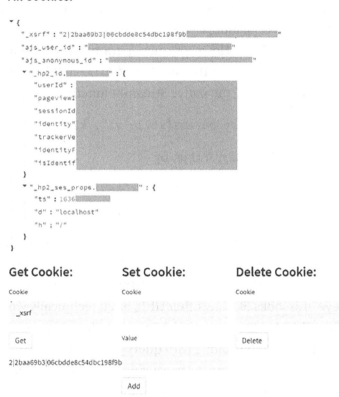

Figure 10-14. *Cookie Manager demo from Extra-Streamlit-Components*

10.4.5 Router

In almost any web application, different URLs exist. This helps in providing two main benefits, modularization of content's code to the developer and an easy access for the user to specific pages. This *STX* component is different than its counterparts, as it doesn't make a ReactJS application, rather uses Python and Streamlit tools to make use of query parameters for routing.

Query parameters is used as Streamlit – as of version 1.1.0 – didn't support URL path modification, as the application by default loads at root http://<DOMAIN>:<PORT>/. However, query parameters are manipulable, as you set the key-value pairs in the URL like http://<DOMAIN>:<PORT>/?key1=v1&k2=value2 by using the native Streamlit function:

st.experimental_set_query_params(key1="v1", k2="value2")

And get them in dictionary format by

st.experimental_get_query_params() # {"key1":"v1", "k2":"value2"}

As we can control the query parameters, nothing is stopping us from mimicking a URL behavior with it, to make something like this: http://<DOMAIN>:<PORT>/?nav=/electronics/computers. To the untrained eye, this looks like any other URL, but it technically works differently by achieving the same goal. Listing 10-23 of this component shows usage of session state along with query parameters as Streamlit's query parameter has some time delay causing problems in navigating between different routes as it is still experimental as of that time. It also calls the view's passed function or class whenever it is asked to by calling show_route_view which checks the current route and if there is an equivalent callable function. Usage of this module can be referred to Listing 10-24.

Listing 10-23. Router/__init__.py

```python
import streamlit as st
from urllib.parse import unquote
import time

def does_support_session_state():
    try:
        return st.session_state is not None
    except:
        return False

class Router:
    def __init__(self, routes: dict, **kwargs):
        self.routes = routes
        if "key" in kwargs:
            st.warning("No need for a key for initialization,"
                       " this is not a rendered component.")
        if not does_support_session_state():
            raise Exception(
                "Streamlit installation doesn't support
                session state."
                " Session state needs to be available in the used
                Streamlit installation")

    def show_route_view(self):
        query_route = self.get_nav_query_param()
        sys_route = self.get_url_route()

        if sys_route is None and query_route is None:
            self.route("/")
            return
```

```python
        elif sys_route is not None and query_route is not None:
            st.experimental_set_query_params(nav=sys_route)
            st.session_state['stx_router_route'] = sys_route
        elif query_route is not None:
            self.route(query_route)
            return

        _callable = self.routes.get(sys_route)
        if callable(_callable):
            _callable()

    def get_nav_query_param(self):
        url = st.experimental_get_query_params().get("nav")
        url = url[0] if type(url) == list else url
        route = unquote(url) if url is not None else url
        return route

    def get_url_route(self):
        if "stx_router_route" in st.session_state and\
                st.session_state.stx_router_route is not None:
            return st.session_state.stx_router_route

        route = self.get_nav_query_param()
        return route

    def route(self, new_route):
        if new_route[0] != "/":
            new_route = "/" + new_route
        st.session_state['stx_router_route'] = new_route
        st.experimental_set_query_params(nav=new_route)
        time.sleep(0.1) # Needed for URL param refresh
        st.experimental_rerun()
```

Listing 10-24. Demo usage of STX's router

```
@st.cache(allow_output_mutation=True, hash_funcs={"_thread.
RLock": lambda _ : None})
def init_router():
    return stx.Router({"/home": home, "/landing": landing})

def home():
    return st.write("This is a home page")

def landing():
    return st.write("This is the landing page")

router = init_router()
router.show_route_view()

c1, c2, c3 = st.columns(3)

with c1:
    st.header("Current route")
    current_route = router.get_url_route()
    st.write(f"{current_route}")
with c2:
    st.header("Set route")
    new_route = st.text_input("route")
    if st.button("Route now!"):
        router.route(new_route)

with c3:
    st.header("Session state")
    st.write(st.session_state)
```

Trying the demo out with multiple routes, we can notice that it acts as expected where the routes having the nav parameter set to either /landing or /home show the equivalent page content as seen in

Figures 10-16 and 10-17, respectively. We can also see the root route returns nothing in Figure 10-15, and the same behavior occurs in Figure 10-18. This module can be further enhanced by adding a not found route, which is something like the infamous 404 page seen quite often on the Internet.

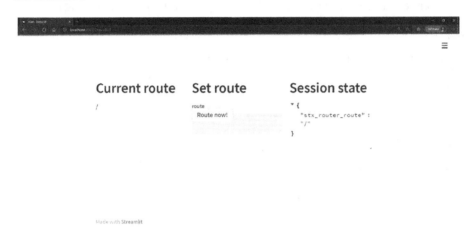

Figure 10-15. *The root route*

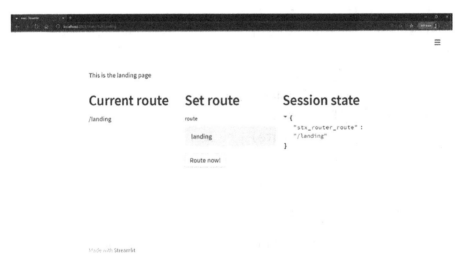

Figure 10-16. */landing route*

10.5 Summary

As you come to the end of this chapter, you are banking on the knowledge needed to render innovative and exciting custom components for Streamlit. By using the simplified version of ReactJS's template and by referring to online resources, you can pretty much not only clone ReactJS's Material UI views to Streamlit but also control some browser functionalities to add a native web application UX to your application. In this chapter, we also discussed how certain aspects of the user interface in Streamlit can be customized to add more versatility and exclusivity to an application. The techniques discussed in building this library can indeed be scaled and implemented by any developer for a multitude of other purposes. It is just worth mentioning that no component is done justice without sharing it with the open source community, to improve it iteratively with feedback and suggestions from other developers.

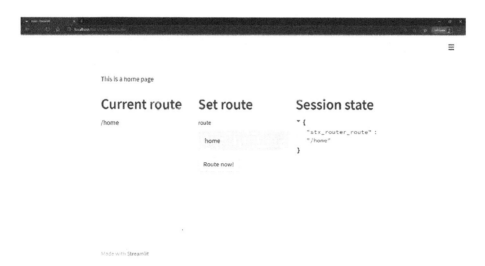

Figure 10-17. */home route*

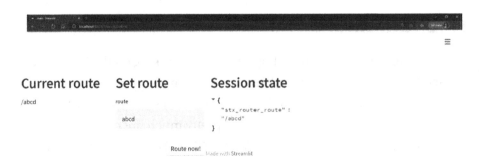

Figure 10-18. *A random unknown route*

CHAPTER 11

Streamlit Use Cases

In this chapter, we will cover several real-world use cases of Streamlit, including but not limited to applications related to data visualization, real-time dashboards, and time-series analysis. Additionally, we will introduce methods to interface our Streamlit application with external subsystems such as an Arduino microcontroller, infrared temperature sensor, and a sonar. Interfacing with physical devices and peripherals will enable us to scale Streamlit into an entirely new dimension where we can develop not only digital applications but also applications for embedded systems. For instance, we can create an operations dashboard to monitor the temperature of a building remotely or to control a valve motor in a factory line. The utility is quite literally endless. And finally as the culmination of everything we have learned thus far in this book, in the final section of this chapter the reader will be guided on how to utilize many of the techniques covered previously, to develop an advanced machine learning application.

11.1 Dashboards and Real-Time Applications

A small yet invaluable niche of web applications are of those related to dashboards with or without real-time devices interfaced with them – the likes of meteorological applications reporting on weather data or interfaces allowing a user to control a motor with real-time feedback. The possibilities are endless and the utility unmitigated. Given Streamlit's

© Mohammad Khorasani, Mohamed Abdou, Javier Hernández Fernández 2022
M. Khorasani et al., *Web Application Development with Streamlit*,
https://doi.org/10.1007/978-1-4842-8111-6_11

versatility specifically with regard to data visualizations and placeholders, we are indeed able to cater to a host of such applications, of which two will be examined in the following sections.

11.1.1 Temperature Data Recorder Application

Given the need for real-time insights of physical parameters, an abundance of entities, the likes of energy firms, research institutions, and meteorological departments, are aggressively implementing SCADA systems, often at exorbitant costs to enhance the accessibility of their data. While large corporations can afford to siphon off large numbers to acquire such systems, smaller enterprises and/or private individuals who do not possess the same means can instead develop their own systems at a fraction of the cost with the help of Arduino microcontrollers, some hobbyist-grade peripherals, and most importantly with Streamlit to create dashboards and control systems.

For this section, we will cover the implementation of a trivial temperature data recording system and application. To that end, an MLX90614 infrared thermometer will be connected to an Arduino UNO microcontroller, as shown in Figure 11-1, to sample the ambient temperature. Before you upload the temperature measurement code to the microcontroller, you must initially download the infrared thermometer's library *Adafruit_MLX90614* in the *Arduino IDE* as shown in Figure 11-2. Subsequently, Listing 11-1 can be uploaded to the microcontroller with a USB cord from the computer through the Arduino IDE. Likewise, the COM port being used to interface with the microcontroller can be determined in the Arduino IDE.

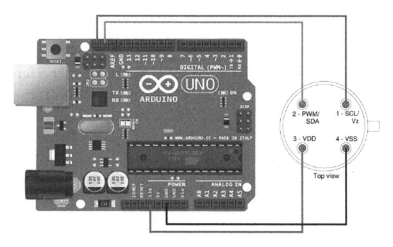

Figure 11-1. *Arduino microcontroller and infrared thermometer wiring schematic [19]*

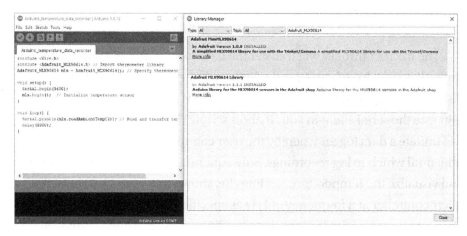

Figure 11-2. *Arduino IDE with library manager*

Listing 11-1. Arduino_temperature_data_recorder.ino

```
#include <Wire.h>
#include <Adafruit_MLX90614.h> // Import thermometer library
Adafruit_MLX90614 mlx = Adafruit_MLX90614(); // Specify
thermometer type

void setup() {
    Serial.begin(9600);
    mlx.begin(); // Initialize temperature sensor
}

void loop() {
    Serial.println(mlx.readAmbientTempC()); // Read and
    transfer temperature data
    delay(1000);
}
```

The microcontroller will transfer the data to our Streamlit application through a serial interface using the Python library *pySerial* shown in Listing 11-2. Please ensure that the correct COM port is being used to initialize the serial client in your Python script. The Streamlit application will imitate a data logger whereby the user can specify an end date and time until which to log recordings. Subsequently, the application will read and visualize the temperature readings (as shown in Figure 11-3) from the microcontroller at a frequency of 1Hz as specified by the duration of the *time. sleep* function. And finally once the recording period has been surpassed, all the temperature readings will be displayed in a table and made available for download.

Listing 11-2. temperature_data_recorder_app.py

```
import serial
import time
import streamlit as st
```

```python
import plotly.graph_objects as go
import plotly.express as px
from datetime import datetime
import pandas as pd

# Plotly temperature gauge visualization function
def temperature_gauge(temperature, previous_temperature, gauge_
placeholder):
    fig = go.Figure(go.Indicator(
        domain = {'x': [0, 1], 'y': [0, 1]},
        value = temperature,
        mode = "gauge+number+delta",
        title = {'text': "Temperature (C)"},
        delta = {'reference': previous_temperature},
        gauge = {'axis': {'range': [0, 40]}}))

    fig.update_layout(
        width=300,
    )
    gauge_placeholder.write(fig)

# Plotly time-series temperature visualization
def temperature_chart(df, chart_placeholder):
    fig = px.line(df, x="Time", y="Temperature (C)")
    chart_placeholder.write(fig)

if __name__ == '__main__':
    st.sidebar.title('Temperature Data Recorder')
    recording = False

    # End date and time form for temperature recording
    with st.sidebar.form('form_1'):
        col1, col2, = st.columns(2)
```

```python
    with col1:
        end_date = st.date_input('Recording end date')
    with col2:
        end_time = st.time_input('Recording end time')
    if st.form_submit_button('Start recording'):
        recording = True
        arduino = serial.Serial(port='COM4', baudrate=9600)

previous_temperature = 0
temperature_record = pd.DataFrame(columns=['Time',
'Temperature (C)'])
gauge_placeholder = st.sidebar.empty()
chart_placeholder = st.empty()

# Recording data while current date and time is less than
specified end
while recording == True and (datetime.now() < datetime.
combine(end_date, end_time)):
    current_time = datetime.now().strftime("%H:%M:%S")
    temperature = round(float(arduino.readline().decode().
strip('\r\n')),1)
    temperature_record.loc[len(temperature_record),
    ['Time','Temperature (C)']] = [current_time, temperature]

    temperature_gauge(temperature, previous_temperature,
    gauge_placeholder)
    temperature_chart(temperature_record, chart_
    placeholder)

    time.sleep(1)
    previous_temperature = temperature
```

```
# Display and download temperature date if end date and
time exceeded
if recording == True and (datetime.now() > datetime.
combine(end_date, end_time)):
    arduino.close()
    if len(temperature_record) > 0:
        st.write(temperature_record)
        st.download_button(
            label="Download data",
            data=temperature_record.to_csv(index=False).
            encode('utf-8'),
            file_name='temperature_record.csv',
            mime='text/csv',
        )
    else:
        st.warning('Please select a future end date and time')
```

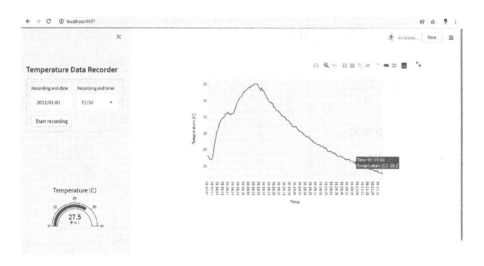

Figure 11-3. *Output of Listing 11-2*

11.1.2 Motor Command and Control Application

Electronic motors are vital for a multitude of industrial or even nonindustrial settings. From controlling operational valves in a factory floor to activating the flight panels on a remote-controlled airplane, the use cases of motors are in abundance. As such, developers often are in need of creating dashboards that provide a means to control motors and also to visualize their performance with the use of gauges.

In this instance, we will control the speed and direction of a motor with a USB joystick and an Arduino UNO microcontroller. The motor used in this example is the *SM-S3317SR* small continuous servo motor that will be connected as shown in Figure 11-4. Both the joystick and microcontroller can be connected to the computer hosting your Streamlit server through a USB cord. Initially, proceed by uploading Listing 11-3 to the microcontroller using the *Arduino IDE*. This script will be used to receive and execute speed commands from our Streamlit application through a serial interface.

Listing 11-3. Arduino_motor_control.ino

```
#include <Servo.h>
Servo motor;
String input;
int target_speed;

void setup() {
    motor.attach(3);
    Serial.begin(9600);
}

void loop()
{
```

```
if(Serial.available()) // Check if data available in
serial port
  {
  input = Serial.readStringUntil('\n'); // Read data
                                        until newline
  target_speed = input.toInt();
  motor.write(target_speed);    // Move motor at target speed
  }
}
```

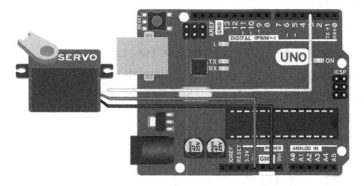

Figure 11-4. *Arduino microcontroller and servo motor wiring schematic [20]*

You may then use the Arduino IDE or alternatively your computer's device manager to identify the serial COM port being used to connect to the microcontroller. Ensure that the same port is used to create the serial client in your Streamlit application using the Python library *pySerial* as shown in Listing 11-4. In this script, we will also use the Python library *Pygame* to interface with the joystick game controller. The values read from the forward axis of the joystick will be used to regulate and reverse the speed of the servo motor. In addition, one of the buttons on the joystick will be used as a kill switch to stop the motor. And finally, a Plotly gauge visualization will be displayed within a Streamlit placeholder to constantly provide an updated target speed as shown in Figure 11-5. And indeed you may scale this method to connect and simultaneously visualize and control other motors, actuators, sensors, and peripherals.

Listing 11-4. motor_control_app.py

```python
import serial
import pygame as pg
import serial
import streamlit as st
import plotly.graph_objects as go
import time

# Plotly speed gauge visualization function
def speed_gauge(target_speed, placeholder):
    fig = go.Figure(go.Indicator(
        domain = {'x': [0, 1], 'y': [0, 1]},
        value = int(target_speed)-90,
        mode = "gauge+number+delta",
        title = {'text': "Speed"},
        delta = {'reference': 0},
        gauge = {'axis': {'range': [-30, 30]}}))

    placeholder.write(fig)

if __name__ == '__main__':
    st.sidebar.title('Motor Command & Control')
    info_bar = st.empty()
    speedometer = st.empty()

    # Create Arduino serial client
    arduino = serial.Serial(port='COM5', baudrate=9600)
    # Create PyGame client
    pg.init()
```

```python
# Create a list of available joysticks to initialize
joysticks = [pg.joystick.Joystick(x) for x in range(pg.
joystick.get_count())]
for joystick in joysticks:
    joystick.init()

if st.sidebar.button('Start motor'):
    info_bar.info('Motor started')
    # Connect to Arduino
    try:
        arduino.open()
    except:
        pass

    if st.sidebar.button('Stop motor'):
        info_bar.warning('Motor stopped')
        arduino.write(bytes('90' +'\n', 'utf-8'))
        arduino.close()
        pg.quit()

    while True:
        # Report all joystick events
        for event in pg.event.get():
            print(event)

        for joystick in joysticks:
            if joystick.get_id() == 0: # Access the first
                                         connected joystick
                axes = joystick.get_numaxes()
                for x in range(axes): # Check all inputs of
                                        the joystick
```

```
                    target_speed = str(int(((joystick.get_
                    axis(1)*-1)*30 + 90)))
                    press = joystick.get_button(0)
                    time.sleep(0.01)

            arduino.flushInput()
            arduino.flushOutput()
            arduino.flush()
            arduino.write(bytes(target_speed +'\n', 'utf-8'))
            # Send speed to Arduino
            speed_gauge(target_speed, speedometer)

            # Disconnect Arduino if joystick button pressed
            if press == 1:
                try:
                    arduino.write(bytes('90' +'\n', 'utf-8'))
                    arduino.close()
                except:
                    pass
                break

    # Disconnect Arduino if 'Stop motor' button pressed
    info_bar.warning('Motor stopped')
    try:
        arduino.write(bytes('90' +'\n', 'utf-8'))
        arduino.close()
    except:
        pass
    pg.quit()
```

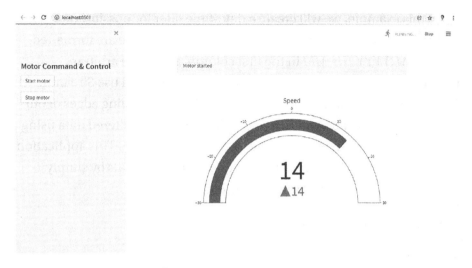

Figure 11-5. *Output of Listing 11-4*

11.2 Time-Series Applications

Perhaps, one of the most profusely used forms of data is time-series data. Anything that is indexed by time, date, or a combination of both can be regarded as being time-series, such as temperature readings from a thermostat or signals from a SCADA system. Such datasets come with their own unique challenges. From filtering to aggregating and visualizing, time-series datasets require bespoke wrangling. Luckily with Streamlit we can create a whole slew of applications to accommodate such needs as shown in the following sections.

11.2.1 Date-Time Filter Application

Filtering data based on a time range is one of those classical functions for practically any data science application. You may only need a subset of the data at hand, and you can do so by selecting a leading or trailing date-time to truncate the dataset with. Given that timestamps come in a variety of formats, or sometimes even separated with date in one column and time in another, it can be rather challenging to create a one-size-fits-all solution.

In this example, we will create a date-time filter for possibly one of the most widely used date-time formats where date and time are formatted as *DD/MM/YYYY HH:MM* in the first column, and some arbitrary measurements are placed in the second column. We will use Streamlit's slider command *st.slider* to truncate the leading and trailing edges of our time-series dataset and will subsequently visualize the filtered data using a Plotly line chart as shown in Listing 11-5 and Figure 11-6. This application can be utilized with datasets using other date-time formats by simply modifying the timestamp format in the code.

Listing 11-5. datetime_filter.py

```python
import pandas as pd
import streamlit as st
from datetime import datetime
import plotly.express as px

# Streamlit slider function used to truncate leading and
trailing edges of dataset
def datetime_filter(datetime_col, df, format):
    lead, trail = st.sidebar.slider('Date-time filter', 0,
    len(df)-1, [0,len(df)-1], 1)
    df[datetime_col] = pd.to_datetime(df[datetime_col],
    format=format)

    sd = df.loc[lead][datetime_col].strftime('%d %b %Y, %I:%M%p')
    ed = df.loc[trail][datetime_col].strftime('%d %b %Y, %I:%M%p')

    st.sidebar.info('Start: **%s**' % (sd))
    st.sidebar.info('End: **%s**' % (ed))

    filtered_df = df.iloc[lead:trail+1][:]

    return filtered_df
```

```python
# Plotly time-series visualization function
def timeseries_chart(df, datetime_col, value_col):
    df[datetime_col] = df[datetime_col].dt.strftime(' %H:%M on
    %B %-d, %Y')
    df = df.sort_values(by=datetime_col)

    fig = px.line(df, x=datetime_col, y=value_col,
                  hover_data={datetime_col: '|%d/%m/%Y %H:%M'})

    st.write(fig)

if __name__ == '__main__':
    st.sidebar.title('Date-time Filter')
    uploaded_file = st.sidebar.file_uploader('Upload a time-
    series dataset')

    if uploaded_file is not None:
        df = pd.read_csv(uploaded_file)
        df_filtered = datetime_filter('datetime', df,
        '%d/%m/%Y %H:%M')

        st.header('Filtered Chart')
        timeseries_chart(df_filtered, 'datetime', 'value')

        st.download_button(
            label="Download filtered data",
            data=df_filtered.to_csv(index=False).
            encode('utf-8'),
            file_name='filtered_data.csv',
            mime='text/csv',
        )
```

323

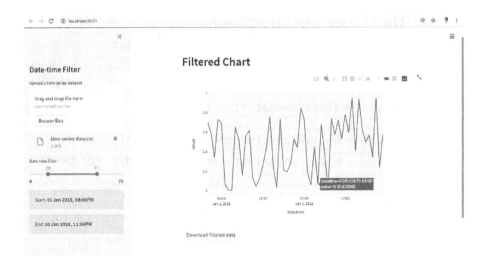

Figure 11-6. *Output of Listing 11-5*

11.2.2 Time-Series Heatmap Application

Another commonly used form of time-series data visualization is the monthly-hourly heatmap. These visualizations allow you to group data points into averages for each hour of each month and can be particularly useful for providing time-series analytics. For instance, one may need to know how much average temperatures are over the course of the year or how many users have visited their website within a one-year period.

In this application, we will initially parse our date-time column from *DD/MM/YYYY HH:MM* into two separate columns for month and hour, that is, *January* and *12AM*, respectively. Subsequently, we will use Pandas's *groupby* command to aggregate our data into monthly and hourly averages for the entire duration of the dataset, and finally we will use Plotly's heatmap visualization to display the data within our Streamlit application as shown in Listing 11-6 and Figure 11-7.

Listing 11-6. timeseries_heatmap.py

```python
import pandas as pd
import streamlit as st
from datetime import datetime
import plotly.express as px

# Month-hours dictionary generator

def month_hours_dict():
    month_hours = {}
    month_names = ['January','February','March','April','May',
    'June','July','August','September','October','November',
    'December']

    for month_name in month_names:
        month = {'%s' % (month_name): {'12AM': None, '01AM':
                                        None, '02AM': None,
                                        '03AM': None, '04AM':
                                        None, '05AM': None,
                                        '06AM': None, '07AM':
                                        None, '08AM': None,
                                        '09AM': None, '10AM':
                                        None, '11AM': None,
                                        '12PM': None, '01PM':
                                        None, '02PM': None,
                                        '03PM': None, '04PM':
                                        None, '05PM': None,
                                        '06PM': None, '07PM':
                                        None, '08PM': None,
                                        '09PM': None, '10PM':
                                        None, '11PM': None}}

        month_hours.update(month)

    return month_hours
```

```
# Aggregating data into monthly-hourly averages
def aggregate(df, datetime_col, format):
    df[datetime_col] = pd.to_datetime(df[datetime_col],
    format='%d/%m/%Y %H:%M')

    for i in range(0,len(df)):
        df.loc[i,'Month'] = df.loc[i][datetime_col].
        strftime('%B')
        df.loc[i,'Hour'] = df.loc[i][datetime_col].
        strftime('%I%p')

    return df.groupby(['Month','Hour'],sort=False,
    as_index=False).mean().round(4)

# Plotly heatmap visualization
def heatmap(df, month_hours, value_col):
    for i in range(len(df)):
        month_hours[df.iloc[i][0]][df.iloc[i][1]] = df.loc[i]
        [value_col]

    data_rows = list(month_hours.values())
    data = []

    for i in range(0,len(data_rows)):
        data.append(list(data_rows[i].values()))

    fig = px.imshow(data,
                    labels=dict(x="Hour", y="Month",
                    color="Value"),
                            x=['12AM','01AM','02AM','03AM',
                            '04AM','05AM','06AM','07AM',
                            '08AM','09AM','10AM','11AM',
                            '12PM','01PM','02PM','03PM',
                            '04PM','05PM','06PM','07PM',
                            '08PM','09PM','10PM','11PM'],
```

```
                              y=['January','February','March',
                              'April','May','June','July',
                              'August','September','October',
                              'November','December']
                              )

    st.write(fig)

if __name__ == '__main__':
    st.sidebar.title('Time-series Heatmap')
    uploaded_file = st.sidebar.file_uploader('Upload a
    time-series dataset')

    if uploaded_file is not None:
        month_hours = month_hours_dict()
        df = pd.read_csv(uploaded_file)

        df_aggregate = aggregate(df, 'datetime', '%d/%m/%Y %H:%M')
        heatmap(df_aggregate, month_hours, 'value')
```

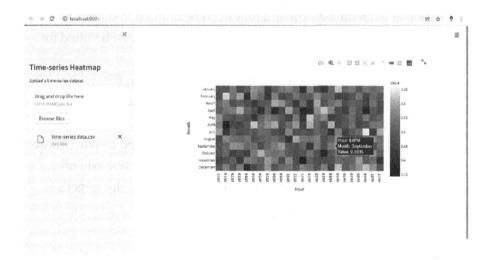

Figure 11-7. *Output of Listing 11-6*

11.2.3 Time Synchronization Application

One of the classical problems when dealing with time-series data is that different datasets might not be synchronized with one another. This means that even when both datasets are representing the same information at the exact same time, they may in fact have different timestamps, and this introduces a whole slew of unintended problems. Such discrepancies can be attributed to a multitude of reasons, namely, the datasets may be in different time zones where one zone has daylight savings while the other does not. Or perhaps the SCADA systems recording the data were subjected to errors during operation. Cause aside, it is absolutely vital to synchronize time-series datasets with one another in order to make accurate use of the data at hand.

To that end, one can make use of a novel technique referred to as "dynamic time warping" (DTW), which synchronizes misaligned datasets by applying dynamic time offsets wherever necessary to maximize the correlation between the two. The advantage of this technique is that it applies as many time offsets as required to achieve the highest possible correlation at each timestamp and may even be applied to datasets with varying lengths. The only caveat is that missing values must be filled for DTW to execute without error.

In this example, we will create a Streamlit application that will synchronize a dataset of readings for power vs. voltage, where voltage is misaligned by two hours. As shown in Listing 11-7, we will define column *power* as the reference dataset, which will be used to synchronize column *voltage*, the target dataset. The synchronize function will take the unsynchronized data shown in Figure 11-8 and offset the target's timestamps to synchronize it as shown in Figure 11-9.

Listing 11-7. timeseries_synchronization.py

```python
import numpy as np
import pandas as pd
import streamlit as st
from fastdtw import *
import plotly.express as px
from sklearn.metrics import r2_score
from scipy.spatial.distance import *

# Dynamic Time Warping synchronization function
def synchronize(df, datetime_col, reference, target):
    x = np.array(df_unsynchronized[reference].fillna(0))
    y = np.array(df_unsynchronized[target].fillna(0))

    distance, path = fastdtw(x, y, dist=euclidean)
    result = []

    for i in range(0,len(path)):
        result.append([df_unsynchronized[datetime_col].
        iloc[path[i][0]],
        df_unsynchronized[reference].iloc[path[i][0]],
        df_unsynchronized[target].iloc[path[i][1]]])

    df_synchronized = pd.DataFrame(data=result,
    columns=[datetime_col,reference,target]).drop_
    duplicates(subset=[datetime_col])

    return df_synchronized

# Plotly time-series visualization function
def timeseries_chart(df, datetime_col):
    df_columns = list(df)
    df[datetime_col] = pd.to_datetime(df[datetime_col],
    format='%d/%m/%Y %H:%M')
```

```python
    df = df.sort_values(by=datetime_col)

    fig = px.line(df, x=datetime_col, y=df_columns,
                  hover_data={datetime_col: "|%d-%m-%Y %H:%M"})

    st.write(fig)

if __name__ == '__main__':
    st.sidebar.title('Time-series Synchronization')
    uploaded_file = st.sidebar.file_uploader('Upload a time-
    series dataset')

    if uploaded_file is not None:
        df_unsynchronized = pd.read_csv(uploaded_file).
        dropna(subset=['datetime'])
        df_synchronized = synchronize(df_unsynchronized,
        'datetime', 'power', 'voltage')

        timeseries_chart(df_unsynchronized, 'datetime')
        st.subheader('Correlation: %s' % (round(r2_score(df_
        unsynchronized['power'],
        df_unsynchronized['voltage']),3)))

        timeseries_chart(df_synchronized, 'datetime')
        st.subheader('Correlation: %s' % (round(r2_score(df_
        synchronized['power'],
        df_synchronized['voltage']),3)))

        st.download_button(
            label="Download synchronized data",
            data=df_synchronized.to_csv(index=False).
            encode('utf-8'),
            file_name='synchronized_data.csv',
            mime='text/csv',
        )
```

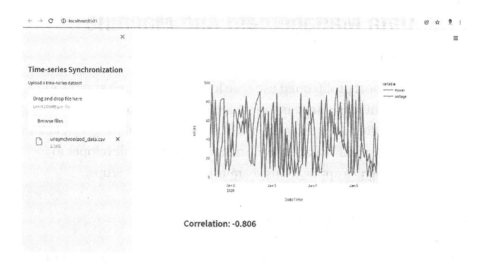

Figure 11-8. *Output of Listing 11-7 (unsynchronized dataset)*

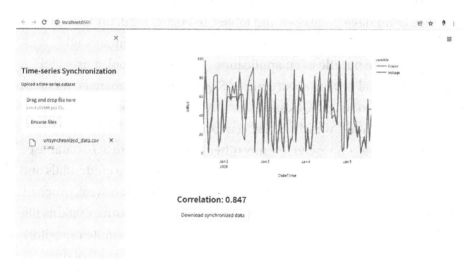

Figure 11-9. *Output of Listing 11-7 (synchronized dataset)*

11.3 Data Management and Machine Learning Applications

Evidently, the most proliferated use case for a Pythonic web application will be for data management and machine learning purposes. Indeed, this is where Streamlit shines the most. With its rich library of widgets related to data wrangling and visualization, Streamlit allows the developer to render data analytics applications seamlessly at their fingertips.

11.3.1 Data Warehouse Application

In this section, we will exhibit the building blocks for a data warehousing application. While warehousing is ostensibly used to refer to the structured storage of data, we will however use Streamlit to provide a rich graphical interface to manage databases and tables; to create, read, update, and delete data; and finally to visualize the stored data on demand, all packaged in one bundle of an application. With such a tool, a user can connect to a local or remote structured SQL database to manage their data without having to write SQL queries or any other code for that matter.

For this instance, we will be using a local PostgreSQL database; however, you may choose to use any other local or remote SQL database as you see fit. All you need to do is to modify the database credentials and client shown in Listings 11-8 and 11-10, respectively. Otherwise, proceed with adding your credentials to a local config file, and ensure that this file is added to your Gitignore file when committing to any remote repositories for added security. Subsequently, use Listing 11-9 to create all of the create, read, update, and delete functions for the databases and tables that you will be working with. In addition, this utilities file will allow you to render the interactive CRUD table widget discussed earlier in Section 4.1 and will also enable you to visualize your data with a line chart.

Listing 11-8. config.py

```
username = '<username>'
password = '<password>'
port = '<port>'
```

Listing 11-9. warehouse_utils.py

```python
from sqlalchemy import create_engine
import psycopg2
from psycopg2.extensions import ISOLATION_LEVEL_AUTOCOMMIT
import pandas as pd
import streamlit as st
from st_aggrid import AgGrid
from st_aggrid.shared import GridUpdateMode
from st_aggrid.grid_options_builder import GridOptionsBuilder
import plotly.express as px

# Function to create a new database
def create_database(database_name, connection):
    connection.set_isolation_level(ISOLATION_LEVEL_AUTOCOMMIT)
    cursor = connection.cursor()

    try:
        cursor.execute("""CREATE DATABASE %s WITH OWNER =
        postgres ENCODING =
        'UTF8' CONNECTION LIMIT = -1;""" % ('warehouse_db_' +
        database_name))
        cursor.close()
        return True
    except:
        return False
```

```python
# Function to return a list of databases
def read_databases(engine):
    result = engine.execute("SELECT datname FROM pg_database")
    result = [x[0].replace('warehouse_db_',") for x in result
    if 'warehouse_db_' in x[0]]
    return result

# Function to rename a selected database
def update_database(database_name_old, database_name_new,
connection):
    connection.set_isolation_level(ISOLATION_LEVEL_AUTOCOMMIT)
    cursor = connection.cursor()
    try:
        cursor.execute("""SELECT pg_terminate_backend (pg_stat_
        activity.pid)
        FROM pg_stat_activity WHERE pg_stat_activity.datname =
        '%s';""" % ('warehouse_db_' + database_name_old))
        cursor.execute("""ALTER DATABASE %s RENAME TO %s;""" %
        ('warehouse_db_' + database_name_old, 'warehouse_db_' +
        database_name_new))
        cursor.close()
        return True
    except:
        pass

# Function to delete a selected database
def delete_database(database_name, connection):
    connection.set_isolation_level(ISOLATION_LEVEL_AUTOCOMMIT)
    cursor = connection.cursor()
    try:
        cursor.execute("""SELECT pg_terminate_backend (pg_stat_
        activity.pid)
```

```
        FROM pg_stat_activity WHERE pg_stat_activity.datname =
        '%s';""" % ('warehouse_db_' + database_name))
        cursor.execute("""DROP DATABASE %s;""" % ('warehouse_
        db_' + database_name))
        cursor.close()
        return True
    except:
        pass

# Function to create a table in the selected database
def create_table(table_name, table, engine):
    table.to_sql(table_name, engine, index=False, if_
    exists='replace', chunksize=1000)

# Function to return a list of tables in the selected database
def list_tables(engine):
    tables = engine.execute("""SELECT table_name FROM
    information_schema.tables
    WHERE table_schema = 'public' ORDER BY table_name;""").
    fetchall()
    return [x[0] for x in tables]

# Function to read the selected table within the selected database
def read_table(table_name, engine):
    try:
        return pd.read_sql_table(table_name,engine)
    except:
        pass

# Function to delete the selected table within the selected
database
def delete_table(table_name, engine):
    engine.execute("""DROP TABLE IF EXISTS %s""" % (table_name))
```

```python
# Function to render an interactive 'create, read, update and
delete' table
def crud(table_name, engine):
    df = read_table(table_name, engine)
    df = df.fillna('None')
    index = len(df)

    # Initiate the streamlit-aggrid widget
    gb = GridOptionsBuilder.from_dataframe(df)
    gb.configure_side_bar()
    gb.configure_default_column(groupable=True, value=True,
    enableRowGroup=True,
     aggFunc="sum",editable=True)
    gb.configure_selection(selection_mode='multiple', use_
    checkbox=True)
    gridOptions = gb.build()

    # Insert the dataframe into the widget
    df_new = AgGrid(df,gridOptions=gridOptions,enable_
    enterprise_modules=True,
    update_mode=GridUpdateMode.MODEL_CHANGED)

    # Add a new row to the widget
    if st.button('-----------Add a new row-----------'):
        df_new['data'].loc[index,:] = 'None'
        create_table(table_name, df_new['data'], engine)
         st.experimental_rerun()

    # Save the dataframe to disk if the widget has been modified
    if df.equals(df_new['data']) is False:
        create_table(table_name, df_new['data'], engine)
        st.experimental_rerun()
```

```python
# Remove selected rows from the widget
if st.button('-----------Remove selected rows-----------'):
    if len(df_new['selected_rows']) > 0:
        exclude = pd.DataFrame(df_new['selected_rows'])
        create_table(table_name, pd.merge(df_new['data'],
        exclude, how='outer',
        indicator=True).query('_merge == "left_only"').
        drop('_merge', 1), engine)
        st.experimental_rerun()
    else:
        st.warning('Please select at least one row')

# Check for duplicate rows
if df_new['data'].duplicated().sum() > 0:
    st.warning('**Number of duplicate rows:** %s' %
    (df_new['data'].duplicated().sum()))
    if st.button('---------Delete duplicates---------'):
        df_new['data'] = df_new['data'].drop_duplicates()
        create_table(table_name, df_new['data'], engine)
        st.experimental_rerun()

# Function to render a line chart for the selected table
def chart(df, columns):
    if len(columns) > 0:
        fig = px.line(df.sort_index(), df.index, columns)
        st.write(fig)
```

Finally, you may use Listing 11-10 to render the frontend interface for your data warehousing application. The output of this script, as shown in Figures 11-10, 11-11, and 11-12, is divided into three sections. Namely, the first section titled *Database Manager* provides the user with the ability to create, read, rename, and delete databases. The next section named *Table Manager* allows the user to upload a table in the form of a CSV file, update it with the interactive CRUD widget, and to delete the table. And finally, the *Data Visualizer* section enables the user to visualize any numeric table by selecting one or more columns to display within a range indexed line chart.

Listing 11-10. warehouse_app.py

```python
from warehouse_utils import *
import config # Credentials file

# PostgreSQL credentials
username = config.username
password = config.password
port = config.port

if __name__ == '__main__':
    # Creating PostgreSQL client
    connection = psycopg2.connect("user=%s password='%s'"
    % (username, password))
    engine = create_engine(
        'postgresql://%s:%s@localhost:%s/' % (username,
        password, port))

    st.title('Data Warehouse')

    st.write('___')

    st.subheader('Database Manager')
    col1, col2 = st.columns(2)

    with col1:
        st.write('**Create database**')
        database_name = st.text_input('Please enter
        database name')
        if st.button('Create database'):
            status = create_database(database_name, connection)
```

```python
        if status is True:
            st.success('Database **%s** created
            successfully' % (database_name))
        elif status is False:
            st.warning('Database with this name already
            exists')

    st.write('**Rename database**')
    database_name_old = st.selectbox('Please select a
    database to rename',
    read_databases(engine))
    if database_name_old is not None:
        database_name_new = st.text_input('Please enter new
        database name')
        if st.button('Rename database'):
            status = update_database(database_name_old,
            database_name_new, connection)
            if status is True:
                st.success('Database renamed from **%s**
                to **%s**'
                % (database_name_old, database_name_new))

with col2:
    st.write('**List databases**')
    database_selection = st.selectbox('Databases
    list',read_databases(engine))

    st.write('**Delete database**')
    database_selection = st.selectbox('Please select a
    database to delete',
    read_databases(engine))
    if database_selection is not None:
        if st.button('Delete database'):
```

```
                status = delete_database(database_selection,
                connection)
                if status is True:
                    st.success('Database **%s** deleted
                    successfully' %
                    (database_selection))

st.write('___')

st.subheader('Table Manager')
st.write('**Select database**')
database_selection = st.selectbox('Please select a
database',
read_databases(engine))

if database_selection is not None:
    engine_database = create_engine("postgresql://%s:%s@
    localhost:%s/%s" %
    (username, password, port,'warehouse_db_' + database_
    selection))

    col1_2, col2_2 = st.columns(2)

    with col1_2:
        st.write('**Create table**')
        table = st.file_uploader('Please upload data')
        if table is not None:
            table = pd.read_csv(table)
            table_name = st.text_input('Please enter
            table name')
            if st.button('Save table'):
                if len(table_name) > 0:
                    create_table(table_name, table, engine_
                    database)
```

```
                st.success('**%s** saved to database' %
                (table_name))
            else:
                st.warning('Please enter table name')

    with col2_2:
        st.write('**Delete table**')
        table_selection = st.selectbox('Please select table
        to delete',
        list_tables(engine_database))
        if table_selection is not None:
            if st.button('Delete table'):
                delete_table(table_selection, engine_database)
                st.success('**%s** deleted successfully' %
                (table_selection))

    st.write('**Read and update table**')
    table_selection = st.selectbox('Please select table to
    reade and update',
    list_tables(engine_database))
    if table_selection is not None:
        crud(table_selection, engine_database)

st.write('___')

st.subheader('Data Visualizer')
st.write('**Select database**')
database_selection = st.selectbox('Please select a database
to visualize',
read_databases(engine))

if database_selection is not None:
    engine_database = create_engine("postgresql://%s:%s@
    localhost:%s/%s" %
```

```
    (username, password, port,'warehouse_db_' + database_
    selection))

col1_3, col2_3 = st.columns(2)
with col1_3:
    table_selection = st.selectbox('Please select table
    to visualize',
    list_tables(engine_database))
    table = read_table(table_selection, engine_
    database)
if table_selection is not None:
    with col2_3:
        columns = st.multiselect('Please select
        columns', table.columns)
        table[columns] = table[columns].apply(pd.to_
        numeric, errors='coerce')

    chart(table, columns)
```

Figure 11-10. *Output of Listing 11-10*

Figure 11-11. *Output of Listing 11-10 continued (1)*

Figure 11-12. *Output of Listing 11-10 continued (2)*

11.3.2 Advanced Application Development: Machine Learning As a Service

The final use case for this chapter will be of a *machine learning as a service*, otherwise known as the MLaaS application. This example will bind together many of the key concepts covered in this book. Specifically, it will provide an overview of how to interface and couple concepts such as databases, caching, session state, user authentication, traffic insights, data visualization, subpages, modularity, and many other features together to render an advanced and production-ready web application in Streamlit.

Before we proceed any further, it is necessary to mention what this application actually performs. Put simply, it will enable the user to train a logistic regression model on an uploaded dataset and subsequently use the model to classify a test dataset. While the utility appears to be rather trivial, the implementation and features will put to use many of the capabilities that Streamlit, PostgreSQL, Pandas, Plotly, and other stacks have to offer. Indeed, this use case is highly scalable and has been expanded to cover other classifiers including decision tree, support vector machine, Naive Bayes, and K-nearest neighbors in *https://dummylearn. herokuapp.com/*.

User Authentication Without a Backend Server

While in Chapter 8 we covered implementing user authentication with a backend server, there is in fact a way to implement authentication without one. With the Streamlit component *Streamlit-Authenticator*, you can create a lighter authentication service locally without a server, analogous perhaps to what SQLite is to SQL Server.

Using Streamlit-Authenticator, you initially need to hash your users' passwords using the *stauth.Hasher* command and then provide the secure hashed passwords to the *stauth.Authenticate* object as shown in Listing 11-11. Afterward, remove ALL references to the plain text passwords in your source code. Each time the user enters their plain text password (Figure 11-13), it is hashed and compared to the hashed password you previously provided, in order to authenticate the user. In addition, you can enable passwordless reauthentication by using the *cookie_expiry_days* argument in the *stauth.Authenticate* command to save a secure JWT on the user's browser to reauthenticate them for the specified number of days before it expires. Subsequently, you may determine a user's authentication status at any stage of your application by accessing the session state *st.session_state['authentication_status']*.

Listing 11-11. Streamlit-Authenticator.py

```python
import streamlit as st
import streamlit_authenticator as stauth

names = ['John Smith','Rebecca Briggs']
usernames = ['jsmith','rbriggs']
passwords = ['123','456']

hashed_passwords = stauth.Hasher(passwords).generate()

authenticator = stauth.Authenticate(names,usernames,hashed_
passwords, 'some_cookie_name','some_signature_key',
    cookie_expiry_days=30)

name, authentication_status, username = authenticator.
login('Login','main')

if st.session_state['authentication_status']:
    authenticator.logout('Logout', 'main')
    st.write(f'Welcome *{st.session_state["name"]}*')
    st.title('Some content')
elif st.session_state['authentication_status'] == False:
```

```
    st.error('Username/password is incorrect')
elif st.session_state['authentication_status'] == None:
    st.warning('Please enter your username and password')
```

Figure 11-13. *Output of Listing 11-11*

Utilities Script

It is a good practice to modularize application development, by relocating commonly used classes, functions, database connections, and other objects to a common file called *Utils.py*. In our use case, we will place the functions for querying the user-insights table, generating a session ID, creating a file upload widget, and creating a PostgreSQL connection function within this file as shown in Listing 11-12. Furthermore, another excellent practice is to use the *st.experimental_singleton* command to cache the database connection object, as this will save a considerable amount of time whenever a call is made to the database.

Listing 11-12. Utils.py

```python
import pandas as pd
from sqlalchemy import create_engine
import streamlit as st
from streamlit.scriptrunner.script_run_context import get_
script_run_ctx
from streamlit.server.server import Server

# Inserting new row in traffic insights table
def insert_row(session_id, engine):
    if engine.execute("SELECT session_id FROM session_state
    WHERE session_id = '%s'" %
    (session_id)).fetchone() is None:
        engine.execute("INSERT INTO session_state (session_id)
        VALUES ('%s')" %
        (session_id))

# Updating row in insights table
def update_row(column, new_value, session_id, engine):
    if engine.execute("SELECT %s FROM session_state WHERE
    session_id = '%s'" %
    (column, session_id)).first()[0] is None:
        engine.execute("UPDATE session_state SET %s = '%s'
        WHERE session_id = '%s'" %
        (column, new_value, session_id))

# Session state function
def get_session():
    session_id = get_script_run_ctx().session_id
    session_info = Server.get_current()._get_session_
    info(session_id)
```

```python
    if session_info is None:
        raise RuntimeError("Couldn't get your Streamlit Session
        object.")

    session_id = session_id.replace('-','_')
    session_id = '_id_' + session_id
    return session_info.session, session_id

# File uploader function
def file_upload(name):
    uploaded_file = st.sidebar.file_uploader('%s' %
    (name),key='%s' % (name),
    accept_multiple_files=False)
    status = False
    if uploaded_file is not None:
        try:
            uploaded_df = pd.read_csv(uploaded_file)
            status = True
            return status, uploaded_df
        except:
            try:
                uploaded_df = pd.read_excel(uploaded_file)
                status = True
                return status, uploaded_df
            except:
                st.error("'Please ensure file is .csv or .xlsx
                format and/or
                reupload file"')
                return status, None
    else:
        return status, None
```

```
@st.cache(allow_output_mutation=True, hash_funcs={"_thread.
RLock": lambda _: None})
def db_engine(username, password, port):
    return create_engine('postgresql://%s:%s@localhost:%s/' %
    (username, password,
    port))
```

Config Script

As discussed in earlier sections, another good practice is to store credentials in dictionaries within a config.py file that is then imported and invoked in your main code. In addition, as shown in Listing 11-13, the hashed passwords generated earlier by Streamlit-Authenticator can also be stored in the config.py file instead of writing them within the main script. Please ensure that the config.py file is added to the *Gitignore* file so that it is not pushed to any remote repositories.

Listing 11-13. config.py

```
# User credentials dictionary
user_credentials = {
'names': ['John Smith','Rebecca Briggs'],
'usernames': ['jsmith','rbriggs'],
'passwords': ['$2b$12$bqO7DBwAIS3rCGyvP2qNN.t6LchM.qGNviocCl
            sjX8fOtdqZgZZyG','$2b$12$48hHezeKpl21oZp2/iMwj.
            bQcP47DAquKe.dYoyRqb9ctyYuyOJei']
                }
```

```
# Traffic insights database credentials dictionary
database_credentials = {
'username': '<username>',
'password': '<password>',
'port': '<port>'
}
```

Main Script

Now that we have gotten the logistics out of the way, we can begin to develop the main script of our application that will serve as the focal point between the various pages and will also cater to some of our housekeeping requirements. As shown in Listing 11-14, we begin by importing scripts for any other pages in the same manner discussed in Section 3.3. Subsequently, we utilize the Streamlit-Authenticator component to authenticate users based on the credentials saved in the config.py file. Next, we enable navigation between pages by using the *st.selectbox* command that calls the function for the selected page from a dictionary of key-value pairs, where the key is the name of the page and the value is the corresponding function. Finally, we invoke the file upload widget from our Utils file and assign the uploaded Pandas dataframes to our session state, where they can be accessed from at any time on demand.

Listing 11-14. main.py

```
import streamlit as st
from Utils import *
import streamlit_authenticator as stauth
import config

# Importing pages
from lr import lr_main
```

```python
def main(engine):
    # Creating pages dictionary
    pages_ml_classifier = {
        'Logistic Regression Classifier': lr_main
        }

    # Creating pages menu
    st.sidebar.subheader('Menu')
    ml_module_selection = st.sidebar.selectbox('Select
    Classifier',
    ['Logistic Regression Classifier'])

    # Creating dataset uploader widgets
    if 'df_train' not in st.session_state:
        st.session_state['df_train'] = None
    if 'df_real' not in st.session_state:
        st.session_state['df_real'] = None

    st.sidebar.subheader('Training Dataset')
    _, st.session_state['df_train'] = file_upload('Please
    upload a training dataset')

    st.sidebar.subheader('Test Dataset')
    _, st.session_state['df_real'] = file_upload('Please upload
    a test dataset')

    # Running selected page
    pages_ml_classifier[ml_module_selection](engine)

if __name__ == '__main__':
    # Creating PostgreSQL client for insights database
    username = config.database_credentials['username']
    password = config.database_credentials['password']
    port = config.database_credentials['port']
    engine = db_engine(username, password, port)
```

```python
# Creating user authentication object
authenticator = stauth.Authenticate(config.user_
credentials['names'],
config.user_credentials['usernames'], config.user_
credentials['passwords'],
'some_cookie_name','some_signature_key', cookie_expiry_
days=30)

# Displaying login bar
name, authentication_status, username = authenticator.
login('Login','sidebar')

if st.session_state['authentication_status']:
    authenticator.logout('Logout', 'main')
    st.write(f'Welcome *{st.session_state["name"]}*')
    main(engine)
elif st.session_state['authentication_status'] == False:
    st.sidebar.error('Username/password is incorrect')
elif st.session_state['authentication_status'] == None:
    st.sidebar.warning('Please enter your username and
    password')
```

Logistic Regression Classifier

The final and undoubtedly most impactful step is to create the script
for our logistic regression classifier page. As mentioned earlier, this
application will provide machine learning-as-a-service, where the user can
train a logistic regression model on an uploaded training dataset and then
use that model to classify a test dataset. The beauty of such an application
is that it is offered as a plug-and-play platform, without the user having to
install any of their own libraries or having to orchestrate a server. To cater
such functionality, we have a whole host of various functions as displayed
in Listing 11-15 that will provide the following:

1. Visualize a confusion_matrix.

2. Visualize an ROC plot.

3. Create an expandable entry form for our model's hyperparameters.

4. Train the logistic regression model and cache the function with *st.cache* to reduce runtime on subsequent reruns.

5. Classify test data using the trained logistic regression model.

6. Visualize accuracy metrics of classified data.

In addition, we will implement the technique described in Section 7.4 to record insights at each step of our application. Specifically, the traffic insights functions imported from Utils.py will be invoked to save into a PostgreSQL database, the date-time when the user reaches various steps of the application, and the size of the uploaded datasets. To wrap it all up, upon completion the user will be allowed to download their hyperparameters and predicted data. The various steps of this application are depicted in Figure 11-14 for your reference.

Listing 11-15. lr.py

```
import streamlit as st
import pandas as pd
from sklearn.model_selection import train_test_split
from sklearn.linear_model import LogisticRegression
from sklearn import metrics
import plotly.express as px
import plotly.graph_objects as go
import plotly.figure_factory as ff
from datetime import datetime
from Utils import *
```

```python
# Plotly confusion matrix visualization
def confusion_matrix_plot(y_test, y_pred):
    cnf_matrix = metrics.confusion_matrix(y_test, y_pred)
    z = cnf_matrix.tolist()[::-1]
    x = ['Negative', 'Positive']
    y = ['Positive', 'Negative']
    z_text = z
    fig = ff.create_annotated_heatmap(z, x, y, annotation_
    text=z_text, text=z,
    hoverinfo='text', colorscale='Blackbody')

    st.write(fig)

# Plotly receiver operating characteristic visualization function
def roc_plot(X_test, logreg, y_test):
    y_pred_proba = logreg.predict_proba(X_test)[::,1]
    fpr, tpr, _ = metrics.roc_curve(y_test, y_pred_proba)
    roc_data = pd.DataFrame([])
    roc_data['True positive'] = tpr
    roc_data['False positive'] = fpr

    fig = px.line(roc_data, x='False positive', y='True positive')
    st.write(fig)

    auc = metrics.roc_auc_score(y_test, y_pred_proba)
    st.info('Area Under Curve: **%s**' % (round(auc,3)))

# Hyperparameters expander function
def lr_hyperparameters():
    with st.expander('Advanced Parameters'):
        col2_1, col2_2 = st.columns(2)
        with col2_1:
```

```python
    penalty = st.selectbox('Penalty', ['l2','l1','elast
    icnet','none'])
    tol = st.number_input('Tolerance (1e-4)',
    value=1)/10000
    fit_intercept = st.radio('Intercept', [True,False])
    class_weight = st.radio('Class weight',
    [None,'balanced'])
    solver = st.selectbox('Solver', ['lbfgs','newton-
    cg','liblinear','sag',
    'saga'])
    multi_class = st.selectbox('Multi class',
    ['auto','ovr','multinomial'])
    warm_start = st.radio('Warm start', [False,True])
with col2_2:
    dual = st.radio('Dual or primal formulation',
    [False,True])
    C = st.number_input('Inverse regularization
    strength', 0.0, 99.0, 1.0, 0.1)
    intercept_scaling = st.number_input('Intercept
    scaling', 0.0, 99.0, 1.0, 0.1)
    random_state = st.radio('Random state',
    [None,'Custom'])
    if random_state == 'Custom':
        random_state = st.number_input('Custom random
        state', 0, 99, 1, 1)
    max_iter = st.number_input('Maximum iterations', 0,
    100, 100, 1)
    verbose = st.number_input('Verbose', 0, 99, 0, 1)
    l1_ratio = st.radio('L1 ratio', [None,'Custom'])
```

```
    if l1_ratio == 'Custom':
        l1_ratio = st.number_input('Custom l1 ratio',
        0.0, 1.0, 1.0, 0.01)

    #Download hyperparameters feature
    hyperparameters = {'penalty':[penalty], 'dual':[dual],
    'tol':[tol], 'C':[C],
    'fit_intercept':[fit_intercept], 'intercept_
    scaling':[intercept_scaling],
    'class_weight':[class_weight],
    'random_state':[random_state],
    'solver':[solver], 'max_iter':[max_iter], 'multi_
    class':[multi_class],
    'verbose':[verbose],'warm_start':[warm_start], 'l1_
    ratio':[l1_ratio]}

    st.download_button(
        label="Download hyperparameters",
        data=pd.DataFrame(hyperparameters).to_
        csv(index=False).encode('utf-8'),
        file_name='Hyperparameters.csv',
    )

    return (penalty, tol, fit_intercept, class_weight, solver,
multi_class, warm_start, dual, C, intercept_scaling,
    random_state, max_iter, verbose, l1_ratio)

# Logistic regression training function
@st.cache
def log_train(df, feature_cols, label_col, test_size, penalty,
tol, fit_intercept, class_weight, solver, multi_class,
    warm_start, dual, C, intercept_scaling, random_state,
    max_iter, verbose, l1_ratio):
```

```
    x = df[feature_cols]
    y = df[label_col]
    x_train,x_test,y_train,y_test=train_test_split(x, y, test_
    size=test_size, random_state=0)

    logreg = LogisticRegression(penalty=penalty, dual=dual,
    tol=tol, C=C, fit_intercept=fit_intercept, intercept_
    scaling=intercept_scaling, class_weight=class_weight,
    random_state=random_state, solver=solver, max_
    iter=max_iter,
    multi_class=multi_class, verbose=verbose, warm_start=
    warm_start, l1_ratio=l1_ratio)

    logreg.fit(x_train,y_train)
    y_pred = logreg.predict(x_test)

    return x_train, x_test, y_train, y_test, y_pred, logreg

# Logisitic regression predictor function
def log_real(logreg, df_real, feature_cols, label_col):
    x_test_real = df_real[feature_cols]
    y_pred_real = logreg.predict(x_test_real)
    x_pred_real = df_real.copy()
    x_pred_real[label_col] = y_pred_real
    return x_pred_real.sort_index()

# Prediction statistics function
def stats(y_test, y_pred):
    accuracy = metrics.accuracy_score(y_test, y_pred)
    precision = metrics.precision_score(y_test, y_pred)
    recall = metrics.recall_score(y_test, y_pred)
    f1 = metrics.f1_score(y_test, y_pred)

    col2_1, col2_2, col2_3, col2_4 = st.columns(4)
```

```python
    with col2_1:
        st.info('Accuracy: **%s**' % (round(accuracy,3)))
    with col2_2:
        st.info('Precision: **%s**' % (round(precision,3)))
    with col2_3:
        st.info('Recall: **%s**' % (round(recall,3)))
    with col2_4:
        st.info('F1 Score: **%s**' % (round(f1,3)))

def lr_main(engine):
    _, session_id = get_session()
    insert_row(session_id, engine)
    update_row('lr1',datetime.now().strftime("%H:%M:%S
%d/%m/%Y"), session_id, engine)

    if st.session_state['df_train'] is not None:
        df = st.session_state['df_train']
        update_row('data1_rows',len(df),session_id,engine)
        update_row('lr2',datetime.now().strftime("%H:%M:%S
%d/%m/%Y"), session_id,
         engine)
        st.title('Training')
        st.subheader('Parameters')
        col1, col2, col3 = st.columns((3,3,2))

        with col1:
            feature_cols = st.multiselect('Please select
            features', df.columns)
        with col2:
            label_col = st.selectbox('Please select label',
            df.columns)
        with col3:
```

```
    test_size = st.number_input('Please enter test
    size', 0.01, 0.99, 0.25, 0.05)

(penalty, tol, fit_intercept, class_weight, solver,
multi_class,
warm_start, dual, C, intercept_scaling, random_state,
max_iter, verbose,
l1_ratio) = lr_hyperparameters()
try:
    x_train, x_test, y_train, y_test, y_pred, logreg =
    log_train(df, feature_cols, label_col, test_size,
    penalty, tol, fit_intercept, class_weight, solver,
    multi_class, warm_start, dual, C, intercept_scaling,
    random_state, max_iter, verbose, l1_ratio)

    st.subheader('Confusion Matrix')
    confusion_matrix_plot(y_test, y_pred)

    st.subheader('Metrics')
    stats(y_test, y_pred)

    st.subheader('ROC Curve')
    roc_plot(x_test, logreg, y_test)

    update_row('lr3',datetime.now().strftime("%H:%M:%S
    %d/%m/%Y"),
    session_id, engine)

    if st.session_state['df_real'] is not None:
        try:
            df_real = st.session_state['df_real']
            st.title('Testing')
            update_row('data2_rows',len(df_real),
            session_id, engine)
```

```python
                    st.subheader('Predicted Labels')
                    x_pred_real = log_real(logreg, df_real,
                    feature_cols, label_col)
                    st.write(x_pred_real)
                    update_row('lr4',datetime.now().
                    strftime("%H:%M:%S %d/%m/%Y"),
                    session_id, engine)

                    st.download_button(
                        label='Download predicted labels',
                        data=pd.DataFrame(x_pred_real).to_
                        csv(index=False)
                        .encode('utf-8'),
                        file_name='Predicted labels.csv',
                    )
                except:
                    st.warning("'Please upload a test dataset
                    with the same feature
                    set as the training dataset"')

            elif st.session_state['df_real'] is None:
                st.sidebar.warning('Please upload a test
                dataset')
        except:
            st.warning("'Please select at least one feature, a
            suitable binary
            label and appropriate advanced paramters"')

elif st.session_state['df_train'] is None:
    st.title('Welcome      ')
    st.subheader('Please use the left pane to upload your
    dataset')
    st.sidebar.warning('Please upload a training dataset')
```

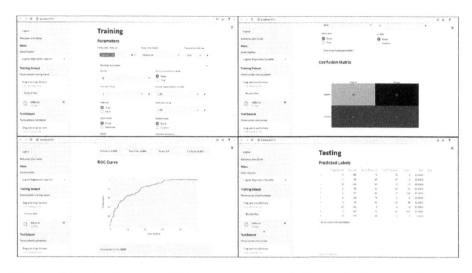

Figure 11-14. *Output of Listing 11-15, with Pima Indians Diabetes training dataset [21]*

11.4 Summary

As you arrive at the end of this chapter and inch closer toward the finish line of the entire book, you are beginning to observe the versatility and impact of Streamlit in real-world use cases. It is becoming ever clearer that a pure Python web framework is indeed able to address and solve various problems at hand. From applications related to data visualization, time-series analysis, SCADA data loggers, motor command and control dashboards, data warehousing, and finally machine learning as a service, we have learned that the mighty Streamlit caters to a breadth of diverse purposes. Furthermore, we saw how it is possible to interface Streamlit with external systems, the likes of Arduino microcontrollers, sensors, and other peripherals, to scale into the world of embedded systems. And perhaps this is only the tip of the iceberg. The point is that Streamlit is what you make of it and whatever your selected tech stack equips you to do.

CHAPTER 12

Streamlit at Work

This final chapter introduces two real-world cases that have taken advantage of Streamlit to develop web applications in some capacity. The first case covers the technical development of a data manager application for wind farms for Iberdrola – a renewable energy firm. We can observe how this application is being used to estimate electrical losses during production and to obtain valuable insights from Iberdrola's SCADA data. The second case divulges the utility of Streamlit for industrial applications with maxon Group – a manufacturer of high-precision electronic motors. Specifically, we can see that Streamlit can be used to create a command and control dashboard application to control the maxon motors of a surgical scope adapter system both locally and remotely.

12.1 Streamlit in Clean Energy: *Iberdrola*

Iberdrola is a multinational electric utility with operations in more than 30 countries in the world. Since its inception, Iberdrola has been dedicated to developing a clean and reliable business model based on investments in renewable energy and is now one of the world's largest renewable energy operators in terms of installed capacity. Iberdrola's renewable energy activities are one of its three strategic business units, alongside networks and wholesale/retail solutions.

© Mohammad Khorasani, Mohamed Abdou, Javier Hernández Fernández 2022
M. Khorasani et al., *Web Application Development with Streamlit*,
https://doi.org/10.1007/978-1-4842-8111-6_12

The renewable business of Iberdrola generates electrical energy from clean resources such as wind (onshore and offshore), hydro, photovoltaic, biomass, and others. In the coming five years, Iberdrola will invest €75 billion in renewable energy and other projects. By the end of the period, renewables will account for 51% of this organic investment (over €34 billion), with a capacity of 60 GW. Similarly, the company forecasts indicate an increase in installed renewable capacity to 95 GW by 2030. The group's commitment will allow it to assist offshore wind technology (reach 4 GW installed by 2025), develop solar photovoltaic (reach 16 GW installed by 2025), and increase its renewable generation capacity to more than 100 GW. This renewable growth is backed by the Paris Agreement which aims to cut greenhouse gas emissions and limit global warming below two degrees Celsius. The agreement was ratified in 2016, at COP21 held in France with 147 countries joining it. It came into force in November 2018 after enough countries joined it for meeting their respective targets of emission cuts. The firm's renewable unit, in addition to generating clean electricity, finances research and development to help advance new technologies that will ensure that green energies continue to play an increasingly crucial role in Iberdrola's portfolio over the next few years.

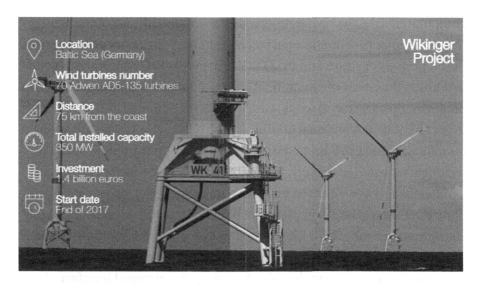

Figure 12-1. Wikinger offshore wind farm. Source: Iberdrola. com [14]

12.1.1 Visualizing Operational Performance of Wind Farms

Daniel Paredes and Jerome Dumont, both members of the Energy Resource department, have spent years developing algorithms and tailor-made software to analyze Iberdrola's wind farms. In particular, the use case being discussed here focuses on a program that analyzes wind farm operational data to obtain energy yield assessment and identify variations. Operational performance studies and energy yield assessments are integral and essential components within the life cycle management of a wind farm. At Iberdrola, the utmost attention is paid to the running and optimization of wind farms, which are constantly inspected for deviations.

To this end, a novel and in-house software solution was rendered to address the needs of operational performance analysis – the Operational Wind Farm data manager hereinafter referred to as OWFdm. The presence of such software adds value by automating and streamlining computations that would be otherwise done manually, accommodating the requirements of operational technicians and engineers alike. Initially developed with Python and the QT GUI framework, OWFdm was able to address the needs of operational analysis; however, a complete deployment to the cloud would provide greater potential and pave the way to accommodate additional utilities for the end users. The justification for migrating the OWFdm to the cloud as a web application included technical reasons (scalability, accessibility, access to network resources and databases) as well as the need for a more powerful visualization library that would largely replace the role of Matplotlib and QT. As all the algorithms were already implemented in Python, a web framework was required to interface with the web browser. For this purpose, Streamlit was introduced to take on the role of creating the frontend interface. As a pure Python package, Streamlit required a very shallow learning curve and reduced the burden of the developers of having to code in HTML or CSS. In addition, Streamlit provided an integrated development environment (IDE) that allowed for rapid development.

In collaboration with Iberdrola Innovation Middle East, a research center devoted to developing innovative solutions in smart grids and distributed renewable energy integration, a redesign and enhancement of the functionality of the OWFdm tool was developed. In the following sections, we will look at some of the Streamlit-based graphical representations utilized by the Iberdrola wind engineers.

12.1.2 Wind Turbine Power Curves

Wind turbines are mechanical devices that convert kinetic energy (energy due to movement) in wind into electrical power. They do this by using three main components: a rotor, a generator, and a tower. The blades of a turbine are connected to the rotor. When the blades move, they cause the shaft of the generator to spin. The type of wire used in wind turbines is known as a multistrand wire and is composed of many individual strands of copper wire twisted together and covered with an outer protective covering.

The power output for a wind turbine depends on the density of the air, which is affected by both altitude and climate. The power output for wind turbines ranges from a few kW to the 14MW of the GE Haliade-X offshore, which is the most powerful turbine available in the market at the time of the writing of this book [17, 18]. A large industrial-type onshore wind turbine such as those populating our countryside usually ranges between 2 and 4MW, with a rotor diameter ranging around 130 meters. The power output for small wind turbines is typically measured in watts (W), while large industrial types are often measured in megawatts (MW). A wind turbine with a 100W power output will meet the needs of an average household, while one that has 3000W can power anything from a small business to an entire neighborhood. A turbine's energy production is proportional to the third power of its blade length, so doubling the blade length would produce eight times as much power. Doubling the blade span (the length of the arc that the blades sweep through when making a full rotation) would produce 16 times as much power.

The power curve of a wind turbine is a graph that shows how much electrical energy the turbine will generate at different wind speeds. Power curves for wind turbines are usually created by testing an actual turbine at specific sites under similar wind conditions and measuring its electrical output at each point either with a wattmeter or a power analyzer. Wind turbines are tested at different wind speeds, and the turbine's power output is measured and recorded as a function of wind speed to generate a wind speed vs. power curve for that particular site. A power curve is typically represented as a graph with wind speed on the x axis and turbine power output on the y axis. The wind speed axis can be given in either actual or average (rated) values. A rated value is the speed at which the turbine's power output matches its maximum capability during normal weather conditions at that site. The typical power curve for a modern industrial three-blade horizontal axis wind turbine is shown in Figure 12-2.

Since the initial wind speed is zero, the turbine's power output begins at zero and gradually increases as wind speeds increase. Wind turbines have to be able to produce electricity even when the wind is blowing below their rated speed – this is called a cut-in speed. The cut-in speed of a turbine will depend on its overall size and design, but there is a minimum speed below which the turbine will not produce any power. As wind speed continues to increase, so does power output until it reaches its rated value. At this point, the power curve flattens and remains constant until wind speeds go beyond the rated value. In the cut-out speed point, where there is a sudden drop in rotational speed and power output, most turbines will enter an automatic braking mode. Wind turbines are designed with an optimum efficiency point (limit point) where all the power in the wind goes into turning the rotor; beyond this limit, no more torque can be converted, and the power output drops dramatically.

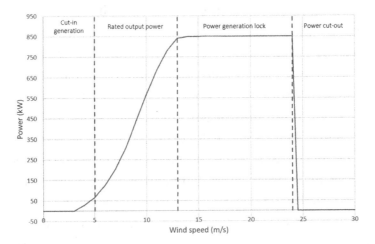

Figure 12-2. Typical wind turbine power output

It is a normal procedure to compare the power curve provided by the turbine manufacturer to the one produced with the observed power during production. This information is useful to wind engineers to perform energy assessment reports, maintenance, or performance evaluations. Figure 12-3 shows three representations in the same graph:

- The power curve as provided by the manufacturer, *operational power curve* in the legend

- The real or measured power curve, *operational power curve (meas)* in the legend

- The three-sigma variance of the real power curve, *operational power curve 3Sigmas* in the legend

- All the data points obtained during the period, *P-v recorded* in the legend

Graphs displayed with Plotly and wrapped with Streamlit can provide an interactive lasso tool that can be used to manually filter outliers. Thanks to the Streamlit framework, a two-way communication between this chart and other components is executed seamlessly.

12.1.3 Wind Roses

A wind rose is a graphical depiction of the frequency with which the wind speed and direction are dispersed at a certain location. Meteorologists use wind roses to give a concise view of how wind speed and direction are typically distributed at a particular location. Modern wind roses normally contain the wind speed, wind direction, time period for which wind data is valid, and other related information. To construct a wind rose, wind observations from anemometers or wind vanes attached to a building or similar structure are plotted on a polar coordinate wind rose. The wind rose contains both the average wind speed and direction during a certain

369

period for a given location. Wind roses typically use 16 cardinal directions, such as NNW (north-northwest), SSW (south-southwest), and so forth, or divide the 360 degrees into sectors.

Figure 12-4 shows a division in eight wind sectors of the wind speed direction of two wind turbines. The graph is displayed using Streamlit's *st.plotly_chart* element with the *go.Scatterpolar* class from *plotly.graph_objects*.

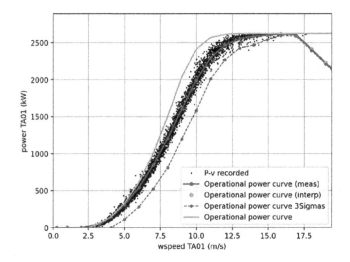

Figure 12-3. *Graph with the different wind turbine power curves*

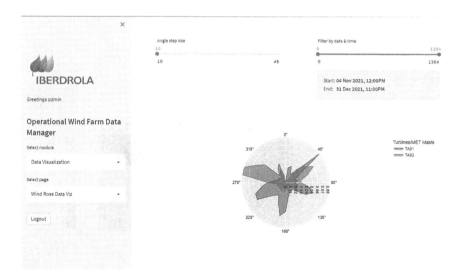

Figure 12-4. *Comparison of two wind turbine wind roses*

12.1.4 Heat Maps

A heat map is a picture that depicts data using colors to represent values. A heat map can depict graphs other than numbers, for example, graphs of graphs. This is more typically known as a matrix plot. The heat map in Figure 12-5 graphs the average active power in watts produced by a wind turbine per hour during each month. Yellow cells signify a higher value (a maximum of 1000 watts), while purple indicates no production. This type of graph offers wind engineers a holistic view of the production patterns per turbine. For instance, and for this specific case, we can infer that November is the windiest month and that the hours around 5 am usually show lower production rates. The graph has been rendered using Plotly and is displayed using Streamlit.

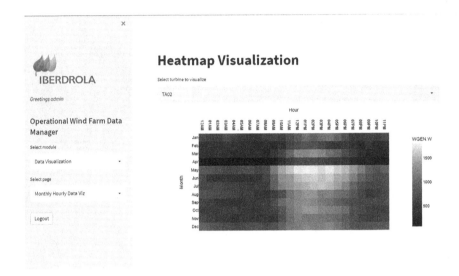

Figure 12-5. *Wind turbine hourly average production per month heat map*

12.1.5 Closing Remarks

Beyond the visualization capabilities, Streamlit has proven to be a highly versatile tool for Iberdrola renewables, enabling us to render multiple datasets on demand by prompting the user to select what data they want to display, as opposed to having to manually program that into the source code. A two-way communication with charts in pure Python is also of great value, for instance, implementing the functionality provided by the lasso tool for manual filtering used in Figure 12-3 would have required some integration efforts with JavaScript or other workarounds. A final advantage is a possibility of rendering charts as HTML on a website, making them interactable with other widgets, as opposed to running it stand-alone locally without any other third-party interactions.

This publication is supported by Iberdrola S.A. as part of its innovation department research studies. Its contents are solely the responsibility of the authors and do not necessarily represent the official views of Iberdrola Group.

12.2 Streamlit in Industry: *maxon Group*

maxon Group is a Swiss manufacturer and distributor of industrial-scale electronic motors used for high-precision and cutting-edge applications. Specifically, maxon's products are utilized extensively for a wide variety of industrial purposes, including but not limited to the healthcare, aerospace, automotive, and packaging industries, to name a few. The versatility of their products, combined with phenomenal build quality and impeccable customer service, enables developers to meet and exceed highly demanding performance requirements, both above and below the atmosphere. Their product catalog hosts a multitude of brushed, brushless, AC, and DC motors, with an assortment of gearboxes, encoders, Hall effect sensors, and most importantly a set of motor controllers that can be commanded via RS232, USB, CANopen, and EtherCAT communication protocols. In addition, maxon offers a high degree of customizability whereby the dimensions, mechanical interfaces, cables, bearings, and other features of the drive disposition can be configured exactly as they are required.

Figure 12-6. *Disposition of a maxon GPX Speed 13 reduction gearbox, ECX Speed 13M brushless motor, and ENX13 encoder*

373

Figure 12-7. maxon EPOS4 Compact 24/1.5 CAN motor controller

12.2.1 Developing a Novel Surgical Scope Adapter System for Minimally Invasive Laparoscopy

Minimally invasive surgery, otherwise known as laparoscopy, is becoming increasingly prevalent as the operation of choice for surgeries on the abdomen. Given the small size of the incisions that are made to the body, laparoscopy affords patients a shorter recovery period and a mitigated possibility of developing complications during and after the surgery. Currently, such operations are conducted manually with a surgical assistant holding and articulating the endoscope that is inserted into the abdomen to view the region being operated on in real time (shown in Figure 12-8). Considering that a human operator is involved in this arrangement, a high level of dexterity and hand-eye coordination is required; any inaccuracy, however slight, may introduce unwarranted error into the operation.

Consequently, a novel scope adapter concept (shown in Figure 12-9) was developed and prototyped by Dr. Nikhil Navkar and Mohammad Khorasani to mitigate the effects of including a human operator in the feedback loop. In this implementation, the endoscope and associated camera head are held and controlled via a UR5 robotic arm offering six degrees of freedom, with an additional two degrees of freedom built into the adapter itself enabling the rotation of the scope and camera head around its axis and the angulation of the scope tip. The rotation is powered by a maxon ECX brushless motor, while the angulation is powered by a maxon brushed DCX motor. Each motor is coupled with a reduction gearbox that offers a top speed of 20 and 16 RPM for the rotation and angulation motors, respectively, and a three-channel optical encoder that provides a resolution of 4096 and 2048 steps per revolution, respectively.

Other advantages associated with the surgical scope adapter include the following:

- Ability to support different endoscopes, camera heads, and robotic arms

- Can be controlled with a variety of inputs including a joystick or by tracking optical markers attached to the surgeon's head

- Can be programmed to reduce human error and unintended movements

- Reduces operator strain and fatigue by eliminating the need to manually hold the scope

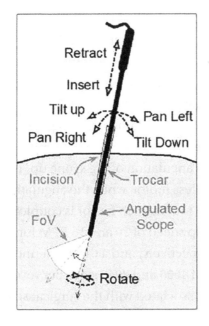

Figure 12-8. *Schematic of an endoscope inserted into the abdomen*

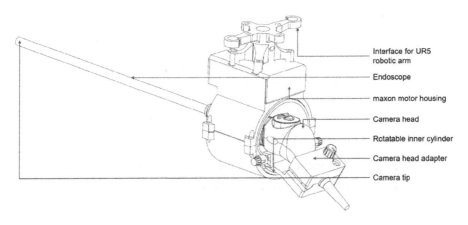

Figure 12-9. *Engineering drawing of the maxon powered surgical scope adapter*

12.2.2 Streamlit Command and Control Dashboard

Upon completion of the mechanical prototype of the surgical scope adapter, a Streamlit application was developed to render a dashboard with the speed and position of the rotation and angulation motors in real time as shown in Figure 12-10. In addition, the Streamlit application was interfaced with a three-axis joystick that was used to control each of the maxon motors as shown in Figure 12-11. Furthermore, by port forwarding the Streamlit application, it was possible to control the motors remotely over the Internet. This is of particular interest for telesurgery, whereby an operator can partake in a surgery without physically being present within the premises of the hospital. Albeit with certain limitations, since with remote control over long distances there is increased latency, which may inhibit the performance of the device.

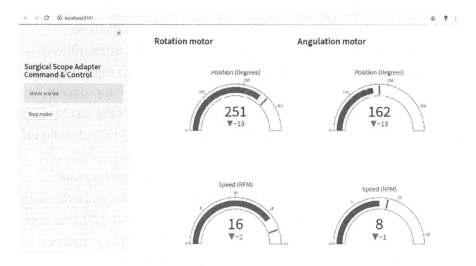

Figure 12-10. *Streamlit command and control dashboard for the surgical scope adapter*

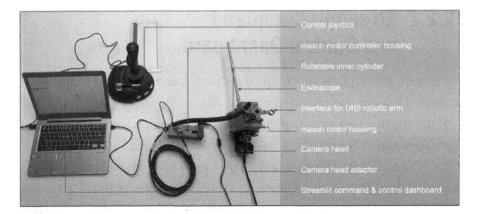

Figure 12-11. *Prototype of the surgical scope adapter with the Streamlit command and control dashboard*

12.2.3 Closing Remarks

While Streamlit is branded as a framework for machine learning and data science applications, it does possess enough versatility to be used for a variety of purposes. As shown in this instance, Streamlit was effectively utilized to bridge several nontrivial subsystems together into one contiguous system. Specifically, Streamlit was used to interface the maxon motors with a joystick, enable remote control over the local area network as well as the Internet, and also to provide a real-time dashboard displaying the motors' position and speed all in a few lines of code.

This work was supported by National Priority Research Program (NPRP) award (NPRP13S-0116-200084) from the Qatar National Research Fund (a member of The Qatar Foundation) and IRGC-04-JI-17-138 award from Medical Research Center (MRC) at Hamad Medical Corporation (HMC). All opinions, findings, conclusions, or recommendations expressed in this work are those of the authors and do not necessarily reflect the views of our sponsors.

12.3 Summary

In this final chapter, we have been acquainted with two real-world instances of Streamlit being utilized effectively for commercial and industrial activities. Namely, the first case demonstrates how Iberdrola – a renewable energy firm – is using Streamlit to create a corporate data management application for their wind farms, to estimate electrical losses during production. The second case expands on an industrial use case whereby high-precision electronic motors manufactured by maxon Group are being commanded and controlled via a Streamlit application, for use within a surgical scope adapter system. Both examples serve to provide evidence of the utility that Streamlit is offering to the corporate world and beyond.

APPENDIX A

Streamlit Application Program Interface

A.1 The Streamlit API

The Streamlit application program interface, hereafter referred to as
the Streamlit API, is the bread and butter of what our formidable web
framework has to offer the world. With several dozen native commands
that cater to rendering text, tables, charts, input widgets, and multimedia
widgets to enacting page layout, data management, state management,
as well as a whole host of other utilities, it is a comprehensive library that
one should acquaint themselves with before proceeding to developing an
application.

A.1.1 Displaying Text

The first series of commands in the Streamlit API accommodate to perhaps
the most primitive need of any web application, namely, that of displaying
text in all of its variety. In this section, we will present the commands that
allow you to display text, rich text, tables, dataframes, plots, markdown,
and more.

© Mohammad Khorasani, Mohamed Abdou, Javier Hernández Fernández 2022
M. Khorasani et al., *Web Application Development with Streamlit*,
https://doi.org/10.1007/978-1-4842-8111-6

Write

Streamlit can display a variety of inputs including but not limited to text, dataframes, and plots using the *st.write(*args, unsafe_allow_html=False)* command. In addition, this command has the following unique attributes:

- You may pass multiple arguments, and all of them will be rendered.

- It will render differently depending on the input.

- The return value of the function is None; therefore, its place in the application cannot be reused.

Table A-1. *st.write parameters*

Parameter	Description
*args(*any*)	Can be used with the following inputs: • string: Renders text, LaTeX expressions, and emoji shortcodes • Data_frame: Displays a dataframe as a table • error: Displays a code exception • func: Displays information about the function • module: Displays information about the module • dict: Displays a dictionary as an interactive widget • mpl_fig: Renders a Matplotlib plot • altair: Renders an Altair plot • keras: Renders a Keras model • graphviz: Renders a Graphviz graph • plotly_fig: Renders a Plotly plot • bokeh_fig: Renders a Bokeh plot • sympy_expr: Displays a SymPy expression formatted as LaTeX • htmlable: displays_repr_html_() for the object if available • obj: Prints the string of an object

(continued)

Table A-1. (*continued*)

Parameter	Description
Unsafe_allow_ html(*bool*)	By default, any HTML detected will be escaped and treated as text. This may be turned off by setting this argument to True, although this is not recommended as it may compromise the users' security.

Displaying text with st.write will be formatted as plain text:

```
st.write('Hello world')
```

Hello world

Markdown format can be used too:

```
st.write('**_Hello_ world**')
```

Outputting:

Hello world

Objects can be passed as arguments, such as dataframes:

```
import pandas as pd

st.write(pd.DataFrame({
    'Column 1': [1, 2, 3, 4],
    'Column 2': [5, 6, 7, 8],
}))
```

The resulting dataframe will be rendered into a nicely formatted table:

	Column 1	Column 2
0	1	5
1	2	6
2	3	7
3	4	8

Several arguments can be passed in the same call and will be printed in order:

```
st.write('A + B =', 'C')
```

$$A + B = C$$

Different objects can be used like the following example with plain text and a dataframe:

```
st.write('Hello world', dataframe)
```

Hello world

	Column 1	Column 2
0	1	5
1	2	6
2	3	7
3	4	8

Charts, figures, and models, such as described in the command parameters, can also be displayed directly using st.write:

```
import pandas as pd
import numpy as np
import altair as alt

dataframe = pd.DataFrame(
    np.random.randn(200, 3),
    columns=['x', 'y', 'z'])

plot = alt.Chart(dataframe).mark_circle().encode(
    x='x', y='y', size='z', color='z', tooltip=['x',
    'y', 'z'])

st.write(plot)
```

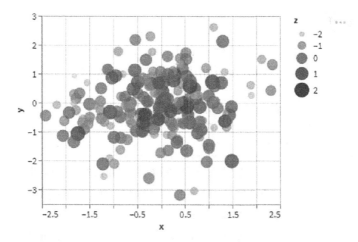

Using st.write is a simple, fast, and convenient way to display data, but more control over the visualization can be obtained using specific API commands. The following subsections will offer a more comprehensive set of tools to display and visualize all types of elements along with the available options to customize the look and feel of the output.

Text

Streamlit displays plain text using the *st.text(str)* command.

Table A-2. *st.text parameters*

Parameter	Description
body(*str*)	The string to display.

Formatted text can be displayed using the *st.text(body)* command:

```
st.text('Hello world')
```

Note that the results are equivalent to the st.write text when inputted as pure text.

```
Hello world
```

385

Markdown

Streamlit can display strings formatted as markdown using the *st. markdown(body,unsafe_allow_html=False)* command.

Table A-3. *st.markdown parameters*

Parameter	Description
body(*str*)	• Can be used to display string as GitHub-style markdown. For additional information, refer to *https://github. github.com/gfm*. • Can also be used with emoji shortcodes. For additional information on all supported shortcodes, refer to *https:// raw.githubusercontent.com/omnidan/node-emoji/ master/lib/emoji.json*. • Can also be used with LaTeX expressions by wrapping them in *$* or *$$*. For additional information, refer to *https://katex. org/docs/supported.html*.
unsafe_allow_ html(*bool*)	By default, any HTML detected will be escaped and treated as text. This may be turned off by setting this argument to True, although this is not recommended as it may compromise the users' security.

Streamlit can display markdown formatted text and easily combine it with LaTeX and emojis:

```
st.markdown('$\overline{ANA}$, **_really_ likes** :doughnut:')
```

As expected, the results are the same that would be obtained using *st. write* with markdown text:

$$\overline{ANA}, \text{ really likes } \bullet$$

Markdown is an easy-to-read and easy-to-write plain text format that gives you the ability to render rich text with formatting that would have otherwise not been possible with normal text. Specifically, it allows you to write bold, italic, hyperlinked, and strike-through text with varying sizes. In addition, markdown permits writing tables, displaying images, and creating bulleted and numbered lists, as well as quotes, code, and checkboxes. For further information, please refer to *https://guides.github.com/features/mastering-markdown/*. An example of each is shown as follows:

- Header sizes can be used to generate headings of various sizes:

```
st.markdown(
"'

# Hello world
## Hello world
### Hello world
#### Hello world
##### Hello world
###### Hello world
"'

)
```

Hello world

Hello world

Hello world

Hello world

Hello world

Hello world

- Text styling can be used to generate bold, italic, and strike-through text:

```
st.markdown('**Hello world**')
st.markdown('_Hello world_')
st.markdown('~~Hello world~~')
```

Hello world

Hello world

~~Hello world~~

- Lists can be used to generate bulleted, numbered, and checkbox lists:

```
st.markdown(
"'

- Hello world
- Hello world
- Hello world
"'
)
st.markdown(
"'

1. Hello world
2. Hello world
3. Hello world
"'
)
st.markdown(
"'
```

```
- [x] Hello world
- [ ] Hello world
" '
)
```

- Hello world
- Hello world
- Hello world

1. Hello world
2. Hello world
3. Hello world

- ☑ Hello world
- ☐ Hello world

- Code can be used to display nonhighlighted and highlighted code according to the programming language specified:

```
st.markdown(
" '
" '
del' hello_world():
    print('Hello world')
" '
" '
)
st.markdown(
" '
"'python
del' hello_world():
```

```
    print('Hello world')
"'

"'

)
```

```
def hello_world():
    print('Hello world')

def hello_world():
    print('Hello world')
```

- Hyperlink can be used to display hyperlinked text:

```
st.markdown('Check out [Streamlit](https://
streamlit.io/)')
```

Check out Streamlit

- Quote can be used to display quoted text:

```
st.markdown('> Hello world')
```

Hello world

- Image can be used to display images:

```
st.markdown('![Image](https://avatars.
githubusercontent.com/u/31454258?v=4)')
```

- Table can be used to display tables:

```
st.markdown(
"""

Name | Score 1 | Score 2
------------ | ------------- | -------------
Jessica | 77 | 76
John | 56 | 97
Alex | 87 | 82
"""

)
```

Name	Score 1	Score 2
Jessica	77	76
John	56	97
Alex	87	82

Title, Header, and Subheader

Typography in Streamlit can be managed using a three-level hierarchy of title, header, and subheader. The commands follow the same naming and accept the same parameterization: *st.title(body, anchor=None), st. header(body, anchor=None)*, and *st.subheader(body, anchor=None)*.

Table A-4. *st.title, st.header, and st.subheader parameters*

Parameter	Description
body(*str*)	The string to display.
anchor(*str*)	The anchor name of the title/header/subheader that can be accessed with #anchor in the URL. If the anchor is not invoked, Streamlit will automatically generate an anchor using the body text.

The format used by Streamlit for the three hierarchical typographies is as follows:

```
st.title('Title')
st.header('Header')
st.subheader('Subheader')
```

Title

Header

Subheader

Caption

Streamlit displays captions with small text using the *st.caption(str)* command.

Table A-5. *st.caption parameters*

Parameter	Description
body(*str*)	The string to display.

Smaller text can be displayed using the caption API for those cases where subheadings or alternative titles are needed:

```
st.title('Title')
st.header('Header')
st.subheader('Subheader')
st.text('Text')
st.caption('Caption')
```

Title

Header

Subheader

Text

Caption

Code

Streamlit renders code with syntax highlighting using the *st.code(body, language='python')* command.

Table A-6. *st.code parameters*

Parameter	Description
body(*str*)	The string to display as code.
language(*str*)	The programming language that the code is written in (used for rendering and syntax highlighting).
	If the language is not set, the code will be left without styling.

The following example displays a block of Python code:

```
code = "'def hello_world(input):
    print(input)"'

st.code(code, language='python')
```

```
def hello_world(input):
    print(input)
```

LaTeX

Streamlit can display mathematical functions formatted as LaTeX using the *st.latex(body)* command.

Table A-7. *st.latex parameters*

Parameter	Description
body(*str or SymPy expression*)	The string and/or SymPy expression to display. For additional information on supported LaTeX functions, refer to *https:// katex.org/docs/supported.html*.

LaTeX can be useful, for instance, for displaying mathematical formulas:

```
st.latex(r"'
    x = \frac{{ - b \pm \sqrt {b^2 - 4ac} }}{{2a}}
    "')
```

$$x = \frac{-b \pm \sqrt{b^2 - 4ac}}{2a}$$

Magic Commands

Magic commands are characterized by Streamlit as functions that enable the developer to render markdown and data to applications in a very concise and easy manner. Whenever Streamlit detects a variable or literal value independently on its own line, it will automatically write that variable to the application using the *st.write* function. In addition, magic commands will ignore docstrings that are located at the beginning of scripts and functions.

Writing text directly without calling any of the Streamlit predefined functions by using the magic command is shown as follows:

Displaying text:

```
" '

# Hello world

Hello _world_
" '
```

Hello world

Hello *world*

Rendering a dataframe:

```
df = pd.DataFrame({'col1': [1,2,3]})
df # <-- Draw the dataframe
```

	col1
0	1
1	2
2	3

Writing the value of a variable:

```
x = 10
'x', x # <-- Draw the string 'x' and then the value of x
```

x 10

If required, you may turn off magic commands by modifying the "/. streamlit/config.toml" file with the following setting:

```
[runner]
magicEnabled = false
```

A.1.2 Displaying Data

Rendering data in all of its variety comes seamlessly with Streamlit. Using a host of native commands, you may display Pandas dataframes, tables, JSON documents, metrics, lists, and other miscellaneous data types.

Dataframes

Dataframes are displayed by Streamlit formatted as an interactive table using the *st.dataframe(data=None, width=None, height=None)* command.

Table A-8. *st.dataframe parameters*

Parameter	Description
data(*pandas.DataFrame, pandas.Styler, pyarrow.Table, numpy.ndarray, Iterable, dict, or None*)	The data to be displayed: • Pandas.Styler: The pandas styling will be used on the dataframe, including most common cell values and colors. Enhanced features such as hovering, captions, or charts are currently not supported. Support for Styler is experimental. • PyArrow tables: PyArrow tables must be enabled by setting config. dataFrameSerialization = "arrow". PyArrow tables are not supported by default by Streamlit's legacy dataframe serialization (i.e., with config.dataFrameSerialization = "legacy").
width(*int or None*)	Width of the UI element in pixels. The default None value will set the width to the one of the page where it is being used.
height(*int or None*)	If the height is set to None, it will equal the height of the page on which it is being used.

The following example displays a dataframe using a heatmap that colors the intensity of the values as compared to other values, using a predefined Matplotlib green colormap and a fixed width of 1000 pixels:

```
df = pd.DataFrame(
    np.random.randn(10, 5),
    columns=('col %d' % i for i in range(5)))

st.dataframe(df.style.background_gradient(), width=1000)
```

	col 0	col 1	col 2	col 3	col 4
0	1.061499	-0.291019	0.149068	1.814765	1.888504
1	-0.752507	0.579338	0.321254	0.339250	0.635232
2	0.379036	-0.145958	-0.325872	0.074630	0.701430
3	2.240969	-1.092776	-0.038628	-1.001478	0.894297
4	1.321030	0.437146	-0.407014	0.077579	-0.264758
5	-1.063232	0.155793	0.240327	-1.651435	0.152272
6	-1.687019	0.080499	0.035114	0.258817	-0.717632
7	0.337745	-0.001519	-1.579446	0.210844	0.589688
8	-0.049692	0.257333	-0.820782	0.205581	0.541947
9	-0.946691	-0.172131	1.125705	0.706602	0.949064

Tables

Static tables are displayed with the *st.table(data=None)* command.

Table A-9. *st.table parameters*

Parameter	Description
data(*pandas.DataFrame, pandas.Styler, pyarrow.Table, numpy.ndarray, Iterable, dict, or None*)	The table data. PyArrow tables must be enabled by setting config.dataFrameSerialization = "arrow". PyArrow tables are not supported by default by Streamlit's legacy dataframe serialization (i.e., with config. dataFrameSerialization = "legacy").

Following the dataframe example, static tables are displayed in the same manner:

```
df = pd.DataFrame(
    np.random.randn(10, 5),
    columns=('col %d' % i for i in range(5)))

st.table(df)
```

	col 0	col 1	col 2	col 3	col 4
0	0.7279	-1.1807	0.1936	-0.6533	-0.3697
1	0.1067	-0.4488	0.3468	0.3638	-0.3759
2	0.3180	0.1942	-0.1919	0.1770	0.2888
3	0.0355	-2.5309	-1.4406	0.3532	0.2755
4	1.2458	-0.2047	-0.1120	0.9540	0.6066
5	0.6839	0.3503	-0.3679	0.6452	2.2059
6	-0.1486	0.3748	-0.6073	1.2363	0.6223
7	-0.2847	-0.1722	1.4219	0.1400	1.2036
8	0.2957	-0.6081	2.8828	0.7309	-0.9761
9	-1.4335	0.3622	-0.7720	2.0623	-1.1737

JSON

An interactive representation of a JSON file can be displayed in Streamlit using the *st.json(body)* command.

Table A-10. *st.json parameters*

Parameter	Description
body(*Object or str*)	The object to be printed as a JSON. The object or string referenced must be serializable to JSON.
expanded(*bool*)	Setting this parameter to True will set the initial state of the JSON element to expanded. By default, it is True.

The following example shows a simple representation of a JSON object. The interactive visualization of Streamlit allows folding and unfolding of the branches.

```
st.json({
    'A': 'a',
    'B': 'b',
    'C': [
        'ca',
        'cb',
        'cc',
        'cd',
    ],
    'D': 'd',
})
```

```
▾ {
    "A" : "a"
    "B" : "b"
    ▾ "C" : [
        0 : "ca"
        1 : "cb"
        2 : "cc"
        3 : "cd"
    ]
    "D" : "d"
}
```

Metric

The *st.metric(label, value, delta=None, delta_color='normal')* command displays in large and bold fonts a metric, indicator, or variable in a dashboard style. An optional change of status indicator can be added.

Table A-11. *st.metric parameters*

Parameter	Description
label(*str*)	The title for the metric.
value(*int, str, or None*)	Value given to the metric. None is rendered as a long dash.
delta(*int, str, or None*)	Small subindicator below the main one showing the change with regard to the last status. For negative numbers (int or float), or strings starting with a minus sign, the arrow will be rendered in red and pointing down; all other options will show in green and the arrow pointing up. If the delta is set to None (the default option), this subindicator will not be presented.
delta_color(*str*)	This attribute inverses the color and the arrow by default for positive and negative values. It is intended for those cases where a negative change might be considered good, and vice versa. If set to "off," the delta will be shown in gray for all cases.

The following example shows a metric indicator of temperature without its delta. The indicator is then adjusted with the delta option to reflect the change from the previous value.

```
st.metric('Temperature', '26.7 C', '2.7 C')
```

Temperature

26.7 C
↑ 2.7 C

A.1.3 Displaying Charts

Another area that Streamlit excels in is in visualizing data. Whether it is rendering a chart using their native command or displaying a third-party chart from Matplotlib, Altair, Vega-Lite, Plotly, Bokeh, PyDeck, or Graphviz, Streamlit allows you to integrate visualizations effortlessly.

Line, Area, and Bar Charts

Simple line, area, and bar charts can be rendered using the *st.line_chart, st. area_chart*, and *st.bar_chart* commands. To display a chart, you may use the following command: *st.line_chart/st.area_chart/st.bar_chart(data, width, height, use_container_width).*

Table A-12. *st.line_chart, st.area_chart, and st.bar_chart parameters*

Parameter	Description
data(*pandas.DataFrame, pandas.Styler, pyarrow.Table, numpy.ndarray, Iterable, dict or None*)	The data to be plotted. Streamlit's legacy dataframe serialization does not include support for PyArrow tables (i.e., config.dataFrameSerialization = 'legacy'). To utilize PyArrow tables, change the config setting to config.dataFrameSerialization = 'arrow'.
width(*int*)	The chart's width dimensions in pixels. If zero, the width is determined automatically.
height(*int*)	The chart's height dimensions in pixels. If zero, the width is determined automatically.
use_container_width(*bool*)	When True, the chart width will adjust to the column width. This argument has precedence over the width argument.

The following example shows the use of the three graphing options stacked and limited in height:

```
chart_data = pd.DataFrame(
    np.random.randn(10, 2),
    columns=['Value 1', 'Value 2'])
st.line_chart(chart_data, height=125)
st.area_chart(chart_data, height=125)
st.bar_chart(chart_data, height=125)
```

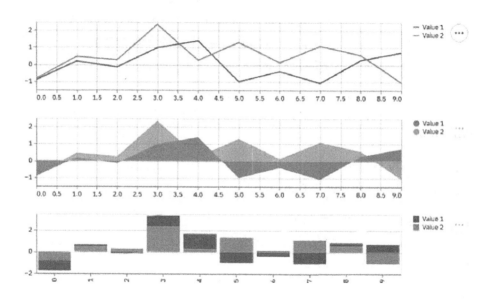

Pyplot

A Matplotlib chart can be rendered using the following command: *st. pyplot(fig, clear_figure, **kwargs)*.

Table A-13. *st.pyplot parameters*

Parameter	Description
fig(*Matplotlib Figure*)	Figure to be plotted.
clear_figure(*bool*)	The figure will be cleared after being rendered when True. The figure will not be cleared after being rendered when False. When left unspecified, we pick a default based on the value of *fig*: • If *fig* is set, it defaults to False. • If *fig* is not set, it defaults to True. Similar to the Jupyter's approach to Matplotlib rendering.
**kwargs(*any*)	Matplotlib's savefig function arguments.

The following example shows how to display a Matplotlib bar chart in Streamlit:

```
import numpy as np
import matplotlib.pyplot as plt

data = np.random.randn(10, 3)
fig, ax = plt.subplots()
ax.hist(data, bins=10)

st.pyplot(fig)
```

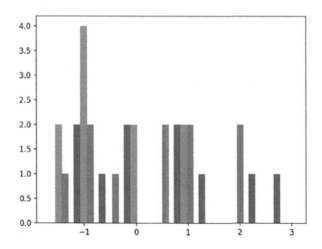

Altair

An Altair chart can be displayed using the following command: *st.altair_chart(altair_chart, use_container_width)*.

Table A-14. *st.altair_chart parameters*

Parameter	Description
altair_chart(*altair.vegalite.v2.api.Chart*)	Altair figure object to render.
use_container_width(*bool*)	If this argument is set to *True*, the chart width will be set to the column width.

The following example shows how to display an Altair scatter plot in Streamlit:

```
import pandas as pd
import numpy as np
import altair as alt

df = pd.DataFrame(np.random.randn(30, 3), columns=['Col1',
'Col2','Col3'])
```

```
fig = alt.Chart(df).mark_circle().encode(
    x='Col1', y='Col2', size='Col3',
    color='Col3',
    tooltip=['Col1', 'Col2', 'Col3']
    )
st.altair_chart(fig)
```

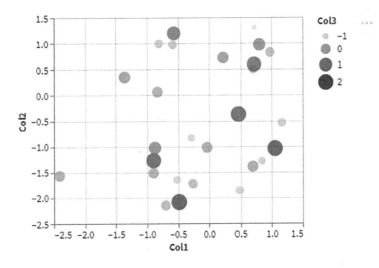

Vega-Lite

A Vega-Lite chart can be displayed using the following command: *st.vega_lite_chart(data, spec, use_container_width, **kwargs)*.

Table A-15. *st.vega_lite_chart parameters*

Parameter	Description
data(*pandas.DataFrame, pandas.Styler, pyarrow. Table, numpy.ndarray, Iterable, dict or None*)	The data to be plotted. Streamlit's legacy dataframe serialization does not include support for pyarrow tables (i.e., config.dataFrameSerialization = 'legacy'). To utilize PyArrow tables, change the config setting to config.dataFrameSerialization = 'arrow'.
spec(*dict or None*)	The specification for the Vega-Lite chart. If the argument has already been set previously, this must be set to None. Please refer to.https://vega.github. io/vega-lite/docs/ for additional information.
use_container_width(*bool*)	When True, the chart width will adjust to the column width. This argument has precedence over the Vega-Lite native argument.
**kwargs(*any*)	Keyword version of spec parameter.

The following example shows how to display a Vega-Lite scatter plot in Streamlit:

```
import pandas as pd
import numpy as np

df = pd.DataFrame(np.random.randn(30, 3), columns=['Col1',
'Col2','Col3'])

st.vega_lite_chart(df, {
    'mark': {'type': 'circle', 'tooltip': True},
    'encoding': {
        'x': {'field': 'Col1', 'type': 'quantitative'},
        'y': {'field': 'Col2', 'type': 'quantitative'},
```

```
        'size': {'field': 'Col3', 'type': 'quantitative'},
        'color': {'field': 'Col3', 'type': 'quantitative'},
    },
}, width=500, height=400)
```

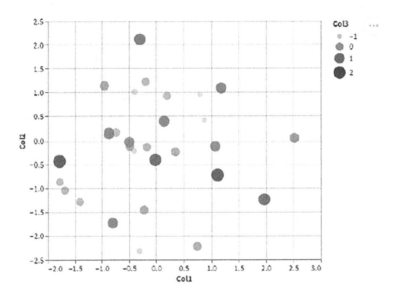

Plotly

A Plotly chart can be displayed using the command *st.plotly_chart(figure_or_data, use_container_width, sharing, **kwargs)*.

Table A-16. *st.plotly_chart parameters*

Parameter	Description
figure_or_data(*plotly.graph_objs.Figure, plotly.graph_objs.Data*)	The Plotly figure object to be rendered. For further information regarding Plotly Python charts, please refer to *https://plot.ly/python/*.
use_container_width(*bool*)	If this argument is set to *True*, the chart width will be set to the column width.
sharing(*{'streamlit', 'private', 'secret', 'public'}*)	This argument will specify the mode of rendering. If it is set to "*streamlit*," the chart will be displayed in Plotly's offline mode. Other modes will require access to a Plotly chart studio account; for further information, please refer to *https://plotly.com/chart-studio/*.
**kwargs(*null*)	Any argument that is accepted by Plotly's *plot()* function may be provided here.

The following example shows how to display a Plotly radar plot in Streamlit:

```
import pandas as pd
import numpy as np
import plotly.express as px

df = pd.DataFrame(np.random.randn(360, 1), columns=['Col1'])

fig = px.line_polar(df, r=df['Col1'], theta=df.index,
line_close=True)
st.plotly_chart(fig)
```

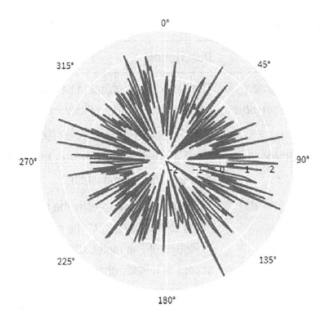

Bokeh

A Bokeh chart can be displayed using the command *st.bokeh_chart(figure, use_container_width)*.

Table A-17. *st.bokeh_chart parameters*

Parameter	Description
figure(*bokeh.plotting.figure.Figure*)	The Bokeh figure object to be rendered.
use_container_width(*bool*)	If this argument is set to *True*, the chart width will be set to the column width.

The following example shows how to display a Bokeh line chart in Streamlit:

```
import pandas as pd
import numpy as np
from bokeh.plotting import figure
```

```
df = pd.DataFrame(np.random.randn(10, 1), columns=['Col1'])

fig = figure(
    x_axis_label='Index',
    y_axis_label='Col1')
fig.line(df.index, df['Col1'], legend_label='Trend',
line_width=2)

st.bokeh_chart(fig)
```

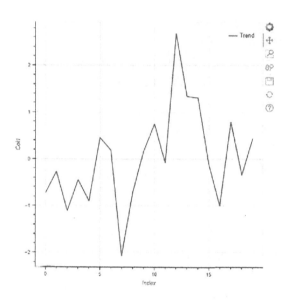

PyDeck

A PyDeck geospatial map can be displayed using the command *st.pydeck_chart(pydeck_obj, use_container_width)*.

Table A-18. *st.pydeck_chart parameters*

Parameter	Description
spec(*pydeck.Deck or None*)	The PyDeck figure object to be rendered.

The following example shows how to display a PyDeck geospatial map in Streamlit:

```python
import pandas as pd
import numpy as np
import pydeck as pdk

df = pd.DataFrame(
    np.random.randn(100, 2)/[50, 50] + [29.76, -95.37],
    columns=['latitude', 'longitude'])

st.pydeck_chart(pdk.Deck(
    map_style='mapbox://styles/mapbox/light-v9',
    initial_view_state=pdk.ViewState(
        latitude=29.76,
        longitude=-95.37,
        zoom=12,
        pitch=40,
    ),
    layers=[
        pdk.Layer(
            'HexagonLayer',
            data=df,
            get_position='[longitude, latitude]',
            radius=200,
            elevation_scale=2,
            elevation_range=[0, 500],
            pickable=True,
            extruded=True,
        ),
    ],
))
```

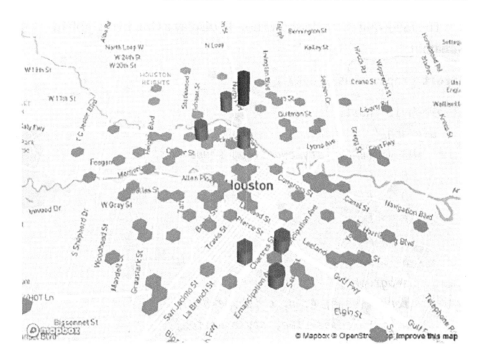

Graphviz

A Graphviz chart can be rendered using the command *st.graphviz_chart(figure_or_dot, use_container_width)*.

Table A-19. *st.graphviz_chart parameters*

Parameter	Description
figure_or_dot(*graphviz.dot.Graph, graphviz.dot.Digraph, str*)	The Graphviz figure object to be rendered.
use_container_width(*bool*)	If this argument is set to *True*, the chart width will be set to the column width.

413

The following example shows how to display a Graphviz graph in Streamlit:

```python
import graphviz as graphviz

st.graphviz_chart("'
    digraph {
        A -> {B C} [style=dotted, shape=box]
        B -> C
        D -> F
        F -> E
        E -> A
        B -> D
        subgraph {
        rank = same; A; B; C [shape=box];
        A -> E [color=blue, style=dotted]
        }
    }
"')
```

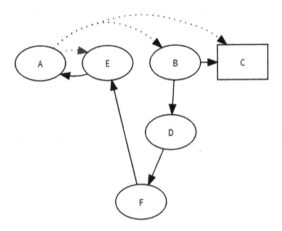

Maps

A Streamlit geospatial map can be displayed using the command *st. map(data, zoom, use_container_width)*.

Table A-20. *st.map parameters*

Parameter	Description
data(*pandas.DataFrame, pandas.Styler, numpy.ndarray, Iterable, dict*)	The *latitude* and *longitude* of the points to be rendered on the map.
zoom(*int*)	The level of zoom when the map is first rendered. For further information, please refer to *https:// wiki.openstreetmap.org/wiki/Zoom_levels*.

The following example shows how to display a geospatial map in Streamlit:

```python
import pandas as pd
import numpy as np

df = pd.DataFrame(
    np.random.randn(100, 2)/[50, 50] + [29.76, -95.37],
    columns=['latitude', 'longitude'])

st.map(df)
```

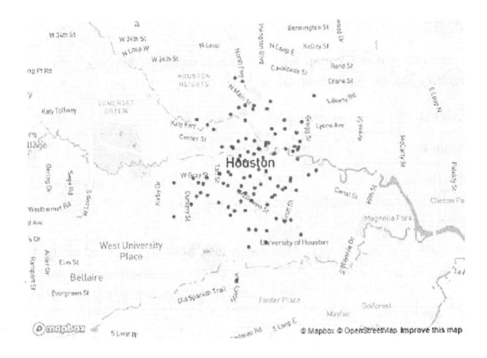

A.1.4 Input Widgets

Streamlit offers a rich and diverse set of input widgets that enable the developer to cater to a wide variety of use cases. From simple buttons, sliders, and forms to color selectors, file uploaders, and select boxes, Streamlit possesses the entire spectrum of inputs.

Buttons

General-purpose buttons can be created for any requirement with the command *st.button(label, key, help, on_click, args, kwargs, disabled=False)* ➤ *bool*.

Table A-21. *st.button parameters*

Parameter	Description
label(*str*)	Label to be displayed in the button.
key(*str or int*)	Unique key, string or integer, to reference the button in the code. The parameter is optional and will be automatically generated if not provided.
help(*str*)	Tooltip to be displayed when the cursor is hovered over the widget.
on_click(*callable*)	Callback function called when the button is clicked.
args(*tuple*)	Tuple of arguments to pass to the callback.
kwargs(*dict*)	Dictionary of keyword arguments to pass to the callback.
disabled(*bool*)	Boolean argument used to disable the widget.

The following example displays the results of a simple arithmetic calculation when the button is clicked:

```
def addition(a,b):
    result = a + b
    return result

if st.button('Not very useful button', key='b1'):
    st.text('Not very useful button clicked')
    st.write(addition(1,2))
```

> Not very useful button

Not very useful button clicked

3

417

Download Button

Download buttons can be added to our websites with the following command: *st.download_button(label, data, file_name, mime, key, help, on_click, args, kwargs, disabled=False)* ➤ *bool*.

Table A-22. *st.download_button parameters*

Parameter	Description
label(*str*)	Label explaining the use of the button.
data(*str or bytes or file*)	The contents of the file to download. Use caching to avoid recomputing on every rerun.
file_name(*str*)	Name of the file to be downloaded. If not specified, a name will be created automatically.
mime(*str or None*)	The data MIME type. The default is "text/plain" for text files or "application/octet-stream" for binary files.
key(*str or int*)	Unique key, string or integer, to reference the button in the code. The parameter is optional and will be automatically generated if not provided.
help(*str*)	Tooltip to be displayed when the cursor is hovered over the widget.
on_click(*callable*)	Callback function called when the button is clicked.
args(*tuple*)	Tuple of arguments to pass to the callback.
kwargs(*dict*)	Dictionary of keyword arguments to pass to the callback.
disabled(*bool*)	Boolean argument used to disable the widget.

The following example displays how a Pandas dataframe can be downloaded as a CSV file using a download button:

```
import pandas as pd

data = pd.DataFrame({'a':[1,2,3],'b':[4,5,6]}).to_csv().
encode('utf-8')

st.download_button(
    label='Download CSV', data=data, file_name='data.csv',
    mime='text/csv')
```

Checkbox

A checkbox can be added to our websites with the following command: *st.checkbox(label, value, key, help, on_change, args, kwargs, disabled=False)* ➤ *bool*.

Table A-23. *st.checkbox parameters*

Parameter	Description
label(*str*)	Label of the checkbox.
value(*bool*)	Chose whether the checkbox is preselected by default when first rendered. Internally, this will be cast to bool.
key(*str or int*)	Unique key, string or integer, to reference the button in the code. The parameter is optional and will be automatically generated if not provided.
help(*str*)	Tooltip to be displayed when the cursor is hovered over the widget.

(*continued*)

Table A-23. (*continued*)

Parameter	Description
on_change(*callable*)	Callback function invoked when the widget's value changes.
args(*tuple*)	Tuple of arguments to pass to the callback.
kwargs(*dict*)	Dictionary of keyword arguments to pass to the callback.
disabled(*bool*)	Boolean argument used to disable the widget.

The checked and unchecked behavior of a checkbox widget is shown as follows:

```
choice = st.checkbox('Healthy choice')

if choice:
    st.write(':broccoli:')
else:
    st.write(':doughnut:')
```

(a) Unchecked checkbox choice   (b) Wise choice

Radio Button

A radio button can be added to our websites using the following command: *st.radio(label, options, index, format_func=special_internal_function, key, help, on_change, args, kwargs, disabled=False)* ➤ *any.*

Table A-24. *st.radio parameters*

Parameter	Description
label(*str*)	Label of the radio group.
options(*Sequence, numpy. ndarray, pandas.Series, pandas. DataFrame, or pandas.Index*)	Radio option labels. It will automatically cast to str. When using pandas.DataFrame, the first column will be selected as a source.
index(*int*)	Preselected option index on first render.
format_func(*function*)	Auxiliary function used to modify the radio option labels. The str values for the labels are passed as arguments, and it returns a modified str as per the function logic. This option is purely cosmetic and has no impact in the operation or return values of the radio widget.
key(*str or int*)	Unique key, string or integer, to reference the button in the code. The parameter is optional and will be automatically generated if not provided.
help(*str*)	Tooltip to be displayed when the cursor is hovered over the widget.
on_change(*callable*)	Callback function invoked when the widget's value changes.
args(*tuple*)	Tuple of arguments to pass to the callback.
kwargs(*dict*)	Dictionary of keyword arguments to pass to the callback.
disabled(*bool*)	Boolean argument used to disable the widget.

The following example displays a two-option radio button and displays the selection:

```
sport_selection = st.radio("What's the best football club in
the World",
('Real Madrid', 'Other team'))

if sport_selection == 'Real Madrid':
    st.write('That was easy :soccer:.')
else:
    st.write('You are clearly wrong.')
```

What's the best football club in the World

◯ Real Madrid
◉ Other team

You are clearly wrong.

Select Box

A select box widget can be added to our websites using the following command: *st.selectbox(label, options, index, format_func=special_internal_ function, key, help, on_change, args=None, kwargs, disabled=False)* ➤ *any.*

Table A-25. *st.selectbox parameters*

Parameter	Description
label(*str*)	Label of the widget.
options(*Sequence, numpy. ndarray, pandas.Series, pandas. DataFrame, or pandas.Index*)	Select option labels. It will automatically cast to str. When using pandas.DataFrame, the first column will be selected as a source.
index(*int*)	Preselected option index on first render.

(continued)

Table A-25. *(continued)*

Parameter	Description
format_func(*function*)	Auxiliary function used to modify the option selection labels. The str values for the labels are passed as arguments, and it returns a modified str as per the function logic. This option is purely cosmetic and has no impact in the operation or return values of the widget.
key(*str* or *int*)	Unique key, string or integer, to reference the button in the code. The parameter is optional and will be automatically generated if not provided.
help(*str*)	Tooltip to be displayed when the cursor is hovered over the widget.
on_change(*callable*)	Callback function invoked when the widget's value changes.
args(*tuple*)	Tuple of arguments to pass to the callback.
kwargs(*dict*)	Dictionary of keyword arguments to pass to the callback.
disabled(*bool*)	Boolean argument used to disable the widget.

The following example displays a select box widget with two options:

```
option = st.selectbox('What would you like to watch?',
('Cricket', 'Baseball'))

st.write('You selected: **%s**' % option)
```

What would you like to watch?

Cricket

You selected: **Cricket**

423

Multiselect Box

A multiple selection widget can be added to our websites with the
following command: *st.multiselect(label, options, default=None, format_
func=special_internal_function, key=None, help=None, on_change=None,
args=None, kwargs=None, disabled=False)* ➤ *str*.

Table A-26. *st.multiselect parameters*

Parameter	Description
label(*str*)	Label of the multiselect widget.
options(*Sequence, numpy.ndarray, pandas. Series, pandas.DataFrame, or pandas.Index*)	Select option labels. It will automatically cast to str. When using pandas.DataFrame, the first column will be selected as a source.
index(*int*)	Preselected option index on first render.
default(*[str] or None*)	Default values.
format_func(*function*)	Auxiliary function used to modify the selection labels. The str values for the labels are passed as arguments, and it returns a modified str as per the function logic. This option is purely cosmetic and has no impact in the operation or return values of the widget.
key(*str or int*)	Unique key, string or integer, to reference the button in the code. The parameter is optional and will be automatically generated if not provided.
help(*str*)	Tooltip to be displayed when the cursor is hovered over the widget.
on_change(*callable*)	Callback function invoked when the widget's value changes.
args(*tuple*)	Tuple of arguments to pass to the callback.
kwargs(*dict*)	Dictionary of keyword arguments to pass to the callback.
disabled(*bool*)	Boolean argument used to disable the widget.

The following example shows a multiselect widget with available four options:

```
options = st.multiselect('What are your favorite seasons?',
['Spring', 'Summer', 'Autumn', 'Winter'])

st.write('You selected: %s' % ', '.join(options))
```

What are your favorite seasons?

You selected: Spring, Autumn

Slider

A slider can be added to our websites using the following command: *st. slider(label, min_value, max_value, value, step, format, key, help, on_ change, args, kwargs, disabled=False)* ➤ *value.*

Table A-27. *st.slider parameters*

Parameter	Description
label(*str*)	Label explaining the use of the slider.
min_value(*a supported type or None*)	The minimum allowed value. It defaults to 0 or 0.0 for int and floats, value – timedelta(days=14) for date/date-time values, time.min if a time.
max_value(*a supported type or None*)	The maximum allowed value. Defaults to 100 or 1.0 for int and float, value + timedelta(days=14) for date/date-time values, time.max if a time.
value(*a supported type or a tuple/list of supported types or None*)	The default value to be used when the widget is first rendered. To use a predefined range, a tuple/list should be passed as an argument with the min and max values. Defaults to min_value.

(continued)

425

Table A-27. (*continued*)

Parameter	Description
step(*int/float/timedelta or None*)	The stepping interval. By default, set to 1 and 0.01 for int and float, timedelta(days=1) for date/datetime values, timedelta(minutes=15) if a time (or if max_value – min_value < 1 day).
format(*str or None*)	A custom format string that specifies how the interface should render numbers in a printf-style format. The return value is not affected by the conversion. %d, %e, %f, %g, and %i are supported for formatting int/float values. For date/time/datetime formatting, use Moment. js syntax: `https://momentjs.com/docs/#/displaying/format/`.
key(*str or int*)	Unique key, string or integer, to reference the button in the code. The parameter is optional and will be automatically generated if not provided.
help(*str*)	Tooltip to be displayed when the cursor is hovered over the widget.
on_change(*callable*)	Callback function invoked when the widget's value changes.
args(*tuple*)	Tuple of arguments to pass to the callback.
kwargs(*dict*)	Dictionary of keyword arguments to pass to the callback.
disabled(*bool*)	Boolean argument used to disable the widget.

The following code implements a slider to select a time between 9.00 and 16.00 hours:

```
from datetime import time

meeting_time = st.slider('Select time:', value = time(11,00),
    max_value = time(16,00), min_value = (time(9, 00)),
    format='hh:mm')

st.write('You are scheduled for: **%s**' % meeting_time)
```

Select time:

11:00

09:00   04:00

You are scheduled for: **11:00:00**

Select Slider

A select slider widget can be added to our websites using the following command: *st.select_slider(label, options, value, format_func, key, help, on_change, args, kwargs) ➤ value.*

Table A-28. *st.select_slider parameters*

Parameter	Description
label(*str*)	Label explaining the use of the slider.
options(*Sequence, numpy. ndarray, pandas.Series, pandas. DataFrame, or pandas.Index*)	Radio option labels. It will automatically cast to str. When using pandas.DataFrame, the first column will be selected as a source.
value(*a supported type or a tuple/list of supported types or None*)	The value of the slider at the time it is first displayed. If a tuple/list of two values is supplied here, a range slider with those lower and upper limits will be created. Defaults to the first option.

(continued)

Table A-28. (*continued*)

Parameter	Description
format_func(*function*)	Auxiliary function used to modify the radio option labels. The str values for the labels are passed as arguments, and it returns a modified str as per the function logic. This option is purely cosmetic and has no impact in the operation or return values of the radio widget.
key(*str or int*)	Unique key, string or integer, to reference the button in the code. The parameter is optional and will be automatically generated if not provided.
help(*str*)	Tooltip to be displayed when the cursor is hovered over the widget.
on_change(*callable*)	Callback function invoked when the widget's value changes.
args(*tuple*)	Tuple of arguments to pass to the callback.
kwargs(*dict*)	Dictionary of keyword arguments to pass to the callback.
disabled(*bool*)	Boolean argument used to disable the widget.

A select slider is a version of the slider widget for nonnumerical, date, or time values. The following example replicates the one from the simple slider but with categorical values:

```
start_time, end_time = st.select_slider('Select time',
    options=['nine', 'ten', 'eleven', 'twelve', 'one', 'two',
    'three', 'four'],
    value=('eleven', 'twelve'))
```

```
st.write('You are scheduled from **%s** to **%s**' % (start_
time, end_time))
```

Select time

eleven   twelve

nine   four

You are scheduled from **eleven** to **twelve**

Text Input

A single-line text input box can be added to our websites with the following command: *st.text_input(label, value, max_chars, key, type='default,' help, autocomplete, on_change, args, kwargs, placeholder, disabled=False)* ➤ *str.*

Table A-29. *st.text_input parameters*

Parameter	Description
label(*str*)	Label explaining the use of this input.
value(*any*)	Chose whether the checkbox is preselected by default when first rendered. Internally, this will be cast to str.
max_chars(*int or None*)	Maximum number of characters permitted in text input.
key(*str or int*)	Unique key, string or integer, to reference the button in the code. The parameter is optional and will be automatically generated if not provided.
type(*str*)	Text input type: regular text input (the "default" option) or masked text (for type input "password").
help(*str*)	Tooltip to be displayed when the cursor is hovered over the widget.

(*continued*)

Table A-29. (*continued*)

Parameter	Description
autocomplete(*str*)	The autocomplete attribute is a new method added to HTML 5. It is intended for websites that want the user to be able to complete a task without having access to their username and password. An optional value will be supplied to the <input> element's autocomplete property. This value will be set to "new-password" for "password" input types and the empty string for "default" input types. More details in `https://developer.mozilla.org/en-US/docs/Web/HTML/Attributes/autocomplete`.
on_change(*callable*)	Callback function invoked when the widget's value changes.
args(*tuple*)	Tuple of arguments to pass to the callback.
kwargs(*dict*)	Dictionary of keyword arguments to pass to the callback.
placeholder(*str or None*)	Optional string to be displayed if there is no text input.
disabled(*bool*)	Boolean argument used to disable the widget.

The example shows the use of mask text in a single-line text box:

```
password = st.text_input('Insert your password:', value='1234',
max_chars = 24,
    type = 'password')

st.write('The entered password is', password)
```

Insert your password:

••••   4/24

The entered password is 1234

Number Input

A numeric input widget can be added to our websites with the following command: *st.number_input(label, min_value, max_value, value=0.0, step=1, format, key, help, on_change, args, kwargs, disabled=False)* ➤ *int or float.*

Table A-30. *st.number_input parameters*

Parameter	Description
label(*str*)	Label for the number input widget.
min_value(*int or float or None*)	The minimum accepted value.
max_value(*int or float or None*)	The maximum accepted value.
value(*int or float or None*)	First render value of this widget. Defaults to min_value, or 0.0 if min_value is None.
step(*int or float or None*)	The stepping interval. By default, set to 1 for int and 0.01 for all other options. For no specified values, it will default to the format parameter.
format(*str or None*)	A custom format string that specifies how the interface should render numbers in a printf-style format. The return value is not affected by the conversion. %d, %e, %f, %g, and %i are supported for formatting int/float values. For date/time/datetime formatting, use Moment.js syntax: `https://momentjs.com/docs/#/displaying/format/`.
key(*str or int*)	Unique key, string or integer, to reference the button in the code. The parameter is optional and will be automatically generated if not provided.

(continued)

431

Table A-30. (*continued*)

Parameter	Description
help(*str*)	Tooltip to be displayed when the cursor is hovered over the widget.
on_change(*callable*)	Callback function invoked when the widget's value changes.
args(*tuple*)	Tuple of arguments to pass to the callback.
kwargs(*dict*)	Dictionary of keyword arguments to pass to the callback.
disabled(*bool*)	Boolean argument used to disable the widget.

A simple 1 to 100 selection, in steps of 1 unit, snippet implementation of the number input command is shown as follows:

```
selection = st.number_input('Choose a number from 1 to 100:',
    min_value = 0, max_value = 100, value = 50, step = 1)

st.write('The current number is ', selection)
```

Choose a number from 1 to 100:

50   −   +

The current number is 50

Text Area

A multiline text input can be added to our websites with the following command: *st.text_area(label, value, height, max_chars, key, help, on_change, args, kwargs, placeholder, disabled=False)* ➤ *str*.

Table A-31. *st.text_area parameters*

Parameter	Description
label(*str*)	Label explaining the use of the input widget.
value(*any*)	Default text shown when the widget is first rendered. Internally, this will be cast to str.
height(*int or None*)	Height in pixels of the UI element.
max_chars(*int or None*)	The maximum number of characters permitted in the text area.
key(*str or int*)	Unique key, string or integer, to reference the button in the code. The parameter is optional and will be automatically generated if not provided.
help(*str*)	Tooltip to be displayed when the cursor is hovered over the widget.
on_change(*callable*)	Callback function invoked when the widget's value changes.
args(*tuple*)	Tuple of arguments to pass to the callback.
kwargs(*dict*)	Dictionary of keyword arguments to pass to the callback.
placeholder(*str or None*)	A string that will be displayed when the text area is empty.
disabled(*bool*)	Boolean argument used to disable the widget.

The multiline text input widget can be used as follows:

```
text = st.text_area(label = 'Insert text:', value = "Hello
world", height = 50)

st.write('Entered text: **%s**' % text)
```

Insert text:

Hello world

Entered text: **Hello world**

Date Input

A date display input widget can be added to our websites using the following command: *st.date_input(label, value, min_value, max_value, key, help, on_change, args, kwargs, disabled=False) ➤ value.*

Table A-32. *st.date_input parameters*

Parameter	Description
label(*str*)	Label explaining the intent of the date selection.
value(*datetime.date or datetime. datetime or list/tuple of datetime. date or datetime.datetime or None*)	Value showed by this widget during the first render. If a list/tuple is provided with zero to two date/datetime values, it will be considered as a range. Today is the default value if nothing is selected.
min_value(*datetime.date or datetime.datetime*)	The default minimum selectable date. If the value is a date, it will be set to 10 years from now. For intervals [start, finish], start − 10 years is assumed.
max_value(*datetime.date or datetime.datetime*)	The maximum selectable date. If the value is a date, it will be updated with 10 years added. If the value is the period [start, end], it will be updated to end + 10 years.

(continued)

Table A-32. (*continued*)

Parameter	Description
key(*str or int*)	Unique key, string or integer, to reference the button in the code. The parameter is optional and will be automatically generated if not provided.
help(*str*)	Tooltip to be displayed when the cursor is hovered over the widget.
on_change(*callable*)	Callback function invoked when the widget's value changes.
args(*tuple*)	Tuple of arguments to pass to the callback.
kwargs(*dict*)	Dictionary of keyword arguments to pass to the callback.
disabled(*bool*)	Boolean argument used to disable the widget.

The following lines of code implement a simple age in days calculator with the date input widget, limiting the lower value to those born after 1920:

```
birth_date = st.date_input('Date of Birth:', value = datetime.
date(2018,12,29), min_value = datetime.date(1920,1,1))

st.write('Your age in days:', datetime.date.today() -
birth_date)
```

Date of Birth:

2018/12/29

Your age in days: 1060 days, 0:00:00

Time Input

A time input widget can be added to our websites using the following command: *st.time_input(label, value, key, help, on_change, args, kwargs, disabled=False)* ➤ *value.*

Table A-33. *st.time_input parameters*

Parameter	Description
label(*str*)	Label of the widget.
value(*datetime.time/ datetime.datetime*)	Value showed by this widget during the first render. Cast internally to str. Current time is the default.
key(*str or int*)	Unique key, string or integer, to reference the button in the code. The parameter is optional and will be automatically generated if not provided.
help(*str*)	Tooltip to be displayed when the cursor is hovered over the widget.
on_change(*callable*)	Callback function invoked when the widget's value changes.
args(*tuple*)	Tuple of arguments to pass to the callback.
kwargs(*dict*)	Dictionary of keyword arguments to pass to the callback.
disabled(*bool*)	Boolean argument used to disable the widget.

The example shows the use of the time input with a default value at render time of 7.00 am:

```
sleep_time = st.time_input('How many hours of sleep are enough? ',
datetime.time(7, 00))
st.write('At least ', sleep_time)
```

How many hours of sleep are enough?

07:00   ▾

At least 07:00:00

File Uploader

A file uploader can be added to our websites using the following command: *st.file_uploader(label, type=None, accept_multiple_files=False, key, help, on_change, args, kwargs, disabled=False)* ➤ *list*. The default value for uploaded files is 200MB. This value is configurable using the server. maxUploadSize config option.

Table A-34. *st.file_uploader parameters*

Parameter	Description
label(*str*)	Label of the widget explaining what files are expected to be uploaded.
type(*str or list of str or None*)	Array of allowed extensions, i.e., ['gif', 'jpg']. To allow all extensions, use None.
accept_multiple_files(*bool*)	When True, it allows the user to upload multiple files at the same time and will return the list of the uploaded files. False is the default option.
key(*str or int*)	Unique key, string or integer, to reference the button in the code. The parameter is optional and will be automatically generated if not provided.

(continued)

437

Table A-34. (*continued*)

Parameter	Description
help(*str*)	Tooltip to be displayed when the cursor is hovered over the widget.
on_change(*callable*)	Callback function invoked when the widget's value changes.
args(*tuple*)	Tuple of arguments to pass to the callback.
kwargs(*dict*)	Dictionary of keyword arguments to pass to the callback.
disabled(*bool*)	Boolean argument used to disable the widget.

The following code can be used to upload multiple files together.

```
files_to_upload = st.file_uploader(label = 'Upload photos:',
accept_multiple_files=True)
```

Upload photos:

Drag and drop files here
Limit 200MB per file   Browse files

Camera Input

The camera input widget can be used to return static footage from the user's webcam using the command *st.camera_input(label, key, help, on_change, args, kwargs, disabled=False)* ➤ *any.*

Table A-35. *st.time_input parameters*

Parameter	Description
label(*str*)	Label of the widget.
key(*str or int*)	Unique key, string or integer, to reference the widget in the code. The parameter is optional and will be automatically generated if not provided.
help(*str*)	Tooltip to be displayed when the cursor is hovered over the widget.
on_change(*callable*)	Callback function invoked when the widget's value changes.
args(*tuple*)	Tuple of arguments to pass to the callback.
kwargs(*dict*)	Dictionary of keyword arguments to pass to the callback.
disabled(*bool*)	Boolean argument used to disable the widget.

The following example shows how to use the camera input command to take a photo with your webcam and read the text in the image using optical character recognition:

```
import pytesseract
from PIL import Image
pytesseract.pytesseract.tesseract_cmd = r'C:\Program Files\
Tesseract-OCR\tesseract.exe'

photo = st.camera_input('Take a photo')

if photo is not None:
    st.subheader('Your text:')
    text = pytesseract.image_to_string(Image.open(photo))
    st.write(text)
```

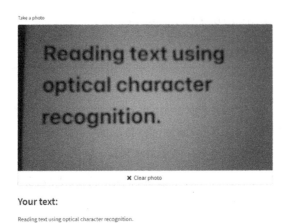

Take a photo

Reading text using optical character recognition.

✕ Clear photo

Your text:

Reading text using optical character recognition.

Color Picker

A color picker widget can be added to our websites using the following command: *st.color_picker(label, value, key, help, on_change, args, kwargs, disabled=False)* ➤ *str.*

Table A-36. *st.color_picker parameters*

Parameter	Description
label(*str*)	Label explaining the use of the widget.
value(*str*)	Hex value showed by this widget during the first render. If None, it will default to black.
key(*str or int*)	Unique key, string or integer, to reference the button in the code. The parameter is optional and will be automatically generated if not provided.
help(*str*)	Tooltip to be displayed when the cursor is hovered over the widget.

(continued)

440

Table A-36. (*continued*)

Parameter	Description
on_change(*callable*)	Callback function invoked when the widget's value changes.
args(*tuple*)	Tuple of arguments to pass to the callback.
kwargs(*dict*)	Dictionary of keyword arguments to pass to the callback.
disabled(*bool*)	Boolean argument used to disable the widget.

The following code shows the color selection widget implementation, with black (hexadecimal value #000000) as the default selection.

```
color = st.color_picker(label = 'Select a Color', value =
'#000000')
```

The current color is #3d0000

Forms

You may encapsulate several widgets together into one form using Streamlit's *st.form(key, clear_on_submit=False)* command. The added benefit of using a form is that Streamlit will not rerun the entire script each time you interact with one of the widgets within it, as it normally would. Instead, Streamlit will only rerun once you click the associated button using the command *st.form_submit_button(label='Submit,' help=None, on_click, args, kwargs)* ➤ *bool*.

441

Table A-37. *st.form parameters*

Parameter	Description
key(*str*)	A unique string that may be used to identify the form.
clear_on_submit(*bool*)	If this argument is set to true, all of the widgets inside the form will be reset to their default values after the form submit widget's value changes.

Table A-38. *st.form_submit_button parameters*

Parameter	Description
label(*str*)	Label to be displayed in the button.
help(*str or None*)	Tooltip to be displayed when the cursor is hovered over the widget.
on_click(*callable*)	Callback function called when the button is clicked.
args(*tuple*)	Tuple of arguments to pass to the callback.
kwargs(*dict*)	Dictionary of keyword arguments to pass to the callback.

The following example shows how a Streamlit form and form submit button may be used together:

```
with st.form('form_1'):
    radio = st.radio('Radio button', ['Hello','World'])
    checkbox = st.checkbox('Hello world')

    if st.form_submit_button('Submit form'):
        st.write('Radio: **%s**' % radio, 'Checkbox:',
        checkbox)
```

```
Radio button
  ● Hello
  ○ World

  ☑ Hello world

  Submit form

Radio: Hello Checkbox: True
```

A.1.5 Displaying Interactive Widgets

Streamlit makes it rather simple to render multimedia content regardless of its source. Whether it is a local image saved on disk, or a video accessed via a URL, or even an array with the raw data of a sound file, you have the ability to display and play multimedia using Streamlit's native commands without any further effort on your behalf.

Displaying Images

We can easily insert images using the following command: *st.image(image, caption, width, use_column_width, clamp, channels='RGB', output_format='auto')*.

Table A-39. *st.image parameters*

Parameter	Description
image(*numpy.ndarray, [numpy.ndarray], BytesIO, str, or [str]*)	One or a list of the following: monochrome image (w,h) or (w,h,1), color image (w,h,3), RGBA image (w,h,4), URL of image, path of a local image, VG XML string.
caption(*str or list of str*)	Image caption. A list of captions should be used if multiple images are displayed (one per image).
width(*int or None*)	Image width. None uses the image size as long as it does not exceed the width of the column. SVG images must use this option as they have no default image width.
use_column_width(*'auto' or 'always' or 'never' or bool*)	"auto" uses the natural image size without exceeding the width of the column. True or "always will use the column width. False or "never" uses the image's natural size. Note: use_column width takes precedence over the width parameter.
clamp(*bool*)	Only applicable for byte array images and ignored for image URLs. Clamp will set the pixel values to a valid range ([0–255] per channel). If required and not set, the image will have out-of-range values, and an error will be thrown.
channels(*'RGB' or 'BGR'*)	For nd.array, this parameter indicates the color information. Defaults to "RGB," or [:, :, 0] for red, [:, :, 1] for green, and [:, :, 2] for blue. Some libraries might use a different coding, like OpenCV that uses "BGR."
output_format(*'JPEG', 'PNG', or 'auto'*)	Parameter to specify the image transfer format. JPEG for photos for lossy compression; PNG for diagrams for lossless compression. The default option "auto" selects the compression based on the image type.

The following example displays a PNG as a static image:

```
st.image('elmo.png')
```

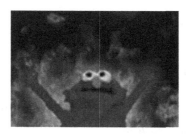

Displaying an Audio Player

An audio player can be displayed using the following command: *st. audio(data, format='audio/wav', start_time)*.

Table A-40. *st.audio parameters*

Parameter	Description
data(*str, bytes, BytesIO, numpy.ndarray, or file opened with*)	Uses the standard io.open() function and accepts raw audio data, a filename, or a URL to an audio file. Raw data formats and Numpy arrays must include the minimum required structure and values for its type.
start_time(*int*)	Time in seconds to set the widget slider to start playing by default.
format(*str*)	Audio file MIME type. "audio/wav" is the default. See `https://tools.ietf.org/html/rfc4281` for more info.

Inserting an audio file can be done in one line of code as follows:

```
st.audio('snoring.mp3', start_time=10)
```

Displaying Video

A video can be added to our websites with the command *st.video(data, format='video/mp4,' start_time)*.

Table A-41. *st.video parameters*

Parameter	Description
data(*str, bytes, BytesIO, numpy.ndarray, or file opened with*)	Uses the standard io.open() function and accepts raw video data, a filename, or a URL to a YouTube or video file. Raw data formats and Numpy arrays must include the minimum required structure and values for its type.
format(*str*)	Video file MIME type. "audio/mp4" is the default. See `https://tools.ietf.org/html/rfc4281` for more info.
start_time(*int*)	Time in seconds to set the widget slider to start playing by default.

A simple example of the insertion of a video is shown as follows:

```
st.video('https://www.youtube.com/watch?v=mOh7ESBEf3U')
```

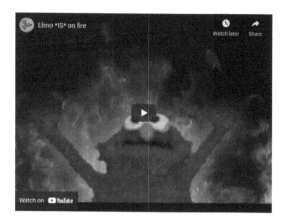

A.1.6 Page Structure

With Streamlit, you have four ways of organizing the web page. Namely, you may utilize a sidebar, multiple columns, expanders, and containers or combinations of them together to customize the user experience. In addition, you may use placeholders to effectively reserve space on your web page in order to use in due course on demand.

Sidebar

Streamlit provides a sidebar with the *st.sidebar* command that may be expanded, contracted, or left to automatically deploy based on the page size. In addition, you may add any other widget or element to it (with the exception of *st.echo* and *st.spinner*) by appending the function to it.

The following example displays how to use a sidebar with another Streamlit element:

```
st.sidebar.title('Hello world')
```

Columns

With columns, you may divide the web page into vertical sections with specified widths using the command *st.columns(spec)* ➤ *list*. This command returns a list of columns that can then be invoked using a *with* statement.

Table A-42. st.columns parameters

Parameter	Description
spec(*int or list of numbers*)	An integer will specify the number of columns of equal width to create. If a list of numbers is used, a column for each number with a width proportional to the number will be created.

The following example displays how to use columns within a Streamlit application:

```
col1, col2 = st.columns([1,2])

with col1:
    st.text_input('Hello')
with col2:
    st.text_input('World')
```

Hello   World

Expander

Streamlit provides an expander widget with the *st.expander(label, expanded)* command that may be expanded or contracted on demand and can host all other widgets or elements within it by using a *with* statement.

Table A-43. *st.expander parameters*

Parameter	Description
label(*str*)	The displayed name of the expander widget.
expanded(*boolean*)	Setting this parameter to True will set the widget to an expanded state on start.

The following example shows how to use an expander with another Streamlit element:

```
with st.expander('Hello world'):
    st.title('Hello world')
```

> Hello world
>
> ## Hello world

Container

Using Streamlit's *st.container()* command, you may group several elements together within an invisible container. Elements can be added to a container using a *with* statement or by appending the Streamlit element after the name of the container. Elements can be added to a container on demand and out of order.

The following example shows how to use a container within a Streamlit application:

```
container_1 = st.container()

container_1.write('Hello')
st.text_input('Hello world')
container_1.write('World')
```

Hello

World

Hello world

Placeholder

Streamlit allows you to reserve places within your web page by using placeholders that can be invoked with the command *st.empty()*. You may add any single element (or group of elements within a container) to the placeholder using a *with* statement or by simply appending the element after the name of the placeholder. You may update the element on demand or replace it with another at any given time, and once you are done, you may empty the placeholder by appending *empty()* to it. Placeholders are particularly useful for generating dynamic or animated content that needs to be updated regularly.

```python
import datetime

clock = st.empty()

while datetime.datetime.now() < datetime.datetime(2022, 1, 12):
    clock.metric(label='Clock', value=datetime.datetime.now().
    strftime('%H:%M:%S'))

clock.empty()
```

Clock
21:05:45

A.1.7 Displaying Status and Progress

Depending on your application, you may need to display the status and/or progress of a certain activity to the user. With Streamlit, we have multiple native methods to communicate to the user as to exactly what stage an operation is at.

Progress Bar

With Streamlit's *st.progress(value)* command, you have the ability to display in real time the progress of any activity.

Table A-44. *st.progress parameters*

Parameter	Description
value(*int or float*)	The value of the progress bar when it renders. Values range from 0 to 100 for int and 0.0 to 1.0 for float.

```
import time

timer = st.progress(0)

for i in range(0,100):
    timer.progress(i)
    time.sleep(1)
```

Spinner

Using Streamlit's *st.spinner(text)* command, you can display a temporary message within a block of executable code.

Table A-45. *st.spinner parameters*

Parameter	Description
text(*str*)	The message to render temporarily while executing the block of code.

```
import time

for i in range(0,100):
    with st.spinner('Time remaining: **%s seconds**'
    % (100-i)):
        time.sleep(1)
```

Time remaining: 86 seconds

Messages

With the commands *st.success(body)*, *st.info(body)*, *st.warning(body)*, and *st.error(body)*, you have the ability to display messages with green, blue, yellow, and red encapsulating boxes, respectively.

Table A-46. *st.success, st.info, st.warning, and st.error parameters*

Parameter	Description
body(*str*)	The message to render.

```
col1, col2, col3, col4 = st.columns(4)

with col1:
    st.success('Hello world')
with col2:
    st.info('Hello world')
with col3:
    st.warning('Hello world')
with col4:
    st.error('Hello world')
```

Hello world   Hello world   Hello world   Hello world

Exception

With Streamlit's *st.exception(exception)* command, you can display a type of exception and a corresponding message.

Table A-47. *st.exception parameters*

Parameter	Description
exception(*Exception*)	The type of exception to render.

```
a = 1
b = 0

try:
    a/b
except:
    st.exception(ZeroDivisionError('Division by zero'))
```

ZeroDivisionError: Division by zero

Balloons

The *st.balloons()* command gives you the ability to render floating balloons should you find it absolutely necessary to do so:

```
st.balloons()
```

Snow

And lastly, the *st.snow()* command gives you the ability to render floating snowflakes in spirit of Streamlit's acquisition by Snowflake:

```
st.snow()
```

A.1.8 Utilities

A host of other functions and added utilities come with Streamlit, such as the ability to configure the web page programmatically, to render code snippets, and to provide object documentation if required.

Page Configuration

You can configure the title, icon, layout, sidebar state, and menu options of your Streamlit application using the *st.set_page_config(page_title, page_icon, layout, initial_sidebar_state, menu_items)* command.

Table A-48. *st.set_page_config parameters*

Parameter	Description
page_title(*str or None*)	The title that will appear on the browser's tab; if not invoked, the script name will be used as the page title.
page_icon(*image, icon, str, or None*)	The favicon that will be displayed on the browser's tab; shortcodes may also be used as an alternative to images.
layout(*'centered' or 'wide'*)	The layout of the page; if not invoked, the page will default to centered.
initial_sidebar_state(*'auto', 'expanded', or 'collapsed'*)	The state of the sidebar when the page starts; if not invoked, it will default to auto.
menu_items(*dict*)	Configuration for the *Get help*, *Report a bug*, or *About* pages within the hamburger menu. For further information, please refer to Section 3.1.

```
st.set_page_config(
    page_title='Hello world',
    page_icon=icon,
    layout='centered',
    initial_sidebar_state='auto',
    menu_items={
        'Get Help': 'https://streamlit.io/',
        'Report a bug': 'https://github.com',
```

```
        'About': 'About your application: **Hello world**'
        }
)
```

Code Echo

You can render code and execute it simultaneously by using the *st. echo(code_location)* command.

Table A-49. *st.echo parameters*

Parameter	Description
code_location(*'above' or 'below'*)	Whether to render the code above or below its execution location.

```
with st.echo():
    st.write('Hello world')
```

```
st.write('Hello world')
```

Hello world

Documentation

You may display the help documentation associated with an object by using the *st.help(obj)* command.

Table A-50. *st.help parameters*

Parameter	Description
obj(*Object*)	The object whose help documentation should be displayed.

```
lst = [1,2,3]
st.help(lst)
```

```
<class 'list'>

Built-in mutable sequence.

If no argument is given, the constructor creates a new empty list.
The argument must be an iterable if specified.
```

Stop Execution

To stop the execution of a Streamlit application at a specific point in your script, you may use the *st.stop()* command to prevent the rest of your code from being executed:

```
st.write('Hello world')
st.stop()
st.write('Bye world')
```

Hello world

A.1.9 Session State Management

Implementing a stateful architecture can be essential for a multitude of web applications. From storing session-specific data such as user credentials to other variables, the absence of such an ability can be a deal breaker for many developers. Just imagine trying to implement logical flow in your application, where a user input in one page is used to generate a visualization in another page. Without storing the input as a session variable, it would be reset once you navigate to the other page or simply rerun the script, leaving you without a visualization. Luckily, Streamlit offers a native and highly intuitive way of managing session state seamlessly that enables developers to cater for an enhanced user experience.

Initializing Session State Variables

Streamlit's session state dictionary is composed of key-value pairs where each key must be initialized before it can be invoked, and each value can consist of a string, integer, list, dictionary, dataframe, object, or other variables. To initialize a variable into your session state, proceed as follows:

```
if 'state_1' not in st.session_state:
    st.session_state['state_1'] = None
```

Accessing Session State Variables

Subsequently, to access the variable initialized within the same session, simply invoke it as follows:

```
state_1 = st.session_state['state_1']
```

To access all of the session state variables, use the following command:

```
st.write(st.session_state)
```

This will return the session state dictionary with all of the key-value pairs stored as follows:

```
▼ {
    "state_1" : NULL
    "state_2" : NULL
  }
```

Updating Session State Variables

To update the value of the session state variable, proceed as follows:

```
st.session_state['state_1'] = 'Hello world'
```

Deleting Session State Variables

To delete a specific session state variable, use the following:

```
del st.session_state['state_1']
```

In order to delete all of the session state variables at once, you may use the following:

```
for variable in st.session_state:
    del st.session_state[variable]
```

Widget Session State

Each widget in Streamlit is automatically associated with its own session state variable, where the key is the same key that is invoked as an argument to the widget, as shown in the following:

```
st.button('Random button',key='random_button_1')
st.text_input('Hello world',key='hello_world_input')

st.write(st.session_state)
```

Random button

Hello world

Howdy

```
▼ {
    "hello_world_text_input" : "Howdy"
    "random_button" : true
}
```

Please note that modifying the value of a widget's session state after instantiating it is not permitted, and should you attempt to do so, a *StreamlitAPIException* error will be thrown. However, setting the state of a widget before it is instantiated is permitted, albeit with a one-time warning message if the default value of the widget has already been set as an argument. In addition, widgets with buttons such as *st.button*, *st.download_button*, and *st.file_uploader* cannot have their session state values modified; by default, they are set to *False* and will be toggled to *True* when they are clicked.

A.1.10 Data Management

Managing data for optimal use of computing resources is of utmost importance for web servers. Given the large scale of data that we are exposed to, it is often essential to cache data, functions, and other objects for prompt reuse when the need arises. To that end, Streamlit offers an in-house capability to cache and reuse data in our applications with tangibly positive outcomes. Furthermore, Streamlit also offers the ability to mutate data natively without any third-party libraries should the need arise.

Caching Data

Streamlit allows you to cache the results and data of a function persistently for later use with the *st.cache(func, persist, allow_output_mutation, show_spinner, suppress_st_warning, hash_funcs, max_entries, ttl)* command. This

461

feature is particularly useful if you are working with large datasets that will take an extended period of time to download or process. With this feature, you can enter your data into the cache by invoking the function written below the *st.cache* decorator and then recall it on demand when needed without having to reexecute the function, even after your script has been rerun.

Table A-51. *st.cache parameters*

Parameter	Description
func(*callable*)	The function to be cached.
persist(*boolean*)	This parameter specifies whether to keep the cached data persistently or not.
allow_output_mutation(*boolean*)	Setting the parameter to True will allow you to override the cached data without receiving a warning from Streamlit.
show_spinner(*boolean*)	If set to True, a spinner will be displayed when there is a cache miss.
suppress_st_warning(*boolean*)	Setting this parameter to True will suppress any warnings about calling embedded functions within a cached function.
hash_funcs(*dict or None*)	With this parameter, you can override the reaction of Streamlit to objects within the cache; when the hasher encounters a specified object within the dict, it will use the associated function in response.
max_entries(*int or None*)	This parameter specifies the maximum number of items to cache, and whenever a new item is added to the list, the oldest item will be removed accordingly.
ttl(*float or None*)	This parameter determines the time in seconds to keep an item in the cache; if not invoked, the cache will not be cleared.

Caching with *st.cache*:

```
@st.cache
def dataframe(rows):
    df = pd.DataFrame(
        np.random.randn(rows, 5),
        columns=('col %d' % i for i in range(5)))
    return df

# Initial invocation to cache dataframe
df = dataframe(100000)

# Subsequent invocation will access the cached dataframe
# without re-executing function
df = dataframe(100000)

# Will re-execute function and recache new dataframe due to
# modified input parameter
df = dataframe(200000)
```

Caching Functions

Streamlit also allows you to cache function executions persistently with the *st.experimental_memo(func, persist, show_spinner, suppress_st_warning, max_entries, ttl)* command. This feature is indeed very similar to the *st. cache* command. And when you no longer need the cache, you may remove it by using the command *st.experimental_memo.clear()*. Please note that commands beginning with *experimental* will have this prefix removed in future releases once the command has matured.

Table A-52. *st.experimental_memo parameters*

Parameter	Description
func(*callable*)	The function to be cached.
persist(*boolean*)	This parameter specifies whether to keep the cached data persistently or not.
show_spinner(*boolean*)	If set to True, a spinner will be displayed when there is a cache miss.
suppress_st_ warning(*boolean*)	Setting this parameter to True will suppress any warnings about calling embedded functions within a cached function.
max_entries(*int or None*)	This parameter specifies the maximum number of items to cache, and whenever a new item is added to the list, the oldest item will be removed accordingly.
ttl(*float or None*)	This parameter determines the time in seconds to keep an item in the cache; if not invoked, the cache will not be cleared.

Caching with *st.experimental_memo*:

```
@st.experimental_memo
def dataframe(rows):
    df = pd.DataFrame(
        np.random.randn(rows, 5),
        columns=('col %d' % i for i in range(5)))
    return df

# Initial invocation to cache function execution
df = dataframe(100000)

# Subsequent invocation will access the cached execution
without re-executing function
```

```
df = dataframe(100000)

# Will re-execute function and recache the new execution due to
modified input parameter
df = dataframe(200000)
```

Caching Objects

Similar to *st.cache*, Streamlit allows you to cache objects persistently with the *st.experimental_singleton(func, show_spinner, suppress_st_warning)* command. And when you no longer need the cache, you may remove it by using the command *st.experimental_singleton.clear()*. It is important to highlight that singleton objects must be thread-safe since they will be shared by all users of the application. Possible use cases for *st. experimental_singleton* are database connections and corpora. However, this is not the case for *st.memo* as each caller will receive their own copy of the cached data.

Table A-53. *st.experimental_singleton parameters*

Parameter	Description
func(*callable*)	The function to be cached.
show_spinner(*boolean*)	If set to True, a spinner will be displayed when there is a cache miss.
suppress_st_ warning(*boolean*)	Setting this parameter to True will suppress any warnings about calling embedded functions within a cached function.

Caching with *st.experimental_singleton*:

```
@st.experimental_singleton
def load_nlp(lang):
    nlp = spacy.load('%s_core_news_sm' % (lang))
    return nlp
```

```
# Initial invocation to cache object
nlp = load_nlp('es')
```

```
# Subsequent invocation will access the cached object without
re-executing function
nlp = load_nlp('es')
```

```
# Will re-execute function and recache new object due to
modified input parameter
nlp = load_nlp('de')
```

Mutate Data

Streamlit allows you to mutate your data and charts in real time by adding a dataframe to the end of a table using the *st.add_rows(data,**kwargs)* command.

Table A-54. *st.add_rows parameters*

Parameter	Description
data(*Pandas dataframe or styler, PyArrow table, Numpy array, dict, None, or iterable*)	The dataframe to be appended to an existing table. If a PyArrow table is used, you must set the *dataFrameSerialization = 'arrow'* in the config file; for further information, please refer to Section 3.1.
**kwargs(*Pandas dataframe, Numpy array, dict, None, or iterable*)	Should you need to do so, you can pass the dataframe to append as a named object, i.e., *'dataset' = df*.

Mutating tables with *st.add_rows*:

```
table = st.table(pd.DataFrame(data={'a':[1,2], 'b':[3,4]}))
df = pd.DataFrame(data={'a':[5,6], 'b':[7,8]})
table.add_rows(df)
```

	a	b
0	1	3
1	2	4
2	5	7
3	6	8

A.1.11 The Hamburger Menu

Streamlit by default is equipped with a hamburger menu at the top-right corner of the web page. This menu provides a host of additional features that may be of use to the user and developer alike. Table A-55 summarizes the available features.

Table A-55. *Hamburger menu features*

Feature	Description
Return	When clicked, Streamlit will rerun the script from top to bottom.
Settings	Opens a window where the user can customize the theme's appearance, color, font, and other associated settings. For further information, please refer to Section 3.1.
Record a screencast	As the name suggests, this feature allows you to record the video and audio feed from your browser window and save it in the *webm* format.

(continued)

Table A-55. (*continued*)

Feature	Description
Report a bug	This option opens a link to the GitHub page where you can report a bug. Alternatively, you may choose to link this option to any other URL you require as shown in Section 3.1.
Get help	Similarly, this option takes you to the Streamlit discussion page where you can raise concerns and ask questions. It may be linked to another URL if required as shown in Section 3.1.
About	This option displays a modal window with the version of Streamlit that you are using. If needed, you may customize the text displayed as shown in Section 3.1.
Clear cache	This feature will clear any data stored by the *st.cache* command. For further information, please refer to Section 4.1.
Deploy this app	Streamlit allows you to deploy your application to their server referred to as Streamlit Cloud directly with this option.
Streamlit Cloud	This link takes you to the home page for Streamlit Cloud that provides further information about their hosting service.
Report a Streamlit bug	Identical to the Report a bug feature, this option will take you to the GitHub page where you can raise bugs and concerns.
Visit Streamlit docs	This link will simply take you to Streamlit's API.
Visit Streamlit forums	Likewise, this link will take you to Streamlit's forum.

Bibliography

[1] A. A. Sutchenkov and A. I. Tikhonov, Active Investigation and Publishing of Calculation Web Based Applications for Studying Process, Journal of Physics 7 (2020).

[2] D. Karade and V. Karade, AIDrugApp: Artificial Intelligence-Based Web-App for Virtual Screening of Inhibitors against SARS-COV-2, 59 (n.d.).

[3] D. M. A. Raheem, S. Tabassum, S. K. Nahid, and S. A. Anzer, A Deep Learning Approach for the Automatic Analysis and Prediction of Breast Cancer for Histopathological Images Using A Webapp, International Journal of Engineering Research 10, 7 (n.d.).

[4] A. N. Habowski, T. J. Habowski, and M. L. Waterman, GECO: Gene Expression Clustering Optimization App for Non-Linear Data Visualization of Patterns, BMC Bioinformatics 22, 29 (2021).

[5] F. M. Torun, S. V. Winter, S. Doll, F. M. Riese, A. Vorobyev, J. B. Mueller-Reif, P. E. Geyer, and M. T. Strauss, Transparent Exploration of Machine Learning for Biomarker Discovery from Proteomics and Omics Data, 11 (n.d.).

[6] R. Shigapov, P. Zumstein, J. Kamlah, L. Oberlander, J. Mechnich, and I. Schumm, Bbw: Matching CSV to Wikidata via Meta-Lookup, 10 (n.d.).

[7] A. R. Kashyap and M.-Y. Kan, SciWING – A Software Toolkit for Scientific Document Processing, ArXiv:2004.03807 [Cs] (2020).

© Mohammad Khorasani, Mohamed Abdou, Javier Hernández Fernández 2022
M. Khorasani et al., *Web Application Development with Streamlit*,
https://doi.org/10.1007/978-1-4842-8111-6

[8] J. Vig, W. Kryściński, K. Goel, and N. F. Rajani, SummVis: Interactive Visual Analysis of Models, Data, and Evaluation for Text Summarization, ArXiv:2104.07605 [Cs] (2021).

[9] Pournaki, A., Felix Gaisbauer, Sven Banisch, and E. Olbrich. "The twitter explorer: a framework for observing Twitter through interactive networks." ArXiv abs/2003.03599 (2020).

[10] A. Saxena, M. Dhadwal, and M. Kowsigan, Indian Crop Production: Prediction And Model Deployment Using Ml And Streamlit, 13 (n.d.).

[11] S. F. N. Islam, A. Sholahuddin, and A. S. Abdullah, Extreme Gradient Boosting (XGBoost) Method in Making Forecasting Application and Analysis of USD Exchange Rates against Rupiah, J. Phys.: Conf. Ser. 1722, 012016 (2021).

[12] A. Aboah, M. Boeding, and Y. Adu-Gyamfi, Mobile Sensing for Multipurpose Applications in Transportation, 16 (n.d.).

[13] Ticlo, I., in *Your guide to the Windows 10 cloud solution provider program*, Insight. Retrieved September 18, 2021, from `www.insight.com/en_US/content-and-resources/2016/12222016-your-guide-to-the-windows-10-cloud-solution-provider-program.html`

[14] Iberdrola S.A, in *Wikinger, the project that consolidates Germany as a strategic market*. Retrieved November 7, 2021, from `www.iberdrola.com/about-us/lines-business/flagship-projects/wikinger-offshore-wind-farm`

[15] Wind Turbine Power Curve Definitions, in *Wind Trubine Power Output with steady wind speed*. Retrieved November 2, 2021, from `https://wind-power-program.com/popups/powercurve.htm`

[16] Veena, R., Mathew, S., and Petra, M.I., Artificially intelligent models for the site-specific performance of wind turbines, Int J Energy

Environ Eng 11, 289–297 (2020). `https://doi.org/10.1007/s40095-020-00352-2`

[17] GE Renewable Energy, in *GE Renewable Energy's Haliade-X prototype starts operating at 14 MW*. Retrieved September 14, 2021, from `www.ge.com/news/press-releases/ge-renewable-energy-haliade-x-prototype-starts-operating-at-14-mw`

[18] Michelle Lewis, in *GE's huge Haliade-X 14 MW offshore wind turbine is now operational*. Retrieved September 14, 2021, from `https://electrek.co/2021/10/05/ge-huge-haliade-x-14-mw-offshore-wind-turbine-is-now-operational`

[19] Khorasani, M. (October 7, 2021). How to build a real-time SCADA system using Python and Arduino. Medium. Retrieved December 31, 2021, from `https://towardsdatascience.com/how-to-build-a-real-time-scada-system-using-python-and-arduino-7b3acaf86d39`

[20] Cornelam, & Instructables. (October 6, 2017). Arduino Servo Motors. Instructables. Retrieved December 30, 2021, from `www.instructables.com/Arduino-Servo-Motors/`

[21] Learning, U. C. I. M. (October 6, 2016). Pima Indians Diabetes Database. Kaggle. Retrieved January 5, 2022, from `www.kaggle.com/uciml/pima-indians-diabetes-database`

[22] GDP per capita. Our World in Data. (n.d.). Retrieved January 9, 2022, from `https://ourworldindata.org/grapher/gdp-per-capita-worldbank`

Index

© Mohammad Khorasani, Mohamed Abdou, Javier Hernández Fernández 2022
M. Khorasani et al., *Web Application Development with Streamlit*,
https://doi.org/10.1007/978-1-4842-8111-6

Printed in the United States
by Baker & Taylor Publisher Services